# A Step Ahead

# A Step Ahead

## Competition Policy for Shared Prosperity and Inclusive Growth

 WORLD BANK GROUP

 OECD

# Contents

## Boxes

## Figures

## Maps

## Tables

# Foreword

Sustainable economic development has played a major role in the decline of global poverty in the past two decades. In emerging and developing countries, we have seen positive impacts when countries share welfare gains with the bottom 40 percent of the population.

There is no doubt that competitive markets are key drivers of economic growth and productivity. They are also valuable channels for consumer welfare. When there is competition in markets, consumers benefit from lower prices, better products and services, and innovation. Good governance, macroeconomic stability, access to infrastructure, investment in human development, and social policies to protect the poor are at the forefront of efforts to promote economic growth and shared prosperity. But are they enough to improve the welfare of the poor?

We acknowledge that competition policy is a powerful tool for complementing efforts to alleviate poverty and bring about shared prosperity. An effective competition policy involves measures that enable contestability and firm entry and rivalry, while ensuring the enforcement of antitrust laws and state aid control. Governments from emerging and developing economies are increasingly requesting pragmatic solutions for effective competition policy implementation and recommendations for pro-competitive sectoral policies.

While the benefits of competition and competition policies on macroeconomic indicators and market outcomes are well documented, their short- and long-term distributional effects on the poor require enhanced research and greater attention from policy makers.

This book puts forward a research agenda that advocates the importance of market competition, effective market regulation, and competition policies for achieving inclusive growth and shared prosperity in emerging and developing economies. It is the result of a global partnership and shared commitment between the World Bank Group and the Organisation for Economic Co-operation and Development (OECD).

Part I of the book brings together existing empirical evidence on the benefits of competition for household welfare. It covers the elimination of anticompetitive practices and regulations that restrict competition in key markets and highlights the effects of competition on low-income households as consumers, small producers, and employees. It also looks at how competition can support inclusive economic growth and sheds light on the links among competition, productivity and innovation, and macroeconomic effects.

Part II focuses on the distributional effects of competition policies and how enforcement can be better aligned with shared prosperity goals. It features novel research and empirical evidence on the impact of anticartel enforcement on consumer welfare, the distributional effects of market power, the distributional macroeconomic effects of merger and cartel decisions, and the impact of competition on innovation in developing and developed economies.

Now is the time to widely disseminate collective knowledge on the benefits of competition for economic development and shared prosperity. We hope this book will start a conversation on competition's role in poverty alleviation and help deliver better competition policy solutions for diverse audiences.

Anabel González
*Senior Director*
*Trade and Competitiveness*
*Global Practice*
*World Bank Group*

Adrian Blundell-Wignall
*Director*
*Directorate for Financial and*
*Enterprise Affairs*
*OECD*

# Acknowledgments

This publication has been prepared by the World Bank Group in partnership with the Organisation for Economic Co-operation and Development (OECD). The Competition Policy Cluster of the Trade and Competition Unit, World Bank Group Trade and Competitiveness Global Practice, led the preparation of this publication, in close coordination with the Competition Division of the OECD Directorate for Financial and Enterprise Affairs. The Markets and Institutions Global Solutions Group of the World Bank Group Poverty Global Practice also provided substantial inputs and reviewed the papers showcased in this publication.

This publication builds on the World Bank Group Global Engagement on Competition Policy for Inclusive Growth and Shared Prosperity and the proceedings of its inaugural conference, organized jointly with the OECD and held at the World Bank Group headquarters in Washington, DC, in June 2015. It also builds on the application of the World Bank Group's Markets and Competition Policy Assessment Tool in low- and middle-income countries.

The main objectives of the Global Engagement on Competition Policy were to (i) increase knowledge on how to promote efficient and contestable markets for shared prosperity; (ii) carry out a series of high-level, peer-to-peer learning events to disseminate best practices on competition policy as an instrument for poverty and shared prosperity; and (iii) prepare and release a publication that showcases empirical evidence and recent policy research on the links to competition, poverty, and shared prosperity.

The World Bank Group Competition Policy Team that led the preparation of this publication includes Georgiana Pop, Senior Economist; Martha Martinez Licetti, Lead Economist and Global Product Specialist; Sara Nyman, Economist; and Tania Priscilla Begazo Gomez, Senior Economist. Martha Martinez Licetti, Sara Nyman, and Tania Priscilla Begazo Gomez coauthored chapter 1, "Introduction," and chapter 2, "Effects of Market Competition and Competition Policies." The OECD team comprising Silvia Carrieri, Policy Analyst; John Davies, former Head of Division; and Ania Thiemann, Global Relations Manager and Competition Expert, coauthored with the World Bank Group sections on dynamic effects and further research in chapter 2, "Effects of Market Competition and Competition Policies." Tanja Goodwin, Economist, World Bank Group Trade and Competitiveness Global Practice; Mariana Iootty, Senior Economist, World Bank Group Trade and Competitiveness Global Practice; Catriona Purfield, Lead

Economist, World Bank Group Macroeconomics and Fiscal Management Global Practice; and Carlos Rodríguez-Castelán, Senior Economist, World Bank Group Poverty Global Practice, provided valuable contributions for the preparation of the report. The advice and suggestions of the peer reviewers of part I of the publication—Paul Brenton, Lead Economist, World Bank Group Trade and Competitiveness Global Practice; and Tara Vishwanath, Lead Economist, World Bank Group Poverty Global Practice—are gratefully acknowledged. Osongo Lenga, Program Assistant, World Bank Group Trade and Competitiveness Global Practice, provided support for the preparation of this publication. The final publication was edited by Martha Martinez Licetti, Georgiana Pop, Sara Nyman, Tania Priscilla Begazo Gomez, and Ania Thiemann. Steve Pazdan, publishing associate in Editorial and Production, General Services Division, coordinated production of the publication.

The team thanks the authors of the selected papers that were submitted to the Call for Proposals "Promoting Effective Competition Policies for Shared Prosperity and Inclusive Growth," notably the following: Marc Ivaldi (Toulouse School of Economics and Centre for Economic Policy Research); Frédéric Jenny (ESSEC Business School, Paris); Aleksandra Khimich (Toulouse School of Economics); Thando Vilakazi (Centre for Competition, Regulation and Economic Development, University of Johannesburg); Sean F. Ennis and Yunhee Kim (OECD); Adriaan Dierx, Fabienne Ilzkovitz, Beatrice Pataracchia, Marco Ratto, Anna Thum-Thysen, and Janos Varga (European Commission); and Tim Büthe and Cindy Cheng (Duke University and Hochschule für Politik at the Technical University of Munich, Germany). These papers were selected from 53 submissions based on a set of pre-established criteria by a committee that included representatives from the World Bank Group (Trade and Competitiveness Global Practice and the Poverty Global Practice), the OECD, and an independent academic. The team is grateful to the selection committee: John Davies, Martha Martinez Licetti, Georgiana Pop, Carlos Rodríguez-Castelán, Professor Daniel Sokol (Levin College of Law, University of Florida), Ania Thiemann, and Tara Vishwanath. Jose G. Reis, Practice Manager, Trade and Competition Unit, World Bank Group Trade and Competitiveness Global Practice; and Klaus Tilmes, Director, World Bank Group Trade and Competitiveness Global Practice, provided strategic oversight.

The publication was prepared under the guidance of Anabel González, Senior Director, Trade and Competitiveness Global Practice, World Bank Group; and Adrian Blundell-Wignall, Director, Directorate for Financial and Enterprise Affairs, OECD.

# Abbreviations

| | |
|---|---|
| ASYCUDA | Automated System for Customs Data |
| AT&T | American Telephone & Telegraph |
| CA | competition authority |
| CAFC | Court of Appeals for the Federal Circuit (United States) |
| CAN | calcium ammonium nitrate |
| CARICOM | Caribbean Community |
| CCPC | Competition and Consumer Protection Commission (Zambia) |
| CCRED | Centre for Competition, Regulation and Economic Development (University of Johannesburg) |
| CEPR | Centre for Economic Policy Research (United Kingdom) |
| CGE | computable general equilibrium (model) |
| CIF | cost, insurance, and freight |
| CMA | Competition and Markets Authority (United Kingdom) |
| COMESA | Common Market for Eastern and Southern Africa |
| DCG | Dar es Salaam Corridor Group |
| DOJ | Department of Justice (United States) |
| DSGE | dynamic stochastic general equilibrium (model) |
| ETG | Export Trading Group |
| EU | European Union |
| FDI | foreign direct investment |
| FISP | Farm Input Subsidy Programme (Malawi); Farmer Input Support Programme (Zambia) |
| FOB | free on board |
| FSSA | Fertiliser Society of South Africa |
| FTC | Federal Trade Commission (United States) |
| GDP | gross domestic product |
| GE | General Electric |
| GIZ | Deutsche Gesellschaft für Internationale Zusammenarbeit (German development agency) |
| GNP | gross national product |
| IBM | International Business Machines Corp. |

| | |
|---|---|
| ICN | International Competition Network |
| IP | intellectual property |
| IPC | Import Planning Committee (South Africa) |
| ISCED | International Standard Classification of Education |
| ISIC3 | International Standard Industrial Classification of All Economic Activities, Rev. 3 |
| IT | information technology |
| LC | liquidity-constrained |
| LCC | low-cost carrier |
| MSP | Minimum Support Price |
| NACE | statistical classification of economic activities in the European Community |
| NBC | Nitrogen Balance Committee (South Africa) |
| NIRA | National Industrial Recovery Act (United States) |
| NLC | non-liquidity-constrained |
| OECD | Organisation for Economic Co-operation and Development |
| OFT | Office of Fair Trading (United Kingdom) |
| OLS | ordinary least squares |
| PCAIDS | Proportionally Calibrated Almost Ideal Demand System |
| PMR | Product Market Regulation (indicators) |
| PPP | purchasing power parity |
| R&D | research and development |
| SADC | Southern African Development Community |
| SME | small and medium enterprise |
| TFP | total factor productivity |
| TFRA | Tanzania Fertilizer Regulatory Authority |
| UNCTAD | United Nations Conference on Trade and Development |
| US$ | U.S. dollars |
| USPTO | U.S. Patent and Trademark Office |
| WAEMU/UEMOA | West African Economic and Monetary Union |
| WDD | wealth distribution data |
| WGI | Worldwide Governance Indicators (World Bank) |
| WIPO | World Intellectual Property Organization |
| WTO | World Trade Organization |

# PART I

Competition Policy, Shared
Prosperity, Poverty Alleviation,
and Inclusive Growth: Empirical
Evidence to Support Policy Action

# 1. Introduction

Reducing poverty and improving the distribution of welfare, while boosting the overall prosperity of the population, is a common goal across most low- and middle-income countries. The decline in poverty rates in recent decades has been significant, with extreme poverty[1] halving between 1990 and 2015. Yet there is still progress to be made: about 900 million people were living in extreme poverty in 2012 (representing 12.7 percent of the global population) and a projected 700 million people in 2015.

As poverty rates decline, a parallel challenge will be to ensure that the bottom 40 percent of the income distribution in every country can share in the nation's prosperity. Shared prosperity has been defined as "expanding the size of the pie continuously and sharing it in such a way that the welfare of those at the lower end of the income distribution rises as quickly as possible" (World Bank 2013).[2] It is measured as income growth of the bottom 40 percent of the income distribution in the population, and in some lower-income countries this goal will coincide with that of reducing poverty (box 1.1).

Increased opportunity for less well-off households in competitive markets has been an essential element in the progress that has been made toward reducing poverty and boosting shared prosperity. With this fact being increasingly acknowledged by governments, this report aims to respond to the following questions that are now being posed by many policy makers in World Bank Group and Organisation for Economic Co-operation and Development (OECD) partner countries:

- To what extent does the degree of competition in domestic markets affect poverty and the distribution of welfare?
- How can competition policy be used to increase competition and affect these outcomes?

A foundation for answering these questions is found in two observations that are prevalent across countries:

1. Growth—and particularly growth in real labor incomes—is the key driver of poverty alleviation, and competition is known to drive growth by increasing total factor productivity.
2. Lower-income groups tend to be overproportionally affected by market outcomes in sectors that
    a. Are particularly prone to anticompetitive behavior by firms; or
    b. Are often subject to restrictive regulations imposed by governments.

## Who Are the Bottom 40 Percent?

The bottom 40 percent may include many possible populations depending on the country. Among developing regions, the income of the richest person among the bottom 40 percent makes that person either extremely or moderately poor, particularly in Sub-Saharan Africa and parts of East Asia (map B1.1.1). In these countries, targeting a reduction in poverty will be equivalent to boosting shared prosperity. In Latin America and the Caribbean and parts of Europe and Central Asia, the richest person in the bottom 40 percent is generally classed as vulnerable. In these countries, reducing poverty and vulnerability will be key for shared prosperity.

MAP B1.1.1 **Income of the Richest Person in the Bottom 40 Percent across Countries**

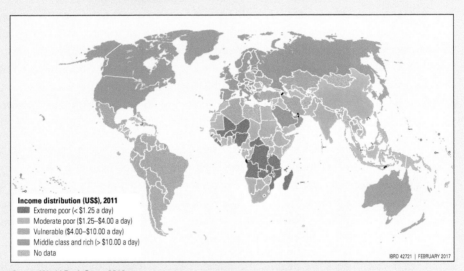

Income distribution (US$), 2011
- Extreme poor (< $1.25 a day)
- Moderate poor ($1.25–$4.00 a day)
- Vulnerable ($4.00–$10.00 a day)
- Middle class and rich (> $10.00 a day)
- No data

IBRD 42721 | FEBRUARY 2017

*Source:* World Bank Group 2016.
*Note:* Based on the $1.25 poverty line and 2005 purchasing power parity (PPP) prices, as full distributional data using 2011 PPP prices were not yet available.

This publication seeks to answer these questions and sheds light on this largely "unexplored" area of research. It highlights empirical research on the importance of competition, and competition policies, for variables that are relevant for poverty and sharing prosperity. Part I builds on a review of the evidence on the relationship between competition, poverty, and the distribution of welfare carried out by the World Bank Group (Begazo and Nyman 2016). Part II presents new research on competition policies and their welfare-enhancing effects, following a call for proposals undertaken as part of the joint cooperation between the World Bank Group and the OECD.

## 1.1 What Is Competition Policy?

Competition policy is the set of policies and laws that ensure that competition in the marketplace is not restricted in such a way as to reduce economic welfare (Motta 2004). In practical terms, competition policy usually involves two pillars: pillar 1 is the promotion of measures to enable contestability, firm entry, and rivalry; and pillar 2 is the enforcement of antitrust laws (typically rules against abuse of dominance and anticompetitive agreements, and merger control) and state aid control (table 1.1).[3] The former involves the improvement of regulations and administrative procedures by government bodies, while the latter focuses on business behavior of all entities that perform commercial functions. It is worth noting that the ultimate aim of competition policies is not to increase the number of firms in a market or to eliminate market power to achieve a theoretical state of perfect competition. Their final goal is to generate the right incentives for firms to improve their economic performance relative to their actual and potential rivals and in so doing deliver the best outcomes for consumers and the economy as a whole.

The competition policy tools available and the extent to which competition policies are implemented vary across countries. Since the competitive environment in any country will be affected by its policies and regulations, there is scope to implement pillar 1 on pro-competition market regulation[4] to varying degrees in any country. Pillar 2 (competition enforcement) on the other hand usually requires a competition law to be

**TABLE 1.1  A Comprehensive Competition Policy Framework**

| Fostering competition in markets | |
| --- | --- |
| **Pro-competition regulations and government interventions: Opening markets and removing anticompetitive sectoral regulations (pillar 1)** | **Competition enforcement: Effectively enforcing competition law and rules economywide (pillar 2)** |
| Reform policies and regulations that strengthen dominance: restrictions to the number of firms, statutory monopolies, bans toward private investment, lack of access regulation for essential facilities | Tackle cartel agreements that raise the costs of key inputs and final products and reduce access to a broader variety of products |
| Eliminate government interventions that are conducive to collusive outcomes or increase the costs of competing: controls on prices and other market variables that increase business risk | Prevent anticompetitive mergers |
| Reform government interventions that discriminate and harm competition on the merits: frameworks that distort the level playing field or grant high levels of discretion | Strengthen the general antitrust framework to combat anticompetitive conduct and abuse of dominance |
| | Control state aid to avoid favoritism, ensure competitive neutrality, and minimize distortions on competition[a] |

*Source:* Adapted from Kitzmuller and Martinez Licetti 2012.

a. This subtopic is included under pillar 2 since it comprises economywide rules. However, it could be considered to be a separate pillar since it is often developed outside of rules on merger control and anticompetitive behavior of firms.

enacted and a competition authority (or other responsible body) to enforce the law. Thus, for countries without a competition law or an authority to enforce the law, the focus of competition policy will lie in pillar 1 in the short to medium run. Pillar 1 comprises not only agriculture policies and regulation of network sectors to set the right environment for competition where it is viable but also government interventions to ensure that trade policy is set in a way that enhances competition in domestic markets and embedding competition principles in industrial policies. Pillar 1 includes also bringing a competition lens to conducting regulatory impact assessments of procedures, regulations, or policies to understand their impact on competition and to identify more pro-competition alternatives.

Where a competition law has been enacted and a functional competition authority is in place, competition enforcement (pillar 2) complements economic market regulation (pillar 1). Competition authorities monitor and punish anticompetitive behavior by firms and prevent mergers that could harm competition. Competition authorities typically support pillar 1 with advocacy efforts, conducting research on the effect on competition of proposed government interventions, and providing opinions on their unintended impacts on market functioning and potential alternatives to minimize market distortions. In some cases, a new competition authority may find it more effective to focus on these advocacy efforts in the early stages of its development while it develops its enforcement capacity.

Integrating competition policy with other policies and introducing competition principles can make those broader policies more effective. There is evidence that the introduction of market-based competitive voucher schemes into subsidy programs has positive effects. Industrial policy can also benefit from being complemented by competition policy. Other studies find that sectoral industrial policies (such as subsidies or tax holidays) have a larger impact on productivity growth when targeted at competitive sectors or where they are allocated in such a way as to preserve or increase competition (for example, by inducing entry or encouraging younger enterprises). Trade policy is another key tool that policy makers can use to enhance competition and welfare in the absence of a competition enforcement framework (see box 2.4 in chapter 2). Finally, competition law enforcement (pillar 2) can complement traditional poverty reduction measures such as direct cash transfers to the poor from the state. Since a large proportion of cash transfers tend to be spent on food and other basic goods, tackling anticompetitive behavior in these sectors is important to prevent these transfers from leaking to firms in the form of anticompetitive profits.

Although the goals of competition enforcement are typically to ensure an effective competitive process, promote consumer welfare, and enhance efficiency, some competition laws include objectives related to reducing poverty and inequality. For example, according to a recent survey of 18 African competition authorities, 12 authorities stated that increasing fairness and equality was an objective of the competition law, while nine had poverty reduction as an explicit objective of their competition law (World Bank and African Competition Forum 2016).

This review of the literature will highlight evidence on the impact of key competition policy measures in reducing poverty and increasing shared prosperity. This evidence largely focuses on the impact of increasing the degree of competition in markets through (i) increases in entry, which can be achieved through policy interventions that remove entry restrictions or that reduce the cost of entry but may also be the result of a more organic process where markets are already contestable; (ii) introduction of pro-competition regulations, which for example reduce the costs of competing for firms that are already in the market, which level the playing field, or which are designed to simulate competitive market outcomes; and (iii) using competition enforcement to tackle anticompetitive behavior by firms, such as cartel agreements that increase prices and reduce output.

## 1.2 How Does the Degree of Competition Affect Poverty, Shared Prosperity, and Inclusive Growth?

This review examines the impact of competition on the welfare of less well-off households in terms of the functions that these households perform in the market—namely as consumers, producers, and employees. This approach has the advantage of being relatively intuitive while also acknowledging the potentially mixed effects that competition can have on households because each function will be affected differently by competition in a specific market. Understanding the links between the degree of competition, poverty, and shared prosperity will in turn assist in understanding how various competition policy tools can be used to achieve these goals by boosting the level of competition.

Analogies can be drawn between this functions-based framework and the channels of impact examined by other strands of the literature on market reforms. For example, the literature linking trade reforms with poverty typically examines policies as having an impact on household welfare and poverty mainly through (i) the price of goods and services and (ii) factor returns. Other studies adopt a related asset-based framework under which the main drivers of income growth in the long term are the level and distribution of physical, financial, social, and human assets that households own and accumulate, as well as the intensity with which they are used and the returns associated.[5] In this review, the effect of the price of goods and services will be captured largely through the examination of the impact of competition on consumers. The effect of returns to endowments will be captured through the impact on producers and employees that, as in the asset-based framework, depends on the accumulation, intensity of use, and returns to physical, financial, human, and social assets.

The sustained fall in poverty and increases in shared prosperity in recent decades have been strongly connected with economic growth. To understand how poverty reduction is driven through the functional framework, it is helpful to identify the key components of historical changes in poverty. Studies that decompose poverty reduction into the effects of growth and distribution[6] show that, in the majority of countries that have been surveyed, economic growth accounts for most of the observed reduction in poverty over the last decade,[7] which reinforces the existing consensus that economic growth is strongly and negatively correlated with changes in poverty.[8] Economic growth was also key for shared prosperity. Over the recent period of 2007–12, most of the variation in bottom 40 percent income growth in 94 countries can be explained by growth in average income for the entire population (rather than in the relative income share of the poorest 40 percent).[9]

When the drivers of poverty reduction are divided into changes in labor income, nonlabor income, and demographics, labor income growth clearly emerges as the most important contributor to poverty reduction. With this alternative decomposition of poverty reduction, it is possible to understand more precisely what is behind increases in welfare beyond simply growth and distribution. In particular, Inchauste et al. (2014) find that, of 21 developing countries studied, labor income growth accounts for more than half of poverty reduction in 12 countries, and in another 6 countries it accounted for more than 40 percent of the reduction in poverty. In this context, labor incomes are driven by the level of employment in salaried jobs or activity as small producers and entrepreneurs, as well as the real returns from those labor activities. In fact, in most cases, it was the growth in real returns to labor that contributed the most to poverty reduction, rather than an increase in employment.

Given these trends it becomes clear that the degree of competition in markets has an important and multifaceted impact on poverty reduction and shared prosperity. First, competition has both a direct and dynamic impact on the variables that form labor income through households' market functions. These are (i) income to producers (as the owners of production factors such as capital and land); (ii) income to employees (as the providers of labor); and (iii) prices faced by consumers. Incomes are impacted through both the number of adults employed in salaried jobs or engaged in other productive activities and the returns to those activities, whereas consumer prices affect the real value of those incomes in terms of consumption possibilities. Second, drawing on the growth-distribution decomposition and linked to the dynamic effects of competition, effective market competition is widely acknowledged to spur economic growth by increasing industry- and firm-level productivity, leading to rises in gross domestic product (GDP) and expansions in jobs and labor productivity. Figure 1.1 outlines the drivers of poverty reduction and increasing shared prosperity.

**FIGURE 1.1  Key Drivers of Poverty Reduction, and How They Relate to Competition**

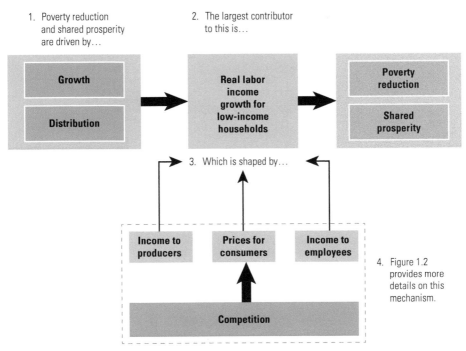

*Source:* World Bank Group, Competition Policy Team.

Figure 1.2 depicts in more detail the mechanisms through which competition affects the variables that drive poverty reduction and shared prosperity, and how they relate to each other. For ease of explanation, in figure 1.2 these mechanisms have been divided into:

1. Mechanisms that can have a more *direct impact on the level and distribution of household welfare*—namely the incomes of producers and employees and the prices, quality, and variety of goods and services available to consumers— by removing inefficiencies in those markets that are particularly relevant to the poor. These mechanisms are more relevant and more frequently observed in markets where poorer citizens produce, work, and purchase. These latter direct mechanisms are directly affected by the degree of competition in the short term but can also be impacted by dynamic effects in the longer term.

2. Mechanisms that primarily *boost growth dynamically in the longer term*— notably increases in firm productivity through the entry, growth, and expansion of more productive firms, as well as by incentivizing firms

FIGURE 1.2
**Mechanisms through Which Competition Affects Poverty Reduction and Shared Prosperity**

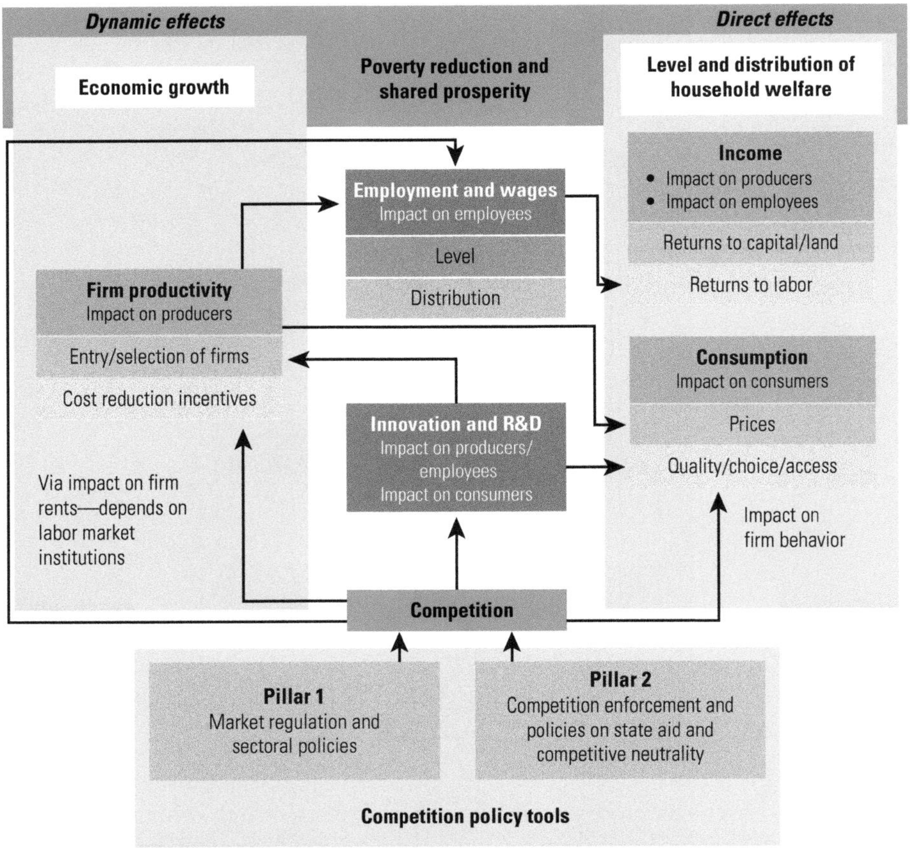

*Source:* World Bank Group, Competition Policy Team.
*Note:* R&D = research and development.

to reduce costs. The link between competition and innovation also has a bearing on long-term productivity through process innovation, for example.

Longer-term shifts in productivity and growth in turn affect market outcomes that have a direct effect on the level and distribution of household welfare:

- Productivity changes affect the level and distribution of jobs and wages.
- Productivity increases lead to more competitive prices if markets are sufficiently competitive for firms to pass on productivity increases to consumers.
- Product innovation has a direct impact on welfare by increasing the variety, quality, and availability of products for consumers.

## 1.3 In Which Sectors Can Safeguarding Competition Maximize Benefits for the Poor?

Competition policy can be most effective in reducing poverty and increasing shared prosperity by boosting competition in sectors that are most relevant for less well-off households. In terms of direct effects, perhaps the clearest way of contributing to these goals is to boost competition in sectors that make up a relatively high proportion of the consumption basket of less well-off households. Where these sectors are relatively more important for the consumption basket of the less well-off compared to richer households, such interventions also have a positive distributional effect. These sectors will form the focus sectors for this review.

Food products and nonalcoholic beverages are by far the most important category of consumption for the poorest households. This is a common trend across 13 countries in Latin America and Africa for which household consumption data were available.[10] In 10 of the 13 countries, food and nonalcoholic beverages made up 40 percent or more of the consumption basket of the lowest income decile. Figure 1.3 summarizes the average proportion of the consumption basket made up by different product categories across the 13 countries. Food and nonalcoholic beverages is also the category that has the greatest relative importance for the least well-off compared to the highest income deciles, suggesting that this is where competition policy interventions would have the most progressive impact. In addition, the elasticity of demand for staple

**FIGURE 1.3  Average Proportion of Different Products in Consumption Baskets across 13 Countries**

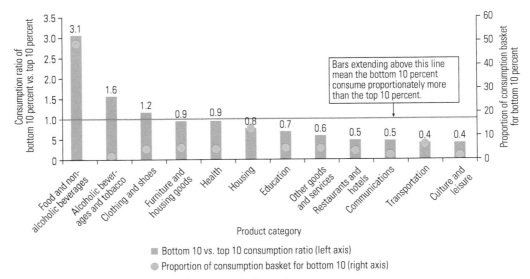

*Source:* World Bank Group elaboration on household survey data for 13 countries.

*Note:* The consumption basket is made up of the product categories across the bottom axis. The 13 countries are Brazil, Chile, Colombia, Ecuador, El Salvador, Guatemala, Kenya, Mexico, Nicaragua, Panama, Peru, South Africa, and Zambia.

foods tends to be low for all income groups but particularly for the lowest income groups,[11] which exacerbates the regressive nature of the welfare costs from high prices. Housing and transportation are also important consumption categories for poor households, although any competition policies that impact prices, quality, or variety for all income groups equally in absolute terms (for example, through a linear change in prices) would be less progressive than with food and beverages because the more well-off generally consume relatively more of these items than the poor.[12] Figures 1.4 and 1.5 contrast the proportion of the consumption basket made up by food and transportation, respectively, over income deciles for the 13 countries.

Services such as transport and telecommunications play an important dynamic role in boosting shared prosperity despite making up a lower proportion of the consumption basket of poorer households and affecting the poor relatively less than the rich in terms of their direct effects. Transport, energy, and telecommunications represent key inputs for producers and entrepreneurs. In addition to the direct effect on consumers, more competitive markets for these input services should directly reduce input costs for small producers and boost producer returns, as well as leading to spillover effects across the economy by boosting overall productivity and growth that dynamically benefit the poor (competition in agricultural input markets is similarly crucial, particularly

**FIGURE 1.4** **Proportion of Consumption Consisting of Food and Nonalcoholic Beverages, by Income Decile**

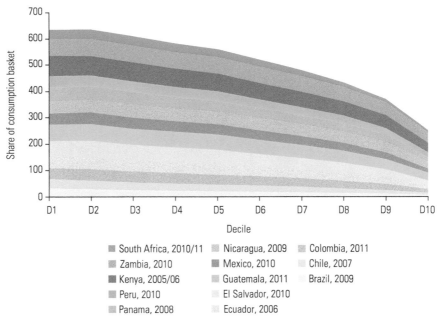

*Source:* World Bank Group computations from various issues of household surveys.
*Note:* D1 is the lowest income decile; D10 is the highest.

A Step Ahead

FIGURE 1.5 **Proportion of Consumption Consisting of Transportation, by Income Decile**

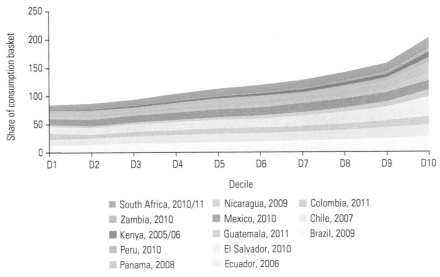

Source: World Bank Group computations from various issues of household surveys.
Note: D1 is the lowest income decile; D10 is the highest.

in agricultural economies and will also be touched upon in this review). Furthermore, better access by poorer households to these services also improves access to information and access to a wider set of markets, which can promote competition in other sectors. Better-informed and more mobile consumers are more able to switch between suppliers, which can allay the market power of the supplier. Thus, lack of access can contribute to inequality and perpetuate poverty across generations.

Introducing a more pro-competition stance in transport, telecommunications, and, to a lesser extent, energy has been on the agenda of many countries in recent decades. However, empirical research on the impact on the poor of competition reforms in these sectors remains very shallow, especially for developing countries. In the transport sectors, substantial easing of economic regulation occurred in a number of transport sectors in OECD countries from the late 1970s and 1980s, opening up the market to a greater number of private players and increasing the ability of those players to compete. A review of evidence on the effects of pro-competition reforms in the air transport sector will be provided here, given that competition in that sector can have direct relevance for the bottom 40 percent, particularly in middle-income countries. It is also an important input for the economy, and has a bearing on the productivity of downstream firms that use air transport as an input, as well as on the growth of a country's tourism sector—an important employment-generating sector. While bus transport has particular relevance for low-income consumers, the nature of the market failures in the sector means that the optimal balance between regulatory intervention and competition is more complex (Estache and Gómez-Lobo 2003; Berechman 1993), and evidence on the impact of opening up the sector to competition tends to be focused on efficiency effects rather than on the effects on consumer welfare. It will therefore not be explicitly covered in this review but is acknowledged as an area for future research. The review will, however, touch upon existing evidence in the telecommunications sector and the energy sector, particularly for those market segments where competition is viable or where economic regulation that simulates the results of competition is implemented.

Other sectors that have a dynamic effect on improving producer and employee incomes include social sectors such as education and health as well as the financial sector. Social sectors are key for building human capital, and the financial sector can increase access to inputs, boost entrepreneurship, and help the less well-off better manage risks. Like bus transport, however, in social sectors the relationship between competition and desired outcomes is complex given that they display significant market failures, arising from information asymmetries and positive externalities associated with these services. This calls for a more nuanced approach to competition in these sectors, and increases the role of ex ante regulation. However, there is some evidence that interventions that increase information available to the consumer and thus enhance competition between providers can help to improve the quality of services delivered. And, in the case of health care, increasing the availability of low-priced generic pharmaceuticals has also been shown to be of particular benefit to price-sensitive consumers—such as those not covered by health insurance plans (Frank and Salkever 1992, 1997). This is particularly pertinent in developing countries, where health insurance coverage is rarer. Creating a competitive public procurement system is also relevant for these sectors; the government acts as a proxy consumer for these goods and can set the rules for tender processes in order to ensure it faces a competitive market and extracts more value for public funds. (Box 2.3 in chapter 2 discusses this further.) The banking sector also has a relatively complex relationship with competition (due to issues around information asymmetries and the nonlinear relationship between bank competition and stability of the financial system). The relevance of competition for these sectors will not be a focus of this review but is nonetheless deserving of further research.

Sectors that are key for the poor tend also to be more susceptible to competition issues. The focal sectors for this review—food, agricultural inputs, telecommunications, and transport—are relevant for this topic not only because they are key for the less well-off but also because they are sectors where a lack of competition appears to be relatively more likely and where competition policy has a key role to play. Sectors like telecommunications and transport that are characterized by natural monopolies and network effects (in some certain market segments) are susceptible to generating dominant players who are then able to abuse their dominance, for example by failing to supply access to essential facilities on a fair and nondiscriminatory basis (see box 2.5 in chapter 2), thus restricting entry opportunities for smaller operators and increasing prices and limiting choice for consumers. Such services are also where a comprehensive competition policy, encompassing strong ex ante regulation (pillar 1) and ex post competition enforcement (pillar 2), are required.

Meanwhile, goods and services that are important for the poor appear to be particularly susceptible to collusive behavior by firms. Figure 1.6 outlines the key factors that facilitate cartel formation and longevity by providing an environment conducive for firms to select a collusive strategy, coordinate behavior, and punish deviations from the strategy. Many of these characteristics are common across goods and services consumed by the poor or used as inputs by small producers—including product homogeneity, regular and frequent transactions, and cost symmetry among firms—by virtue of the fact that the poor tend to consume basic daily necessities that have less scope for product differentiation. In fact, in some cases it may be that it is precisely because the poor are more engaged in these sectors that suppliers may be in a better position to exercise their market power through collusion. Poorer households, for example, are more likely to have more inelastic demand and

**FIGURE 1.6 Factors That Facilitate Cartels, and How They Relate to This Review's Focal Sectors**

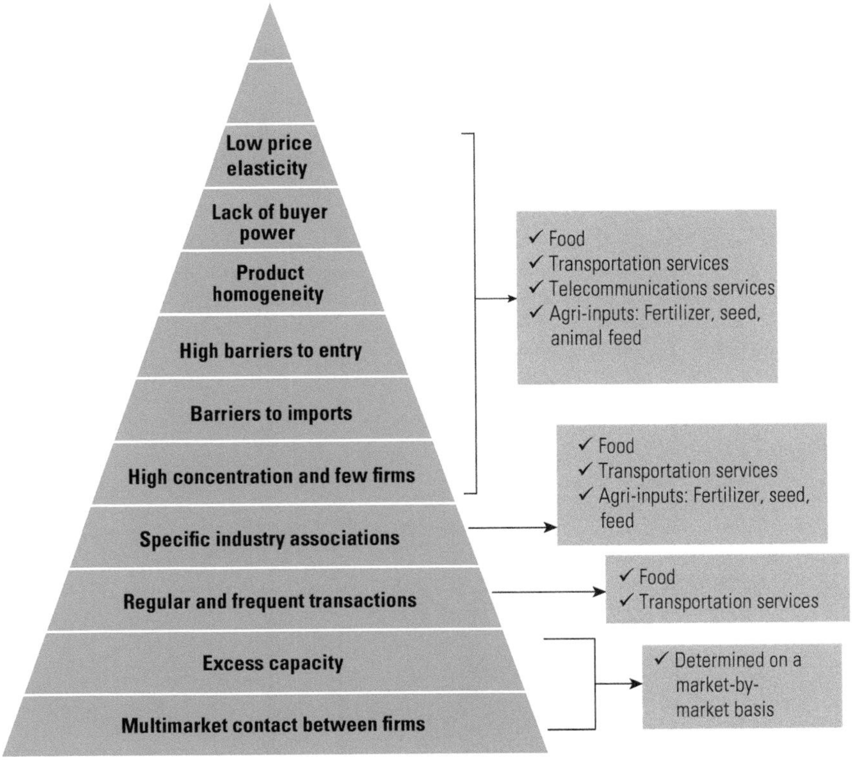
Low price elasticity
Lack of buyer power
Product homogeneity
High barriers to entry
Barriers to imports
High concentration and few firms
Specific industry associations
Regular and frequent transactions
Excess capacity
Multimarket contact between firms
✓ Food
✓ Transportation services
✓ Telecommunications services
✓ Agri-inputs: Fertilizer, seed, animal feed
✓ Food
✓ Transportation services
✓ Agri-inputs: Fertilizer, seed, feed
✓ Food
✓ Transportation services
✓ Determined on a market-by-market basis

*Sources:* Motta 2004; World Bank Markets and Competition Policy Assessment Tool 2016.

to lack buyer power. Moreover, a legacy of anticompetitive regulations and current import barriers are most likely to be present in sectors like agriculture where they are justified as protection for low-income producers.

Existing evidence from low- to middle-income countries suggests that cartels in the focal sectors of this review are relatively common—particularly in transport and food. A World Bank Group Competition Policy Team[13] database of 227 cartels that have been detected and sanctioned in the Latin American region between 1995 and 2015 shows that the food/beverages and transport/logistics sectors have registered the highest number of cartels, with 39 and 48 cartels, respectively (figure 1.7). Meanwhile, a further World Bank Group database of cartels that have been sanctioned in South Africa shows that, of the 76 cartels sanctioned in the last decade (excluding the construction sector), 12 were in food sectors, 11 were in transportation, five were in agricultural inputs, and seven cartels were in the health care sector (World Bank 2016). And these results only account for the proportion of cartels that have been detected by competition authorities—a proportion that has been estimated at a maximum of 24 percent in developing countries according to recent research (see chapter 3).

Governments in developing countries could prioritize competition policy efforts in sectors that are most effective in reducing poverty and increasing shared prosperity. Particularly when resources are limited, this could be a good approach for governments to maximize the impact of competition policy. For young competition authorities, this approach can also help to build support for their enforcement and advocacy efforts.

FIGURE 1.7 **Product and Service Groups in Which Latin American Competition Authorities Sanctioned Cartels, 1995–2015**

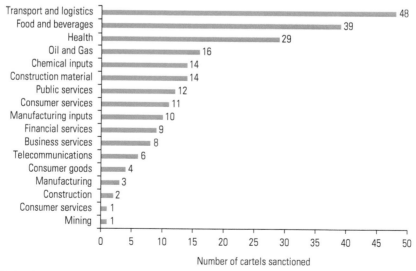

Source: Martinez Licetti and Goodwin, forthcoming.

A Step Ahead

This review aims to increase the understanding of the costs of competition in terms of the welfare of low-income groups, the tools that can increase competition, and the sectors in which this can be most valuable. The findings can inform policy decisions and enable governments to use the power of competitive rivalry between firms to achieve their development goals more effectively. Furthermore, it is hoped that acknowledging the current status of research in this area, particularly for emerging and developing economies, will help encourage additional research to cover current gaps.[14]

## Notes

1. The rate of extreme poverty is the share of the population whose income is below the international poverty line, which the World Bank Group currently defines as being $1.90 a day.

2. Both the World Bank Group and the Organisation for Economic Co-operation and Development (OECD) share a common vision in this area. The World Bank Group has set two goals to be achieved by 2030: end extreme poverty and promote shared prosperity. For the OECD, promoting an inclusive growth agenda to help tackle unemployment and ensure that the benefits of growth are shared equally is a top strategic objective.

3. For more details on competition advocacy, see ICN 2009.

4. Pro-competition regulations are those that are designed to achieve public policy objectives while minimizing the extent to which the regulations hinder competition, or those that are set with the explicit objective of increasing entry or the degree of rivalry in a market. See the glossary at the end of this report for further details.

5. An asset-based conceptual framework has been extensively used in studies that have analyzed the determinants of progress of poverty reduction and shared prosperity around the world (for these issues, see, for instance, Attanasio and Székely 1999; Carter and Barrett 2006). Recent policy applications that briefly discuss the interactions between competition policy and welfare within this framework include Bussolo and López-Calva 2014, and López-Calva and Rodríguez-Castelán 2016.

6. See, for example, Inchauste et al. 2014.

7. See Inchauste et al. 2014. They use the Datt-Ravallion decomposition method to split the change in poverty into distribution-neutral growth and redistribution effect. Their analysis shows that economic growth accounts for most of the reduction in moderate poverty in 17 of the 21 countries that have presented substantial declines in poverty over the 1996–2010 period. Redistribution, which can be interpreted as a proxy of inequality reduction, was found to be more important in four countries. Specific decomposition for Latin America and the Caribbean suggests that growth accounts for 8.7 percentage points out of the 13.6 percentage point reduction in poverty rate between 2003 and 2013 (see LAC Equity Lab as of June 3, 2015). In the Eastern Europe and Central Asia region the contribution from growth to poverty reduction was predominant. For instance, in Belarus, Georgia, Poland, and Serbia, growth accounted, respectively, for 84.9, 78.8, 77.5, and 70.1 percent of poverty reduction (source: ECATSD calculations using ECAPOV and EUSILC data as of March 3, 2016).

8. For a survey in this area see Ferreira 2010. See also Chen and Ravallion 2007.

9. Shared prosperity, or growth in average incomes of the bottom 40 percent, consists of growth in average incomes of the entire population plus growth in the income share of the poorest 40 percent. Therefore, variation of growth in average incomes of the bottom 40 percent across countries and over time can be decomposed into the variation due to growth in average incomes of the entire population, and the variation due to growth in the income share of the bottom 40 percent.

10. The countries are Brazil, Chile, Colombia, Ecuador, El Salvador, Guatemala, Kenya, Mexico, Nicaragua, Panama, Peru, South Africa, and Zambia.

11. See, for example, Dubihlela and Sekhampu 2014.
12. For transport this is the case for all countries.
13. Martha Martinez Licetti, Global Lead for Competition Policy and Lead Economist; Tanja Goodwin, Economist; and Sara Nyman, Economist.
14. While this chapter focuses on developing country evidence to the extent possible, much of the existing literature relates to developed countries. It is important to note that results from developed countries may not be directly transferable to developing countries, given the differences in the level of market development, as well as the degree of market and institutional failures that are more common in developing economies. The presence of these market and institutional failures is likely to mean the effect of competition policy may not be realized to its full potential. Therefore parallel reforms—for example, in the spheres of transport infrastructure, investment in skills, and development of land, financial, and insurance markets—can help to enhance the impact of competition reforms.

## Bibliography

Attanasio, O. P., and M. Székely. 1999. "An Asset-Based Approach to the Analysis of Poverty in Latin America." Research Department Publications 3075, Inter-American Development Bank, Washington, DC.

Begazo, T., and S. Nyman. 2016. "Competition and Poverty: How Competition Affects the Distribution of Welfare." Viewpoint: Public Policy for the Private Sector Note 350, World Bank, Washington, DC, April.

Berechman, J. 1993. *Public Transit Economics and Deregulation Policy*. Amsterdam: North Holland.

Bussolo, M., and L. F. López-Calva. 2014. *Shared Prosperity: Paving the Way in Europe and Central Asia*. Washington, DC: World Bank.

Carter, M. R., and C. B. Barrett. 2006. "The Economics of Poverty Traps and Persistent Poverty: An Asset-Based Approach." *Journal of Development Studies* 42 (2): 178–99.

Chen, Shaohua, and Martin Ravallion. 2007. "Absolute Poverty Measures for the Developing World, 1981–2004." Proceedings of the National Academy of Sciences of the United States of America 104 (43): 16757–62.

Dubihlela, Dorah, and Tshediso J. Sekhampu. 2014. "The Impact of Price Changes on Demand among Poor Households in a South African Township." *International Business and Economics Research Journal* 13 (3): 463–74.

Estache, Antonio, and Andrés Gómez-Lobo. 2003. "The Limits to Competition in Urban Bus Services in Developing Countries." Working Paper wp205, University of Chile, Department of Economics.

Ferreira, Francisco. 2010. "Distributions in Motion: Economic Growth, Inequality, and Poverty Dynamics." Policy Research Working Paper 5424, World Bank, Washington, DC.

Frank, R. G., and D. S. Salkever. 1992. "Pricing Patent Loss and the Market for Pharmaceuticals." *Southern Economic Journal* 59 (2): 165.

———. 1997. "Generic Entry and the Pricing of Pharmaceuticals." *Journal of Economics and Management Strategy* 6 (1): 75–90.

ICN (International Competition Network). 2009. "Report on Assessment of ICN Members' Requirements and Recommendations on Further ICN Work on Competition Advocacy." Presented at the 8th Annual Conference of the ICN, Zurich, June.

Inchauste, Gabriela, João Pedro Azevedo, B. Essama-Nssah, Sergio Olivieri, Trang Van Nguyen, Jaime Saavedra-Chanduvi, and Hernan Winkler. 2014. *Understanding Changes in Poverty*. Directions in Development Series. Washington, DC: World Bank.

Kitzmuller, M., and M. Martinez Licetti. 2012. "Competition Policy: Encouraging Thriving Markets for Development." Viewpoint: Public Policy for the Private Sector Note 331, World Bank, Washington, DC, August.

López-Calva, Luis Felipe, and Carlos Rodríguez-Castelán. 2016. "Pro-growth Equity: A Policy Framework for the Twin Goals." Policy Research Working Paper 7897, World Bank, Washington, DC.

Martinez Licetti, M., and T. Goodwin. Forthcoming. "International Cartel Database: Cartel Trends, Networks, and Impacts in Latin America." World Bank, Washington, DC.

Motta, Massimo. 2004. *Competition Policy*. Cambridge, U.K.: Cambridge University Press.

World Bank. 2013. "Shared Prosperity Links to Growth, Inequality, and Inequality of Opportunity." Policy Research Working Paper 6649, World Bank, Washington, DC.

———. 2016. *South Africa Economic Update: Promoting Faster Growth and Poverty Alleviation through Competition*. South Africa Economic Update, issue no. 8. Washington, DC: World Bank Group.

World Bank and African Competition Forum. 2016. *Breaking Down Barriers: Unlocking Africa's Potential through Vigorous Competition Policy*. Washington, DC: World Bank Group.

World Bank Group. 2016. *Global Monitoring Report 2015/2016: Development Goals in an Era of Demographic Change*. Washington, DC: World Bank.

# 2. Effects of Market Competition and Competition Policies

## 2.1 Direct Welfare Effects on the Level and Distribution of Household Welfare

The effects of the level of competition on the welfare of low-income households—and the benefits of employing competition policy—are examined here in terms of the functions that these households perform in the market: namely as consumers, producers, and employees. Because a lack of competition in a specific market affects these functions differently, competition can have mixed effects on household welfare. It is acknowledged that there may be some trade-off in the short term between the benefits of lower prices for consumers and the returns to producers or employees, where less productive firms and their employees may lose out. Although in the long term the dynamic effects of competition should benefit all functions, as resources tend to shift to more productive firms and higher growth industries leading to economywide gains, there are likely to be short-term costs involved in this adjustment that are worth considering in any transition. This holds regardless of whether the impact is from foreign or domestic competition. These costs can be a real concern for developing economies and raise the importance of cost-mitigating policies during the adjustment phase.

### 2.1.1 The Costs of Market Power and the Benefits of Competition and Competition Policy for Consumers

A lack of competition in essential goods and services markets makes those products more costly, or even unaffordable, and potentially contributes to an increase in poverty. Stern and Dixit (1982) were among the first to develop theoretical models of oligopoly that allow for empirical evaluation of welfare losses arising from the exercise of market power by firms. Since then, a general finding in the literature is that lower competition (or higher market power) is associated with higher prices, lower quality, and limited product variety, and that policies that encourage market entry and competition ultimately benefit consumers, for instance through lower prices.[1] Since poorer consumers spend a greater share of their income than do wealthier consumers on basic provisions such as food staples (see figure 1.4 in chapter 1), it is intuitively appealing to look toward competition policy as an agent to deliver better deals for consumers in these staple markets to contribute to poverty reduction. This section presents studies on the absolute and distributional effects of a lack of competition on low-income consumers, with a particular focus on the effect of competition in food and retail markets that are essential for low-income households.

Exercise of market power in food processing markets is costly for households. Through simulations of the U.S. food industry, Sexton and Zhang (2006) show that modest exercise of oligopoly market power at successive stages of the marketing chain in conjunction with processor oligopsony power reduces consumer surplus by 46 percent relative to the competitive outcome.[2] If the oligopoly power rises to the level of a Cournot duopoly, consumer surplus is reduced by 75 percent. The magnitude of deadweight losses (that is, excluding surplus transferred from consumers to firms) under modest exercise of successive oligopoly power is 7 percent. For modest exercise of successive oligopsony power the deadweight loss is 5 percent. Peterson and Connor (1995), examining the impact of the theoretical developments of the 1980s, found that estimates of average consumer overcharges due to market power in U.S. food industries varied between 6.0 percent and 815.9 percent, and estimates for deadweight welfare loss varied between 0.11 percent and 289.1 percent, depending on the empirical approach being taken.[3]

The consumer impact of market power in services sectors such as telecommunications and energy has also been studied for some countries. Stryszowska (2012) calculates the loss in consumer surplus caused by the low degree of competition in the Mexican telecommunications sector through a cross-sectional study. The consumer harm in Mexico is estimated at an average of US$25.8 billion per year over the period 2005–09, equivalent to 1.8 percent of Mexican gross domestic product (GDP) per year. The estimated loss in consumer surplus consists of two components: loss in consumer surplus caused by overcharging existing consumers (52 percent of total loss in consumer surplus) and loss in consumer surplus caused by a lower number of subscriptions than would have been in place in the absence of market power (48 percent of total loss). One of the few studies conducted on energy market competition for developing countries, using panel data for 51 developing countries over the period from 1985 to 2000, found that competition raises economic performance in electricity generation (more so than privatization) and that competition lowers industrial prices; however, it did not find evidence for an effect on residential prices (Zhang, Parker, and Kirkpatrick 2008).

In retail energy markets, even in a situation in which competition is possible, customer stickiness is a well-known hindrance to competitive market outcomes and can be more prevalent among the poorest deciles. In the United Kingdom a Retail Market Review by the sector regulator estimated that about 40–60 percent of energy customers are "sticky" and that low-income customers are likely to be disproportionately represented in this group (OFGEM 2011). This may partially explain why firms charge about 10 percent more in the area where they are the former incumbent (OFGEM 2008).

## Poorer Households Often Bear the Burden of Uncompetitive Markets

Households with lower income suffer relatively larger welfare losses from monopoly and imperfect competition in staple goods markets than do wealthier households. As we saw in chapter 1, this regressive distributional effect stems from the varying composition of the consumption basket across the income spectrum. This is highlighted by a handful of studies that have emphasized the distribution of welfare loss rather than the absolute amount of loss (Creedy and Dixon 1998, 2000; Urzúa 2013; Argent and Begazo 2015; World Bank 2016).

There is evidence of this distributional impact from both developing and developed economies, such as for Mexico, Australia, and New Zealand. For example, in the case of Mexico, Urzúa (2013) examines the distributional and regional effects of the existence of high market power for seven markets—consisting of food, beverages, and medicines—relative to a situation where markets are perfectly competitive.[4] While all income groups lose out as consumers from the existence of high market power, for the lowest income decile the associated net consumer welfare loss is 20 percent higher than that for the highest income deciles. For the rural sector, the welfare loss for the lowest income decile is 23 percent higher than that of the highest income decile and 26 percent higher than the second highest decile. The poor therefore suffer disproportionately from a lack of competition (box 2.1). In Australia, Creedy and Dixon (1998) estimated the relative burden of monopoly for different household income levels for 14 commodity groups (including food, beverages, and housing costs) and found that the welfare loss associated with monopoly power is higher for low-income households compared with high-income households. The loss is 46 percent higher for the lowest decile compared to the highest. Creedy and Dixon (2000) make a similar finding for New Zealand.

Other studies have examined the distributional effects of market power more generally, particularly with reference to the division of returns to labor and capital. A frequent theme of these studies is that the final distributional outcome depends on the initial position of market players. Comanor and Smiley (1975) find that the exercise of market power can have major impacts on the degree of inequality in the distribution of household wealth. They estimate that up to one-half of wealth holdings by the richest 2.4 percent of American households were due entirely to capitalized monopoly gains. Rognlie (2015) suggests that increases in inequality due to increases in the income share of capital relative to labor results from a residual increase in profits, which reflects increases in markups and market power. Ennis and Kim (in chapter 5 of this report) build on Comanor and Smiley's methodology to show that, for eight Organisation for Economic Co-operation and Development (OECD) countries, market power may account for a substantial amount of wealth inequality, with market power accounting for between 10 and 24 percent of the wealth of the top income decile. On the basis that the degree of market power determines the distribution of income between workers and owners of capital, Dutt (1984) shows that economic growth and income

## Mexico: Poor and Rural Households Are Disproportionately Affected by Monopolies

Using data from Mexico's National Survey of Income and Expenditure of Households, a study sponsored by the Organisation for Economic Co-operation and Development (OECD) examined the impact of market power on levels of household spending on staple products like tortillas, chicken, and milk. The data showed that the harm caused by monopoly power is greatest among the poorest 10 percent of households. In urban areas, those households suffer a relative welfare loss that is nearly 20 percent higher than that suffered by the wealthiest 10 percent of households owing to the larger share of staples in the consumption basket of poorer households. This discrepancy is even more pronounced in rural areas and in poorer regions. The southern states—many of which are among the poorest in Mexico—are hit the hardest (map B2.1.1).

**MAP B2.1.1    Relative Welfare Losses Resulting from Uncompetitive Market Structures, by State**

Welfare loss relative to the state with the lowest welfare loss (Baja California)

High (> 2.5)
Medium
Low (< 2.0)

*Source:* Urzúa 2013.

distribution may not be conflicting goals, and that policies that reduce market power can have positive effects on both growth and income distribution.[5] More recently, Assous and Dutt (2013) examine the interaction between monopoly power, economic growth, and income distribution and find that the dynamics of income distribution between wages and profits depend on changes in power relations in both the labor and goods markets. Rodríguez-Castelán (2011), meanwhile, examines the theoretical link between product market concentration and poverty. He finds conditions for which higher market concentration could either lower or raise the poverty index, though the conditions for higher market concentration leading to higher levels of poverty are more realistic.[6]

## Cartels Are Costly and Harmful for Consumers

Various surveys have sought to estimate the average increase in costs to buyers caused by a sellers' cartel; the mean overcharge varies between 16 and 49 percent. These studies compare the actual price set by the cartel to an estimate of the competitive price or the price that would have prevailed in the absence of the cartel. Such price-fixing overcharges can be seen as a transfer of income or wealth from buyers to the members of the cartel. Box 2.2 provides an overview of the methodologies often used to calculate overcharges. Table 2.1 summarizes the findings of recent economic surveys of cartel overcharges, while figure 2.1 shows the regional distribution of cartel episodes and overcharges according to 485 legal decisions by competition authorities as provided in Connor (2014).

Additional observations also emerge regarding the differences between the effects of international cartels, bid rigging, and food cartels, and the magnitude of the effects depending on the prevalent legal framework. Bolotova (2009) finds that international cartels impose higher overcharges than domestic cartels. Boyer and Kotchoni (2014) find that the antitrust law regime has no impact on the overcharge. Bolotova, Connor, and Miller (2009) find that the average overcharge imposed by food industry cartels is about 8 percentage points lower than cartels in the overall sample. Connor (2014) finds that bid-rigging conduct displays 25 percent lower markups than price-fixing cartels.

---

### BOX 2.2

### Calculating Overcharges from Anticompetitive Behavior

Overcharges are a measure of the damages caused to customers—either consumers or downstream firms—by anticompetitive conduct by firms (usually for cartel conduct). Methodologically, the key issue to be faced in order to properly measure overcharges is to identify the proper counterfactual or "but-for" scenario, that is, what would have happened to the variable of interest (typically price) had the anticompetitive activity not taken place. The counterfactual sets a baseline against which the actual effects of the anticompetitive conduct can be measured. There are several possible methods that make different assumptions about the counterfactual. Komninos et al. (2009) describe 15 different techniques to calculate overcharges. Broadly these methods can be divided into three groups: comparator-based, financial analysis–based, and market structure–based.

The most commonly used and credible are comparator-based approaches. These use data from sources that are external to the infringement to estimate the counterfactual. This can be done through (i) cross-sectional comparisons (comparing different geographic or product markets); (ii) time-series comparisons (analyzing prices before and after an infringement); or (iii) a combination of the two in "difference-in-differences" models (for example, comparing the change in price for a cartelized market over time to the change in price in a noncartelized market over the same time period).[a] Econometric techniques are usually used to isolate, as far as possible, the impact of the anticompetitive conduct on the price being studied by controlling for influences unrelated to the conduct. However, the results will likely depend on the controls used and various other assumptions—thus estimation should be tested for such sensitivities.

*(Box continues on the following page.)*

### Calculating Overcharges from Anticompetitive Behavior *(continued)*

Financial analysis–based and market structure–based approaches can also be used, but they are typically seen as less reliable. Financial analysis–based approaches use financial information on comparator firms and industries, benchmarks for rates of return, and cost information to estimate the counterfactual. Practical challenges relating to the use and interpretation of accounting data, and to the issue of cost allocation when there are common costs, are the reason that this approach is less popular than the comparator-based approach. Market structure–based approaches—which are based on deriving a theoretical model of firm behavior to assess the counterfactual situation—are rarely used because of the difficulties in identifying models that fit the data convincingly.

There is a need to build stronger methodologies for estimating overcharges, especially in developing countries. Although calculating overcharges is usually not necessary in proving a case given that cartels are treated as per se anticompetitive, estimates of overcharges can be helpful (i) in providing a basis for civil damages, which can help to increase the deterrent effect of competition enforcement, and (ii) for demonstrating impact and value for money of enforcement to support advocacy efforts. In some cases they may also be used to calculate administrative fines. Building suitable methodologies and identifying data requirements for calculating overcharges can thus help improve the effectiveness of competition enforcement.

a. The difference-in-differences technique allows one to control for unexplained factors that are common between the comparator and the data of interest to avoid a shortcoming of cross-sectional and time-series approaches—that is, the assumption that any unexplained difference is due solely to the infringement.

**TABLE 2.1    Summary of Recent Economic Survey Findings of Cartel Overcharges**

| Survey | Mean overcharge (%) | Median overcharge (%) |
| --- | --- | --- |
| Connor and Bolotova (2006)[a] | 29 | 19 |
| Connor and Lande (2008) | 31–49 | 22–25 |
| Boyer and Kotchoni (2014)[b] | 15.76 | 16.43 |
| Connor (2014) | 49 | 23 |

a. Figures given are those under the most conservative evaluation approach.
b. Correct for the fact that overcharge estimates are potentially biased.

This report presents new research on cartels that expands the focus of analysis to a greater range of developing countries. Although developed country cartels are overrepresented in existing research given the greater availability of information, Ivaldi et al. (in chapter 3 of this report) attempt to assess cartel damages to developing country economies using a database of over 200 major cartel episodes in more than 20 developing countries over 1995–2013. The harm, in terms of cartels' excess profits resulting from price overcharges, is up to almost 1 percent of GDP (affected sales reach about 6.4 percent of GDP). Furthermore, Ivaldi et al. estimate the maximal annual probability of uncovering an existing cartel to be about 24 percent; the actual damage appears to be at least 4 times bigger than the detected harm.

FIGURE 2.1 **Distribution of Cartel Episodes and Overcharges Determined by Competition Authorities, by Region**

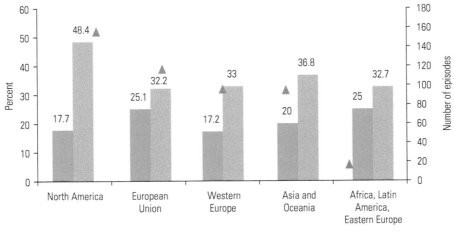

Legend: ■ Median  ■ Mean  ▲ Number of episodes (right axis)

*Source:* Elaboration on data from Connor 2014.

Cartels occur at various levels of the value chain, causing harm to both intermediary customers and end consumers.[7] While direct purchasers of a cartelized product are the immediate losers, if the cartel comprises intermediaries such as manufacturers or distributors, then the loss can be passed on to other buyers farther down the distribution channel, in particular, to the end consumer. For example, in South Africa, Mncube (2013) estimates that collusion between major bread manufacturers, which allowed them to fix the price of flour, bread, and maize meal from 1996 to 2007, led to an overcharge of independent bakeries by 7–42 percent on the price of wheat flour. This harmed not only small independent bakeries through an increase in their costs but also consumers of bread, assuming that some of this cost increase would have been passed through to the final consumer.

When estimating the exact loss to the end consumer from cartel overcharge, two factors need to be considered. First, the cartelized product is often only one component of a finished product; and, second, intermediary buyers will not always pass on 100 percent of the overcharge to their own buyers by raising the price of the product they sell. In fact, depending on demand and supply conditions at each part of the supply chain, the final consumer may end up bearing less than or more than 100 percent of the overcharge. The impact of anticompetitive behavior on small producers is further explored in section 2.1.2.

Cartel behavior can also occur in public procurement markets in the form of bid-rigging cartels. In this case, the harm manifests as a lower ability for governments to deliver public goods and services (box 2.3). This is particularly detrimental to government delivery of social goods and services such as health and education, as well as for other government schemes such as agricultural input subsidy programs.

## Competition in Public Procurement Allows Governments to Deliver Key Goods and Services for Poverty Alleviation

In the case of social sectors and public goods, the government often acts as a consumer of goods and services, making purchases on behalf of its citizens. When competition is suppressed in procurement markets through collusive tendering or bid rigging, the purchasing power of public funds is eroded because of higher costs. Given the size of the public procurement market—often up to 10 to 15 percent of the GDP of developed countries and up to 30 to 40 percent of the economies of least developed countries—these losses have the potential to be particularly substantial and can have significant impacts on the budget available to governments to increase access to essential goods and services.[a,b]

Because responsibility for setting tender rules lies on governments, rules can be set in such a way that ensures that government faces a competitive market and can extract more value for public funds. Clarke and Evenett (2003) showed that the resource savings that could be generated by only a conservative reduction in bid rigging (for example, leading to a price reduction of 15 percent on 1 percent of government contracts in 2000) was greater than the average annual operating budget of the competition agency in a number of countries—including India, Kenya, South Africa, Tanzania, and Zambia—often by a factor of several times over.[c] In South Africa in 2008, four pharmaceutical distributors were found guilty of bid rigging against hospitals from 1998 to 2007. A report of the Competition Commission estimated price effects, from 2001 during a brief noncollusive period, to be 10–15 percent. According to Khumalo, Mashiane, and Roberts (2014), a South African cartel in precast concrete products (pipes, manholes, channels and drains, railway sleepers, poles, toilets, bus shelters, and palisade fencing) that affect government and private tenders rendered an overcharge in the range of 16.5–28 percent in Gauteng, and 51–57 percent in KwaZulu-Natal. In 2005, the Russian Federation's public procurement system was reformed through a new modern public procurement law and laws making bid rigging sanctionable by imprisonment for up to three years.

It is estimated that the reform of the Russian system in the five-year period from 2006 to 2010 has resulted in budgetary savings of more than €26.5 billion. Furthermore, a stark increase in participants per auction was observed. It is reported that, in 2008, the average number of suppliers taking part in open procurement auctions was 26, versus nine participants per auction when the auction form of procurement was implemented.[d]

### Examples of cost-savings in developing countries based on the implementation of more transparent and competitive procurement systems

A 2003 Organisation for Economic Co-operation and Development (OECD) study of the benefits of transparent and competitive procurement processes refers to the following examples of benefits achieved:

- In Bangladesh, a substantial reduction in electricity prices due to the introduction of transparent and competitive procurement procedures
- In Colombia, a saving of 47 percent in the procurement of certain military goods through the improvement of transparency and procurement procedures
- In Guatemala, a 43 percent saving in the cost of purchasing medicines, due to the introduction of more transparent and competitive procurement procedures and the elimination of any tender specifications that favor a particular tender

*(Box continues on the following page.)*

**Competition in Public Procurement Allows Governments to Deliver Key Goods
and Services for Poverty Alleviation *(continued)***

- In Nicaragua, a substantial reduction in the budget for expenditures on pharmaceuticals
  due to the establishment of a transparent procurement agency accompanied by the effective implementation of an essential drugs list
- In Pakistan, a saving of more than Rs 187 million (US$3.1 million) for the Karachi Water
  and Sewerage Board through the introduction of an open and transparent bidding process
- In Japan, a decline in prices across 18 tenders by approximately 20 percent after competitive bidding was restored to the procurement process
- In the United States, a saving of 23.1 percent on prices paid by the U.S. Department of
  Defense from combating bid rigging
- In South Africa, a decline of approximately 27 percent in prices of health care products
  after antitrust intervention.

*Sources:* OECD 2003. See also Anderson 2008 and OECD 2009.

a. Kirton 2013.

b. As well as preventing bid rigging, an inclusive government procurement policy exists where there is a "level playing
field," in which policy and regulations ensure that there is equality of opportunity in the pursuit of contracts to fully reap
the benefits of competitive bidding procedures, to ensure efficiency, and to ensure that foreign firms and small and medium
enterprises are not excluded for competing on the basis of these characteristics.

c. See Clarke and Evenett 2003.

d. From: http://unctad.org/meetings/en/SessionalDocuments/ciclpd14_en.pdf.

There is also deadweight loss associated with cartelization due to the reduction in
output under the cartel. As pointed out by Hüschelrath (2008), overcharges refer to
the income transfer between consumers and firms. However, the deadweight loss to
society that comes from contraction in output that occurs under a cartel would not
be captured by estimates of consumer loss using the overcharge and the observed
level of sales. This deadweight loss includes, for example, the damage to consumers
who do not buy the product in the presence of a cartel but who would have bought it
if there were no cartel. Connor and Helmers (2006) approximate that deadweight
loss may add additional harm of 10 to 30 percent. This loss is equivalent to the deadweight loss that would occur in the presence of monopoly pricing (for example,
Posner 1974).

The observed effects of detected cartels capture only a fraction of the actual harm
that occurs because of anticompetitive behavior. Many violations of the competition
law are never detected, and thus the loss in consumer welfare is often unobserved. For
example, an early study from Bryant and Eckard (1991) suggested that, in a given year,
only about 15 percent of cartels are detected in the United States, whereas Combe,
Monnier, and Legal (2008) confirmed that this figure is about 13 percent for Europe.

This highlights the need for competition authorities to continuously enhance their ability to monitor markets for anticompetitive behavior and to build evidence to successfully sanction cartels, and ultimately to deter anticompetitive behavior. It also underlines the need to ensure that market regulations are not set in a way that facilitates collusion between firms.

### Anticompetitive Regulations and Policies Harm Low-Income Consumers

Focusing solely on the conduct of private firms addresses only part of the problem caused by a lack of competition. State-imposed barriers to competition can also lead to the same effects as cartels or schemes by dominant firms to exclude competitors. In other cases, it is the lack of mechanisms to enable competition in markets that might cause harm, for example a lack of rules or information to allow consumer switching. These regulatory barriers to competition can take several forms. They include (i) rules that reinforce dominance or limit entry; (ii) rules that are conducive to collusive outcomes or increase costs to compete in the market; and (iii) rules that discriminate, distort the level playing field, and protect vested interests.[8]

Such policies and regulatory restrictions can lead to higher prices, less competition in nonprice dimensions like quality and service, and diminished incentives to innovate. They are usually beyond the reach of competition laws, and the government itself enforces the restraint. Below are some examples of the impact on consumers of these obstacles to competition for various sectors where studies are available. This review does not claim to be exhaustive but is intended to give an overview of the type of evidence that is available in key sectors.

Government interventions in food markets, such as the imposition of import tariffs or minimum support prices, are often justified as mechanisms to increase the incomes of agricultural producers, but instead they ultimately harm the poor. This is because these interventions clearly also have the effect of raising food prices for consumers, and most empirical analyses suggest that the poor are often net consumers of food, including of imported goods, rather than net producers (see Christiaensen and Demery 2007; Wodon et al. 2008; and Wodon and Zaman 2010).[9] In fact, it is the largest farmers, rather than smallholder farmers, who stand to gain most from food price increases, which means that the distributional effects of such policies are a particular cause for concern (Barrett and Dorosh 1996).

Restrictions on retail markets can generate losses for consumers of food products. Griffith and Harmgart (2012) evaluate the impact of restrictive planning regulation on entry into the UK grocery retail industry. They find that more restrictive planning regulation reduces the number of large format supermarkets and leads to a loss to consumers of up to £10 million per annum.[10] In Italy, Schivardi and Viviano (2011) find that prices of goods in the food and beverages retail subsector are higher with more stringent government restrictions on the entry of large stores.

## Entry in Retail Markets Boosts Welfare through Prices, Quality, and Variety of Goods

Greater competition through entry in retail markets of food products and other necessities boosts the welfare of low-income households through its effect on prices, quality, and variety of goods, although the progressiveness of the impact depends on the context of the reform. Experimental evidence from a conditional cash transfer program for the poor in the Dominican Republic shows that entry into the retail market led to a significant and robust reduction in prices (about 6 percent) while maintaining quality of the products or services provided by grocery stores (Busso and Galiani 2014). In this case, broadening the number of outlets that were able to participate in conditional cash transfer programs had a positive effect on low-income households. Similarly, entry of foreign supermarkets in Mexico, following the lifting of restrictions on foreign direct investment (FDI), led to significant welfare gains for the average household equal to 6.2 percent of initial household income, with the greatest contributor to this effect being the direct price index effect of foreign supermarkets offering cheaper prices, new varieties, and different shopping amenities to consumers. However, in this case, the richest groups gained about 50 percent more than the poorest because the poor substitute less of their retail consumption to foreign stores (Atkin, Faber, and Gonzalez-Navarro 2015).

In retail markets in the United States, substantial consumer gains from entry have come in the form of quality and variety improvements, as well as from price reductions; and low-income households experienced greater consumer welfare gains from increased competition compared to their higher-income counterparts. Hausman and Leibtag (2007) consider consumer benefits from increased competition in a differentiated product setting. They estimate consumer benefits from entry and expansion of nontraditional retail outlets that compete with traditional retail outlets for food. They find substantial benefits for consumers, in terms of spending on food and nonfood items. The direct welfare gain[11] that arises from the increase in product variety because of the entry and expansion of supercenters is on average 20.2 percent of average food expenditure, whereas the indirect welfare gain from the reduction in prices that arises because of increased competition from supercenters is on average 4.8 percent. Thus, the total average welfare gain is 25 percent of food expenditure. The authors also consider the distribution of these welfare gains. Households with income below US$10,000 benefit by approximately 50 percent more than the average household because lower-income households tend to shop more at the new low-priced outlets. Minorities also gain significantly more than nonminorities.

## Competitive Introduction of New Brands or Products Also Benefits Consumers

A number of studies have highlighted the positive effect on consumer welfare from higher competition via the introduction of new brands or a new product in food and beverages markets. Hausman (1997a) was one of the first to estimate the increase in consumer welfare from the introduction of a new brand of cereal. He finds that the increase in consumer welfare in the case of imperfect competition is only 85 percent as high as in the perfect competition case (Hausman 1997a). Nevo (2001 and 2003) also quantified the positive effects of new brands in the ready-to-eat cereals market. Xiao (2008) finds that the introduction of a new variety of soft drink in the United States led to an increase in consumer welfare, with 89 percent of consumer benefits coming from the increased price competition and 11 percent coming from the new variety effect. Kim (2004) estimated the effects of new brands on incumbents' profits and consumer welfare in the U.S. processed cheese market and found that the observed increase in consumer welfare was attributable mainly to an increase in the number of brands in the sample market.

There is also evidence of the effects of new drug entry (or threat of entry), particularly generics, on consumer welfare and prices (for instance Bokhari and Fournier 2013; Tenn and Wendling 2014). Experimental evidence from Uganda showed that new entry in the market for the supply of antimalarials by a player committed to supplying authentic drugs at a price below those of incumbents led to a 50 percent fall in the amount of fake drugs being sold by incumbents and a 15–20 percent fall in the prices of incumbents. In the United States, the overall annual consumer welfare effect of new entry in the U.S. market for anticholesterol drugs for consumers in the lowest income decile is about 40 percent of the effect for those in the highest income decile in absolute terms (Dunn 2012). However, the annual income of those in the lowest decile is considerably lower than 40 percent of the income of the highest, implying that gains for the lowest decile are proportionally greater than for the highest decile. This is partially driven by the fact that lower-income households tend to be more price sensitive than their higher-income counterparts.

Positive effects of new product entry have been quantified for various other goods and services beyond food and pharmaceuticals. Hausman and Leonard (2002) break the overall competitive benefit to consumers from the introduction of a new brand of bath tissue in the United States into two parts that have roughly equal impact: the effect on the prices of existing products due to increased competition and the effect of additional product variety. Petrin (2002) estimated consumer welfare and producer surplus from the introduction of the minivan into the automobile market in the 1980s and found that overall consumer benefits far outweighed the costs of development and the profits obtained by the innovator. Almost half of consumer benefits came from increased price competition and accrued to non–minivan purchasers. In the U.S. passenger airline industry, Goolsbee and Syverson (2008), using data for 1993–2004, find that incumbents cut fares significantly in response to the threat of the entry of Southwest Airlines, and these lower prices appear to increase the number of passengers that were flying on the incumbents prior to entry. Gebreab (2002) found that the entry of an additional operator increased mobile subscriptions by an average 57 percent across a sample of more than 40 African countries. Other examples of seminal studies that look to quantify the consumer welfare gains from new product introduction include Hausman (1997b) for the U.S. telecommunications sector and Brynjolfsson and Smith (2003) for online books.

## Consumers Gain from the Enforcement of the Competition Law

Enforcing a competition law is one way to alleviate the costs of a lack of competition for consumers. Three key mechanisms through which the enforcement of competition law can help foster gains to consumers are the following: (i) through the detection and removal of cartels; (ii) by deterring firms from engaging in anticompetitive practices; and (iii) by preventing mergers that will significantly affect competition.[12] These are explored further below.

## Dismantling and Deterring Cartels Can Benefit Low-Income Consumers

Effective anticartel enforcement delivers direct benefit to consumers by removing price overcharges. The costs of cartel behavior for consumers also represent the potential benefits to consumers of anticartel enforcement in terms of lower prices. Impact assessments carried out by competition authorities for their enforcement activities have sought to quantify the direct benefits of competition law enforcement resulting from direct changes in prices. The European Commission, for example, has estimated the observable customer benefits from cartel decisions adopted in 2014 to be between US$2.0 billion and US$2.9 billion (European Commission 2015). In the United Kingdom, the competition agency estimated that, from April 2011 to March 2014, it generated direct savings for consumers of an average of £151 million per year as a result of its competition enforcement activities.[13] In the United States, the Federal Trade Commission (FTC) estimated that, for the four years from 2010 to 2013, it has generated US$1.8 billion of consumer savings through its nonmerger actions.[14]

When enforcement is targeted at sectors that are key for low income consumers, it can be particularly beneficial in reducing poverty and boosting shared prosperity. In South Africa, for example, enforcement action to tackle cartels in four cartels in wheat, maize, poultry, and pharmaceuticals led to income gains for the poorest 40 percent that were 3.4 times those for the richest 40 percent (World Bank 2016). Overall poverty stood to fall by 0.4 percentage points by tackling cartels in the wheat, maize, poultry, and pharmaceuticals sectors, under the conservative assumption that this led to a 10 percent decrease in prices across products. Comparing this poverty impact per U.S. dollar spent on the Competition Commission's budget to the poverty impact per South African rand spent on cash transfers reveals that anticartel enforcement is an effective instrument, with potential poverty impact from anticartel enforcement being many times higher, about 38 times in this case. And, because the risk of cartel behavior is often particularly high in sectors that are important for the poorest groups, as we saw in section 1.3 in chapter 1, it is likely that such results would hold in other countries.

The effects of competition enforcement on inequality have recently been a topic of consideration for the antitrust community. Baker and Salop (2015) hypothesize that market power is likely to contribute to inequality by raising the return to capital relative to the rate of economic growth and by discouraging innovation and productivity. They discuss the implications of this on the design of competition policy in terms of both the potential need for more aggressive antitrust enforcement and in terms of the possibility of setting the reduction of inequality as a higher priority for antitrust enforcement and regulatory agencies.

The direct effects of cartels and anticartel enforcement discussed so far do not account for the effects of deterrence. Some have argued that, when assessing the impact on consumer welfare of enforcing competition rules, it is important to account not only for increases in competition as a result of detecting and sanctioning cartels but also the unobserved impact that a credible enforcement regime can have in deterring others from behaving anticompetitively. A recent paper by Davies and Ormosi (2014) estimates that cartel deterrence is at least twice as effective as cartel detection as a means for removing harm, and undetected harm is at least twice as large as detected harm. Under less cautious, but plausible, assumptions, deterred harm is nearly 10 times higher than the harm detected by competition authorities. Clarke and Evenett (2003) provide evidence that a widespread international vitamins cartel increased prices significantly more in countries without an effective cartel enforcement regime, suggesting that the presence of an enforcement regime moderated the harm from the cartel.

### Merger Control Also Prevents Adverse Effects on Consumers

Merger enforcement can benefit consumers by prohibiting anticompetitive mergers. These mergers, if allowed to go ahead unchecked, would result in either an increase in market power (the so-called "unilateral effects") or a market environment that would be more favorable to collusion (the so-called "coordinated effects"). In both cases, lower competition would cause higher prices and less favorable conditions for consumers and/or suppliers.

Merger control and remedies can prevent price increases. In the United Kingdom, an evaluation of the competition agency's conditional clearance of the Shell-Rontec merger—which required the divestment of 12 forecourts—found that this prevented price increases, saving drivers £150,000 in potentially affected areas.[15] Postema, Goppelsroeder, and Bergeijk (2006) measure the costs and benefits of merger control in the Netherlands by using merger simulation tools. The results show that—for four selected markets—a weighted average price increase of about 14 percent would have prevailed in the absence of merger control between 1998 and 2002. Applying this figure to all nine cases in which a merger was prohibited or allowed subject to remedies during that period provides an estimated figure for welfare gains of merger enforcement of roughly €770 million between 1998 and 2002. A retrospective by Kwoka (2013) on U.S. merger control found that, for the sample of mergers that have been permitted, on average, prices increased after the transaction, suggesting a relatively lenient antitrust stance.[16]

By averting potential price increases, merger remedies prevent a transfer of surplus from consumers to firms. In South Africa, the imposition of conditions on the acquisition of the Infant Nutrition Business of Pfizer by Nestlé would have led to a price increase of 1 to 9 percent, depending on the assumptions used, according to a study by Sithebe, Barzeva, and Mncube (2014). Meanwhile, Hüschelrath (2008) examines evidence from the Nuon-Reliant merger case in the Netherlandic electricity market to determine its contribution to consumer welfare. In 2003, Nuon, a Netherlandic energy utility operating in electricity wholesale and retail markets in the Netherlands, sought to acquire the assets of Reliant, one of the major electricity generators in the Netherlands. The Netherlandic competition authority found that a combination of the two firms' generation assets would raise competition concerns and cleared the merger subject to the remedy that Nuon would undertake a series of power plant auctions.[17] It is estimated that, although the deadweight losses from the merger would have been small (between 0.60 and 1.36 percent of the overcharge effect) because of the typically low demand elasticity in electricity markets, in the absence of these remedies the redistribution of surplus from consumers to firms due to the merger would have been between 6 and 12 percent (or between about €280 million and €612 million of postmerger sales).[18]

Competition authorities have also attempted to estimate the direct benefits of their merger control activities on consumers. The European Commission (2015), for example, estimated that its merger control interventions in 2014 delivered consumer savings of at least US$2.2 billion–US$5.7 billion. In the United Kingdom, the competition agency estimates that, from April 2011 to March 2014, it generated direct savings for consumers of £11 million per year as a result of merger control activities.[19] In the United States, the FTC estimates that, for the four years from 2010 to 2013, it generated US$2.2 billion of consumer savings through its merger control actions.[20]

### Embedding Competition Principles in Sectoral Policies Lowers Prices and Increases Access

What follows are some examples of the impact of obstacles to competition on consumers for various sectors where studies are available. This review does not claim to be exhaustive but is intended to give an overview of the type of evidence that is available in key sectors. Box 2.4 meanwhile provides an overview of how trade policy provides a tool for countries to boost competition and increase consumer welfare across sectors, as long as the right competitive conditions are present in domestic markets.

### Food

In the case of Kenya, market reforms in the sugar and maize markets would increase the disposable income of consumers, especially the poorest. For example, Argent and Begazo (2015) use household survey data to estimate welfare effects of price changes for sugar and maize across the income distribution in Kenya, while taking into account the dual role of households as producers and consumers of maize. They find that allowing sugar prices to fall by 20 percent by relaxing trade barriers that shield the domestic sugar industry from competition would lead to welfare gains for all income deciles, leading to a 1.5 percent fall in poverty, with the proportionate gains for the poorest

## Pro-Competition Effects of Trade Reform and Its Interaction with Competition Policy

Opening markets to trade can lower prices for consumers via reductions in the price-cost margin. Treichel et al. (2012) estimate that removing import bans on 24 products in Nigeria that increase prices, and replacing them with tariffs set at the same level as similar products, could lift more than 4 million Nigerians out of poverty. Edmond, Midrigan, and Yi Xu (2011) find that, for the Taiwanese manufacturing sector, by increasing competition, trade reduces markups and so reduces distortions in labor and investment decisions. Not only does this lead to a welfare gain equal to a 25 percent permanent increase in consumption but it also directly raises total factor productivity. For the manufacturing sector in Bulgaria, the Czech Republic, Estonia, Hungary, Poland, the Slovak Republic, and Slovenia, Marinov (2010) finds that the degree of trade liberalization and toughness of competition policy enforcement both have a significantly negative effect on firms' markups, although the magnitude of the effect is greater in the case of competition policy. Hoekman and Javorcik (2004), using a sample of 41 industrial and developing countries, find that the larger a country the less important are tariffs and the more important are domestic entry regulations in determining markups. Badinger (2007) and Boulhol (2010) show that for manufacturing industries in the United States and in Organisation for Economic Co-operation and Development (OECD) countries, respectively, increasing import penetration lowers markups.

Other studies explore how the interaction between domestic competition and the degree of openness to trade across countries affects the gains for trade. In 24 U.S. food processing industries, imports and export intensity lower price-cost margins, and this effect is more likely the lower the degree of domestic competition (Lopez and Lopez 2003). This reflects the findings of McCorriston (2006) that in the presence of imperfect competition, the welfare gains from trade are higher than under perfect competition. On the other hand, Epifani and Gancia (2011) note that, when trade opening has an asymmetric effect on markups across sectors (for example, in traded versus nontraded sectors), the resulting intersectoral misallocations may reduce welfare. Thus, promoting competition, particularly in nontraded sectors, may be a prerequisite to ensuring positive gains from trade.

Several studies have pointed out that market power at immediate stages of the value chain, including in transport services, can hinder the gains from trade from being fully realized. Arkolakis, Costinot, and Rodríguez-Clare (2012) and De Loecker et al. (2016), for example, both examine the interaction between the gains from trade and variable markups. Similarly, concentration in the distribution sector acts as an import barrier by increasing trading costs, thus reducing the benefits of market access for the poor from tariff reductions (Francois and Wooton 2010). The positive effects of reducing transport costs by increasing competition in transport are discussed in this report.

The effects of market power of intermediaries are also found in intranational trade. A recent study suggests that the gains from intranational trade in remote regions of Ethiopia and Nigeria tend to be captured by intermediaries, thus highlighting the importance of the distribution sector in influencing the extent to which the rural poor benefit from trade (Atkin and Donaldson 2014). Anticompetitive behavior in transport and distribution networks, for example, is often identified as one of the reasons behind intranational transport costs being higher than international transport costs in many countries (Kunaka 2011).

income decile being 4.4 times higher than for the highest income decile. Similarly, reducing maize prices in Kenya by 20 percent by limiting government interventions that distort price, such as the price-inflating purchasing activities of the National Cereals and Produce Board, would have approximately the same effect as a real income increase of 1.2 percent on average, with the gains for the poorest income deciles being 7.4 times larger than for the highest income deciles. This would result in a net decline in poverty of 1.8 percent. Also in Kenya, Jayne and Argwings-Kodhek (1997) found that eliminating controls on prices and private trade in maize in Kenya accounted for US$10.1 million of savings a year for consumers in Nairobi.

## Transport

Air transport liberalization has a positive impact on prices, traffic and access, and overall consumer welfare. Maillebiau and Hansen (1995) examine the impacts of liberalization of the international air transport market on demand, fares, accessibility, and consumer welfare in the North Atlantic, based on data for markets between the United States and five European countries.[21] It is found that liberal international airline bilateral agreements—which prohibited either country from restricting airlines of the other country with respect to capacity or fares, allowed each country to designate more than one airline to serve routes to the other, and increased the number of authorized routes and gateways between the two countries—have resulted in fare reductions of approximately 40 percent, while accessibility increased by 55 percent. Combining the estimated impacts of liberalization on yields and accessibility, they estimate that, in the year 1989, passenger traffic between the United States and the five countries studied was 40–60 percent greater as a result of liberalization, and that liberalization produced consumer welfare increases of US$3 billion–US$5 billion, or US$400–US$600 per traveler.

Price reductions in response to regulatory reforms have been estimated also for other countries such as Armenia, Mexico, Pakistan, and several African countries. A 2013 World Bank study found that air connectivity with Armenia was relatively low, whereas prices were relatively high because of the restrictive regulatory environment in which the sector operated. Estimates suggest that reducing concentration on a certain route by half as a result of changes in the enforcement of sector regulation will reduce prices for the economy class segment by between 20 and 28 percent. Assuming a price reduction of 25 percent welfare gains for the consumer could add up to 1.4 percent of GDP.[22] In Pakistan, in 2009 the competition authority determined that a 1972 bilateral agreement between Pakistan and Saudi Arabia had created an unduly severe barrier to competition and recommended opening up the routes to other airlines.[23] After the modification of the bilateral service agreement, the market now includes four competitors offering more choices for passengers in flights, scheduling, and fares. Fares for passengers decreased from 2008 rates, reflecting an aggregate US$60 million in consumer savings in the year 2013 alone. Passengers each saved approximately US$491 (50,000 rupees) off 2007 rates.[24] In Mexico, Ros (2010 and 2011) finds policies adopted to open up the air transport sector since 2000 have significantly benefited consumers. In particular, new concessions awarded to low-cost carriers (LCCs) since 2005 have significantly changed the competitive landscape. Indeed, by 2008, LCCs had already obtained 30 percent of the market. Using data on approximately 500 domestic routes in Mexico, Ros (2011) finds that LCCs' lowest-quoted fares are approximately 25 percent lower than those of incumbent carriers. The presence of LCCs on a route is associated with reductions in the fares of one of the two principal incumbent carriers. Furthermore, a lack of pro-competitive methods to allocate slots at the Mexico City airport has resulted in fares being between 40 and 80 percent higher than comparable routes within Mexico (Ros 2010). Meanwhile, based on the observed effects of liberalizing air services in the Southern African Development Community (SADC) region, the ComMark Trust (2006) analyzed price changes on 56 routes within SADC. Air fares on liberalized routes declined by an average of 18 percent. In cases where an LCC entered the market, airfares were generally 40 percent lower than before liberalization.

In some cases, benefits from regulatory reforms accrue in the form of quality improvements. For instance, by measuring the effects of liberalization in 20 intra-Africa routes to and from Addis Ababa, Abate (2013) concludes that, while there was no evidence of a reduction in fares, the quality improving effect (measured in terms of increased departure frequencies) of liberalization is substantial. Routes that experienced some type of liberalization compared to those governed by restrictive bilateral arrangements experienced an increase in departure frequency of up to 40 percent.

### Telecommunications

Lack of pro-competition regulation in telecommunications increases the prices of services, lowers their quality, and limits access. Gupta (2013) shows that, following deregulation, consumer welfare in the telecommunications market increased by US$96 billion–US$111 billion across OECD countries for the period 1998–2008, partly due to a decline in quality-adjusted prices. Part of this increase results from consumers without a strong willingness to pay beginning to consume existing products and services because of the lower prices. Meanwhile, Lee and Lee (2006) estimate consumer surplus for the Korean mobile telecommunications market and find that the introduction of competition through a facilities-based competition policy was accompanied by a price decrease and an increase in the number of subscribers.[25]

### Energy

Theory suggests that energy market reforms would raise prices for residential consumers relative to industrial consumers, although this has not been borne out in empirical studies. Empirical research is very shallow on the impact on the poor of competition reforms in the energy sector, especially for developing countries, and the theoretical effects of competition in the energy sector are generally complex. However, studies from the United Kingdom and Italy on both gas and electricity markets have found in fact that there is little evidence of a continuing disadvantage for lower-income consumers from competitive reforms (Price 2005; Miniaci, Scarpa, and Valbonesi 2008). These studies evaluate whether deregulation and a more competitive environment lead to higher relative prices for residential (and in particular rural or low-income) consumers versus industrial consumers—as theory would suggest because of their relatively higher costs and the fact that competition undermines the feasibility of cross-subsidization. Using data from electricity industries in 19 OECD countries from 1987 to 1996 to test for the effects of privatization, competition, and regulation, Steiner (2001) provides evidence that market liberalization led to lower prices but that gains were realized disproportionately by industrial consumers.

### Pharmaceuticals

Elimination of antisubstitution laws to enable widespread use of generic drugs resulted in significant savings for consumers. Until the mid-1980s, antisubstitution laws in the United States prohibited pharmacists from dispensing a lower-cost generic drug for a prescription written for a brand-name drug. An extensive investigation conducted by the FTC determined that antisubstitution laws imposed substantial costs on consumers by restricting price competition between large manufacturers producing the same drug. It was reasoned that providing pharmacists with the option of choosing between a brand drug and its generic equivalent would stimulate price competition, without compromising the quality of health care. A study on the economic impact of this reform showed that generic substitution on eligible prescriptions rose after the passage of these laws, and that generic substitution reduced consumer expenditures (Masson and Steiner 1985). Although traditionally prescriptions have predominantly been written using brand names (Steinman, Chren, and Landefeld 2007), by 2012 84 percent of all prescriptions written in the United States were filled with a generic drug, and a generic version of a drug, when available, was dispensed 95 percent of the time (IMS Institute for Healthcare Informatics 2013). Generics substitution laws are estimated to have saved consumers more than US$1 trillion in just 10 years (Engelberg 2014). In India, the potential consumer welfare loss that would have occurred if the patent system for quinolone (an antibiotic) had been more restrictive of competition than it was in practice was estimated at about US$400 million between 1999 and 2000 (Chaudhuri, Goldberg, and Jia 2006).

### Social Sectors

The relationship between competition and consumer welfare in social services is complex, but interventions that increase the information available to consumers may help to improve outcomes. For example, increased information on quality of education by school boosts competition and improves welfare. A study by Andrabi, Das, and Khwaja (2015) highlights both the across-firm and within-firm effects of raising competitive pressure and the subsequent benefits for consumers, by increasing information available to consumers in educational markets in Pakistan on the quality of education. In general, information about product prices and quality allows consumers to make more-informed decisions about their choice of provider. In this case, the authors find that information provision improves consumer welfare by lowering markups and inducing lower-quality schools to improve quality (within-firm effect) or shut down (across-firm effect). There are also certain circumstances where the efficacy of social interventions can be improved by incorporating market-based systems that promote competition between providers. For example, there is evidence that the introduction of market-based competitive voucher schemes into health care subsidy programs can improve efficiency in service delivery through competition while also ensuring better targeting to the poor (Bhatia and Gorter 2007; Gorter et al. 2003; Bellows, Bellows, and Warren 2011). The level of competition fostered by public procurement rules is also relevant for the ability of governments to deliver social goods and services to low-income households. In particular, eliminating bid rigging can increase the purchasing power of public funds (see box 2.3 earlier in this chapter).

### 2.1.2 The Costs of Market Power and the Benefits of Competition and Competition Policy for Small Producers

Two key mechanisms through which small producers can be affected by a lack of competition are through an increase in input costs and the depression of prices that producers receive for their produce. In light of this, the remainder of the section focuses on how input and buyer markets can be made more competitive through competition enforcement or through pro-competitive regulatory reforms. Opportunities for entry and expansion by small producers can also be compromised by anticompetitive behavior and discriminatory treatment of firms under government regulation. Evidence on these two latter effects is currently lacking, although there is some evidence of regulatory reform having an unintentionally differential impact on large versus small producers, which is presented later in this section.

The impact of downstream buyer power on smallholder agricultural producers has been examined by a handful of authors. Porto, Chauvin, and Olarreaga (2011) use a model of supply chains in export crops[26] to simulate the effect of competition in a number of African countries.[27] They find that increases in competition among processors benefit farmers by increasing the farm gate price of the crop and therefore improve their livelihood. For instance, in the case where the firm with the largest market shares splits, there is an average income increase for producing households of 2.8 percent across all case studies.[28] The entry of a small entrant, on the other hand, is found to be unlikely to increase competition sufficient to affect farmers' livelihoods, with the income of households increasing by an average of only a quarter of a percentage point across all cases. Swinnen and Vandeplas (2006), meanwhile, studied a number of agricultural markets and concluded that competition between buyers in the supply chain results in better returns to producers who are able to capture a larger percentage of the export price, and increases their likelihood of being offered inputs and credit as buyers attempt to secure their supplies.

## Anticompetitive Practices Negatively Affect Small Producers

Collusion among buyers can depress prices for small producers. Although it could be argued that lower prices for producers could be passed on to lower prices for end consumers, the presence of buyer power coupled with high market power in selling to customers limits this pass-through to consumers and means that it is instead monopsonistic intermediaries who would benefit from lower prices (see, for example, OECD 2012).[29] Collusion between buyers can be the cause of a reduction in prices received by agricultural producers. Banerji and Meenakshi (2004) find evidence of collusion between three large buyers in wheat auctions in India, and determine that this depressed prices paid to farmers to close to the Minimum Support Price (MSP) paid by government. Without collusion the market price would be 1 to 4 percent more (Rs 5–20 more) than the Rs 550 (US$8.3) per quintal MSP. Mehta, Nayak, and Aggarwal (2012) present a case study of cartelization along the vertical global banana value chain with downward monopsonistic pressure from retailers (in economies such as the United Kingdom) depressing prices for small farmers in banana-producing countries (in Latin America, for example), with supermarkets taking about 40 percent of the final price and farmers about 1–2 percent.

Anticompetitive behavior can have significant negative impacts for low-income agricultural producers when it occurs in agricultural input markets, such as fertilizer, seed, and pesticide. In the fertilizer sector, for example, Jenny (2012) finds that the projected price of potash between 2011 and 2020 under the Canpotex Potash cartel[30] is double what it would be under a competitive scenario. He estimates that 80 to 100 percent of the annual subsidy that would be paid by the Indian government to make fertilizer more affordable to farmers during this period would, in fact, go toward paying cartel profits to potash producers.

Agricultural producers and other small producers are also negatively affected by anticompetitive practices in the transport sector. The breakup of anticompetitive practices in international shipping services, such as rate-fixing practices of maritime conferences, would cause transport prices for goods shipped to the United States from developing countries to decline by 25 percent and lead to cost savings of up to US$2 billion[31] (Fink, Mattoo, and Neagu 2002). Meanwhile, transitioning from a situation where a cartel controls transit freight allocation to an efficient trucking market (which decreases truck turnaround time) would reduce the truck and labor components of transport costs for landlocked economies by over 30 percent. They develop a quantitative model of a transit supply chain model to simulate the impact of changes in freight market organization in landlocked developing countries (Arvis, Raballand, and Marteau 2010).

## Enforcement of Competition Law Can Benefit Small Producers

Anticompetitive behavior often occurs in upstream segments of a value chain—raising costs for small producers. Vilakazi (chapter 4 of this report) adds to the evidence in this area by examining how the structure of fertilizer markets in Malawi, Tanzania, and

Zambia—including vertical integration and integration with import and distribution facilities—may facilitate anticompetitive behavior. In the case of Zambia, where a bid-rigging cartel was found to be operating between the two largest players between 2007 and 2011, ending the cartel and opening up the market to more competition is estimated to have led to annual consumer savings of at least US$21 million, assuming that Zambian fertilizer markups over Tanzanian prices had remained constant rather than falling. In South Africa, Govinda, Khumalo, and Mkhwanazi (2014) estimate that the price difference between the price charged by a cement cartel during collusive and non-collusive periods, controlling for cost drivers, was 7.5–9.7 percent. They estimate the total savings to South African customers due to the breakup of the cartel—assuming an overcharge of 9.7 percent—to be in the range of US$79 million to US$100 million between 2010 and 2013.

### Pro-competition Sectoral Reforms Can Boost Small Producers' Returns

Opening transport markets to competition reduces the prices of transportation services, a key input for producers and traders. Transport deregulation in Rwanda in 1994—where road freight services had previously been a monopoly of a parastatal trucking company—led to a decline in prices of 75 percent in real terms and growth in the Rwandese fleet. In Mexico, road transport prices fell by 23 percent in real terms in the five years following deregulation of the trucking industry between 1989 and 1990 (Teravaninthorn and Raballand 2009). Removing restrictive government policies in international shipping services, such as restrictions on competition from foreign suppliers of shipping services, would lead to an average reduction in transport prices for goods shipped to the United States from developing countries by 9 percent and cost savings of up to US$850 million (Fink, Mattoo, and Neagu 2002).

Lifting anticompetitive government regulations has positive effects on input costs faced by producers, such as in construction materials. For example, in Zambia the price of cement—an essential input in construction—fell by almost 10 percent after 2008, coinciding with the opening of the national cement market to allow a new entrant to compete with the incumbent state monopolist (Ellis and Singh 2010). This happened during a period when cement prices rose in all the other countries studied in the paper (Bangladesh, Ghana, Kenya, and Vietnam). A report prepared by the African Competition Forum on the cement markets in Botswana, Kenya, Namibia, South Africa, Tanzania, and Zambia also illustrates that markets where barriers to entry are higher and competition is stifled are faced with higher levels of cement prices (Mbongwe et al. 2014).

Competition reforms in the agricultural sector, including those that seek to address restrictive government regulations and market failures, often have positive effects on agricultural producers, but the distribution of those effects can vary. A household's net position as a producer or consumer matters. The elimination of Madagascar's monopsony/monopoly vanilla marketing board, and its replacement with imperfectly competitive domestic vanilla traders, had a large positive effect on the purchase price paid to vanilla farmers (from 2–11 percent of the free on board [FOB] price to 22 percent), lifting about 20,000 individuals out of poverty. The impact on income distribution was limited, however, because cash made up a small proportion of rural households' overall income, and much of their consumption was self-produced (Cadot, Dutoit, and de Melo 2009). Also in Madagascar, Barrett and Dorosh (1996) found that first-order gains from higher rice prices through market-oriented reforms accrued mainly to large farmers producing a marketable surplus because farmers below the poverty line made substantial net purchases of rice and therefore experienced first-order losses. Similarly, an effective ban on rice imports in Indonesia—introduced in part to raise the incomes of poor farmers—benefited only the richest farmers and raised the incidence of poverty by just under 1 percent of the population because of high household expenditure on rice (Warr 2005).

In Australia, the early effects of the implementation of the country's National Competition Policy benefited business, but larger firms to a greater extent. This microeconomic reform program introduced in the 1990s[32]—aiming to minimize restrictions on competition and promote competitive neutrality in publicly provided goods and services—was found to have larger positive effects on larger businesses rather than on smaller businesses, and metropolitan areas more than rural areas. The Productivity Commission (1999) used a computable general equilibrium (CGE) model along with interviews with 1,000 individuals to illustrate the long-term effects of National Competition Policy on rural and metropolitan areas. Significant price reductions were seen in the infrastructure sectors. For example, between 1991–92 and 1995–96, the average real price for services provided by 73 state enterprises fell by 15 percent, although the price reductions were generally greater for large business than for small business users. Furthermore, while the analysis found that Australia as a whole would benefit from reform, more variation in the incidence of benefits and costs was expected among rural regions compared with metropolitan areas in terms of output, employment, and income.

### 2.1.3 The Costs of Market Power and the Benefits of Competition Policy for Employees

Both theoretical models and empirical work tend to suggest that a lack of competition in product markets stifles employment in the long term and/or on aggregate. The basic intuition is that less intense competition raises prices above marginal cost, reducing output demanded by consumers and, therefore, reducing labor demanded by producers. An increase in prices also reduces real wages, which can reduce the supply of labor. OECD (2015) presents a review of literature on the relationship between competition and employment.

The impact of competition on wages and income inequality is less examined—and existing studies are more mixed in their findings. Guadalupe (2007) finds that product market competition, measured via two quasi-natural experiments—that is, the European Union (EU) Single Market Program and the appreciation of sterling in 1996—contributed to increased wage inequality between skill levels in the British manufacturing sector. On the other hand, Borjas and Ramey (1995) find that, among industries that have opened to foreign competition in the United States, the relative wages of less-skilled workers are higher in those industries that are less concentrated sectors.

### Anticompetitive Regulation and Policies Affect Employment Growth

A new area of research has found that discriminatory application of policies among firms can also hinder employment growth. In the Arab Republic of Egypt a lack of competition due to capture by firms that were connected to the former Mubarak regime had a negative effect on job creation (Schiffbauer et al. 2015). Entry by connected firms in new previously unconnected sectors reduced aggregate employment growth by 1.4 percentage points per annum in those sectors. Increases in employment from the entry of connected firms do not outweigh the declines in employment in unconnected firms that cannot compete in light of distortive policy privileges for connected firms, including energy subsidies and trade protections.

Among sectors, retail stands out as a sector that employs a significant number of lower-income workers and one that is often subject to anticompetitive regulation. In an analysis of over 100 countries, the World Bank (2013a) found the services sector (including retail) to be the leading sector for job creation in developing countries. The retail sector is seen as relatively favorable toward women as well (World Bank 2012a; Bardasi, Sabarwal, and Terrell 2011; Amin and Islam 2014). Some evidence from Europe shows a negative impact on employment in the sector as a result of government regulations that restrict entry of large retail stores. For example, Bertrand and Kramarz (2002) find that retail employment could have been 7 percent higher in France had entry regulation not been introduced in the early 1970s.

### Competition through Firm Entry May Positively Impact Employees

Available studies on firm entry and employment point to a positive or neutral effect. From a theoretical perspective, Spector (2004), using a general equilibrium model, finds that greater competition, measured by an increase in the number of firms allowed to sell a good, has a positive employment effect in both the short run and the long run. In this model, entry can either increase or decrease wages depending on various parameters but is more likely to raise wages if workers hold low bargaining power initially. In Mexico, foreign retail store entry had adverse effects on employment and labor incomes for workers in the traditional retail sector over the medium-to-long run (Atkin, Faber, and Gonzalez-Navarro 2015). The compensating effect of employment in the nontraditional sector meant that overall there was no effect on municipality-level employment rates and labor incomes. Negative employment effects applied only to a fraction of households and so were muted in the aggregate by reductions in the overall cost of living that benefit all households.

## Competition Law Enforcement May Also Benefit Employees

Novel research included in this report provides insight into this underexamined topic. Dierx et al. (chapter 6 of this report) simulate the effect of EU merger control and cartel policy interventions on employment. They find that the net employment effect is positive in both the short run and long run: namely a 0.17 percent increase after one year and a 0.26 percent increase after five years. In addition, shocks from competition enforcement increased demand for both non-liquidity-constrained, high-skilled households and liquidity-constrained, high-skilled households' labor. The two types of workers experience similar wage increases, albeit the increase for high-skilled households is slightly higher.

## Pro-competition Sectoral Reforms May Have a Positive Impact on Jobs and Wages

Both theoretical models and empirical work tend to suggest a positive effect of product market reform on employment in the long term and/or on aggregate. Examples of theoretical work include Spector (2004) and Blanchard and Giavazzi (2003),[33] while Griffith, Harrison, and Macartney (2007); Fiori et al. (2012); and Nicoletti and Scarpetta (2005) provide examples of empirical work focused on OECD countries.[34]

Findings on the impact of competition on jobs are dependent on a number of parameters, including the type of reform, whether outcomes are observed at the firm level or on aggregate, and the stance of labor regulations. In addition, employment outcomes in the short run are less clear-cut than in the long run. For example, Cacciatore, Duval, and Fiori (2012) find a negative short-run employment effect (but positive wage effect) from product market reform that reduces entry barriers. Profitable investment opportunities in new firms induce households to save more and consume less, which outweighs the job creation effect of increased entry. It could also be argued that the exit of less productive firms due to increased competition could lead to job losses. For a sample of 80 countries, including developing countries, Feldmann (2012) finds that a one standard deviation increase in the restrictiveness of product market regulation is associated with a rise in the unemployment rate of about 1.0 percentage point, a rise in the female unemployment rate of 1.2 percentage points, and a rise in the youth unemployment rate of 1.7 percentage points. In the retail sector in Italy, less restrictive regulations on large store entry are associated with fewer small retail owners, but this is compensated for by additional employment of workers in both small and large retail outlets so that moving to a free entry scenario would increase the employment rate by 0.8 percentage points (Viviano 2008).

As with the effect of a lack of competition, evidence is mixed on the effect of the introduction of more pro-competitive regulation on wages and income inequality. Braconier and Ruiz-Valenzuela (2014) find that a reduction in product market regulation contributed to increased wage inequality across OECD countries. On the other hand, Causa, de Serres, and Ruiz (2014) show that more pro-competitive product market regulation is associated with higher average household disposable income, with higher gains for the poor[35] and lower income inequality in OECD countries.

In summary, available empirical studies support the finding that competition policy is an instrument to increase the welfare of low-income households and producers; however, research in various areas could be expanded. A lack of competition affects poor households disproportionately. Consumers benefit from competition law enforcement, particularly from anticartel enforcement and merger control. Furthermore, the removal of anticompetitive regulations in key markets for low-income consumers and producers and in sectors that generate employment for households at the bottom of the pyramid delivers positive outcomes. Indirectly, competition in public procurement increases the effectiveness of government offerings of services needed by low-income populations. Nonetheless, there is still need to develop more studies that analyze the distributional effects of increased competition across income groups. More rigorous studies can also be conducted for emerging and developing economies to measure the costs of limited competition, and the potential benefits of firm entry, enhanced antitrust enforcement, and removing regulations that restrain competition on low-income consumers.

## 2.2 Dynamic Effects: Competition as a Driver of Productivity, Innovation, and Economic Growth

Competition contributes to higher economic growth that has been the main driver of poverty reduction and shared prosperity in recent decades. This section focuses on evidence to support the ways in which competition impacts firm productivity, innovation, and ultimately economic growth.

### 2.2.1 The Level of Competition Significantly Affects Firm- and Sector-Level Productivity

The economic evidence that a lack of competition hinders productivity[36] growth is overwhelming. The evidence to support the links between competition and productivity arises from all levels: starting with empirical analyses of firm-level data, through sector-level studies, to comparisons of national policy.[37] Greater competition leads to an improvement in allocative efficiency by allowing more efficient firms to enter and gain market share, at the expense of less efficient firms (the so-called "across-firms" effect). This conclusion—that productivity growth is largely driven by reallocation from less to more productive firms—is discussed at length in Arnold, Nicoletti, and Scarpetta (2011), in the context of the effect of anticompetitive regulation, and also in the report *Supporting Investment in Knowledge Capital, Growth and Innovation* (OECD 2013).[38] The studies mentioned in the paragraphs that follow demonstrate a clear empirical link between competition and productivity growth. As productivity growth is the main component of *per capita* GDP growth, this microlevel analysis makes a solid and convincing case that a lack of competition impedes growth.

A classic paper from Nickell (1996) finds that higher competition is statistically significantly associated with faster productivity growth, and various other studies arrive at similar findings. In the context of the United Kingdom, Nickell presents "evidence that competition, measured either by increased numbers of competitors or by lower levels of rents, is associated with a significantly higher rate of total factor productivity growth" (Nickell 1996, 724). Nickell's paper suggests that product market competition works to increase productivity in part because it increases managers' incentives to work hard in shareholders' interests. A large-scale survey on the link between competition and productivity growth can be found in Ahn (2002, 5), who concludes, "A large number of empirical studies confirm that the link between product market competition and productivity growth is positive and robust.... Empirical findings from various kinds of policy changes ... also confirm that competition brings about productivity gains, consumers' welfare gains and long-run economic growth."

Most convincingly, detailed firm-by-firm and even plant-by-plant analysis demonstrates that suppliers facing more competition have higher productivity and faster productivity growth. One of the largest studies, by Disney, Haskel, and Heden (2003), uses a panel of 140,000 separate manufacturing firms in the United Kingdom between 1980 and 1992. The authors conclude, "Market competition significantly raises both the level and growth of productivity" (Disney, Haskel, and Heden 2003, 691). Blundell, Griffith, and Van Reenen (1999), by examining a set of data on manufacturing firms in the United Kingdom, also find a positive effect of product market competition on productivity growth. Januszewski, Köke, and Winter (2002) similarly report a positive link between productivity growth and competition for a survey of 500 German firms. Syverson (2004a) has carried out a series of studies in the United States, using data across 443 U.S. manufacturing industries, finding that those facing more competitive conditions had higher and less dispersed productivity. Another study by Syverson (2004b) finds similar effects *within* a particular industry (ready-mixed cement).

Higher levels of competition are also associated with higher productivity growth and GDP growth in Turkey. A study by the World Bank (2013c) using a panel of Turkish firms for the period 2005–08, suggests that lower markups, as a result of a more competitive environment, would have positive consequences for productivity growth. In particular, a 10 percent decrease in the average price-cost margins in the Turkish economy would lead to a 4.5 percent increase in the annual rate of productivity growth. Similarly World Bank (2014a) finds that a 5 percentage point decrease in price-cost margins in Tunisia driven by an increase in competition could increase labor productivity by 5 percent, on average, translating into additional GDP growth of about 4.5 percent per year.

Studies for Egypt, Jordan, Morocco, and South Africa also show a positive relationship between competition and productivity. Sekkat (2009) uses manufacturing sector data at the three-digit level to examine whether the degree of competition improves total factor productivity (TFP) and labor productivity in Egypt, Jordan, and Morocco. Higher markups have a significant and negative impact on productivity growth in Jordan and Morocco (though not in Egypt). In Egypt, a decrease in the share of state-owned enterprises in a given industry—representing a reduction in obstacles to competition—has a significant and positive impact on productivity growth. Also for the manufacturing sector, in South Africa, Aghion, Braun, and Fedderke (2008), using three different panel datasets, show that there is a strong positive effect of competition—again measured by price cost margins—on productivity growth. In particular, a 10 percent reduction in South African markups would increase manufacturing productivity growth in South Africa by 2 to 2.5 percent per year.

Competition can render policies to support firms more effective, generating larger effects on firm productivity. Aghion et al. (2015) find that sectoral industrial policies (such as subsidies or tax holidays) have a larger impact on productivity growth when targeted at competitive sectors or where they are allocated in such a way as to preserve or increase competition (for example by inducing entry or encouraging younger enterprises). They argue that industrial policy can be designed to enhance competition in a sector and to serve the dual role of increasing consumer surplus and growth.

### 2.2.2 Increased Competition Is Associated with Better Management

Competition improves the productive efficiency of firms (the so called "within-firm" effects[39]) as firms facing competition appear to be better managed. There might be several reasons why this is the case. Schmidt (1997) proposes that the higher risk of bankruptcy in competitive markets might drive better performance within firms, as well as through the across-firms effect. Nalebuff and Stiglitz (1983) suggest that comparisons against rivals in competitive product markets give shareholders better information about managers' performance. More recently, Van Reenen and colleagues have examined links between product market competition and quality of management. In several papers (see, for example, Bloom and Van Reenen 2007) these authors have demonstrated that differences in productivity between countries depend on differences in management quality (measured through a survey), and in particular on how many *badly* managed firms there are. Countries with low productivity growth often have a long "tail" of very badly managed firms at the bottom of the distribution (as opposed to being worse all across the distribution), in a similar pattern to the productivity differences illustrated above. These inefficient firms are particularly prevalent in emerging economies. Strong product market competition appears to boost average management practices through a combination of eliminating the tail of badly managed firms and pushing incumbents to improve their practices, according to the authors.

Bloom, Kretschmer, and Van Reenen (2009) have demonstrated that this relationship holds in a dynamic setting too: they find that increases in competition result in better management scores. The positive effect of competition appears to be even stronger when endogeneity is taken into account. It is the case, for example, for Bloom et al. (2015), who use political competition as an instrumental variable for competition among hospitals in some areas of the United Kingdom, because hospitals are rarely closed down in politically marginal constituencies. Van Reenen (2011) provides a review of recent studies that prove both from a theoretical and empirical perspective that (i) competition increases management quality and (ii) improved management quality boosts productivity.

### 2.2.3 Promoting Competition Stimulates Innovation in Firms

There is evidence that promoting competition serves to encourage innovation, which feeds into higher firm and industry productivity. Much of the initial analysis on this subject, particularly that associated with Aghion, Bloom, Blundell, Griffith, and Howitt (see for example Aghion et al. 2005), related to research and development investments for patenting new products in the United Kingdom and restored Scherer's (1967) conception of the relationship as an "inverted U." Aghion et al. argue that, at low competition levels, the incremental profits from innovating are higher, and this encourages innovation aimed at "escaping competition." This explains the "rising" side of the inverted-U, where more competition leads to more innovation. In contrast, at high levels of competitive intensity, firms have little incentive to innovate and produce new patented products because competition with the existing technological leaders will eliminate the profits from doing so. Some subsequent studies[40] have obtained results that are similar or at least consistent with the theory identified by Aghion et al. Given that pro-competition policy interventions do not focus on making moderately competitive markets hypercompetitive, but rather on introducing or strengthening competition in markets where it does not work well, policies to encourage competition will help boost innovation.

More recent empirical research points to a positive relationship between competition and innovation. Correa (2012), using the same dataset as Aghion et al. (2005), calls into question their results by finding a structural break in the data in the early 1980s, which coincides with establishment of the U.S. Court of Appeals for the Federal Circuit (CAFC) in 1982. Modifying the model in order to take into account the structural break, Correa shows a positive relationship between innovation and competition during the pre-CAFC period 1973–82, and no statistically significant innovation-competition relationship during the post-CAFC period 1983–94. One potential explanation is that after the establishment of the CAFC a more pro-patent environment might have changed the incentives to patent. This change might in turn have induced some less competitive industries to become more patent-intensive than before the reform, with a consequent change in the relationship between innovation, measured as patents, and competition after the CAFC reform.

### 2.2.4 Pro-competition Regulations Can Help Mitigate Negative Effects of Macroeconomic Downturns

One may ask if the long-run gains from increased competition are achieved only at the expense of short-term outcomes, that is, whether for instance it is the case that firms that experience productivity gains shed labor. If so, one could argue that governments may be justified in retaining restrictions on competition during downturns, at least temporarily. We observe in both developed and developing countries that industries often seek such "temporary" protection from their governments, whether from domestic or foreign competition, particularly when the economy slows down. In practice, temporary relief often becomes permanent, as firms face very few incentives to improve while under state protection (while having every incentive to devote resources to lobbying for extensions).

Evidence is somewhat mixed, but OECD analysis of structural reform in product and labor markets suggests that any losses arising from moving to more competitive product markets are transitory at worst. For example, Cacciatore, Duval, and Fiori (2012) find that pro-competition product market reform stimulates GDP immediately but can lead to some increase in unemployment, typically for a period of one to two years. This is perhaps unsurprising, if the labor-shedding effects of increased competition are immediate while the gains from new entry and from smaller competitors expanding capacity take some time to emerge. Similarly, updating earlier work by Duval, Elmeskov, and Vogel (2007) to take account of the recent recession, Sutherland and Hoeller (2013) conclude that less-regulated product markets reduce the time required for recovery from a macroeconomic shock (particularly supply shocks). This connection involves a rather complex link with labor market reform. For example Cacciatore, Duval, and Fiori (2012) find that product market and labor market reforms act as substitutes for one another (product market competition becomes more important in the absence of flexible labor markets), whereas Bassanini and Duval (2009) find that they are complements (reforming both policies produces larger gains than the combined effect of reforming one but not the other).

One illuminating source of evidence on the effects of competition law and policy on recovery is the different responses to the downturn of the 1930s. Few countries actively enforced competition laws as early as the 1930s, but one of the few that did—the United States—made the policy decision to roll back its antitrust enforcement in the depth of the depression. The National Industrial Recovery Act (NIRA) of 1933 legalized cartels in participating sectors, as part of a deal in which price-fixing was exchanged for agreements to maintain wages and employment. Thus, in contrast to the studies of product and labor market reform described above, the U.S. government deliberately sought to reduce both product and labor market flexibility. The effect seems to have been a reduction in output of the order of 10 percent,[41] although the relative contribution of product price-fixing and union wage bargaining cannot be distinguished. During the 1930s, the United States experienced some periods of inflation at a time when output was more than 30 percent below trend, an outcome to which the NIRA seems to have contributed, although demand-side factors were also important as the recovery gathered pace.[42] One controversial study—Cole and Ohanian (2004)—concludes that the NIRA delayed recovery by as much as seven years,[43] although this extraordinarily large effect has been challenged.[44] However, the basic point is well established. As Romer (1999, 197) noted, "By preventing the large negative deviations of output from trend in the mid-1930s from exerting deflationary pressure, it prevented the economy's self-correction mechanism from working. Thus, the NIRA can be best thought of as a force holding back recovery, rather than as one actively depressing output."

There is scant evidence for emerging and developing economies on the advantages of competitive markets to manage negative macroeconomic shocks. However, such a strand of the literature would be relevant to understand how the degree of competition affects transmission of negative macro shocks on poverty and income of households at the bottom of the income distribution. In Tunisia, estimates imply that an increase in competition equivalent to a reduction of price-cost margins of 5 percentage points in all sectors of the economy would boost labor productivity growth by 5 percent on average and would translate into additional GDP growth of about 4.5 percent per year and approximately 50,000 new jobs per year (World Bank 2014a). The Central Bank of Mexico has estimated concentrated markets, restrictive regulation, and anticompetitive behavior cost the economy around 1 percentage point of GDP growth each year (World Bank 2012b). Distortions due to GDP volatility and various crises and the downgrading of competition policy as a public policy priority are proposed as explanations for the breakdown in the relationship.

### 2.2.5 Regulations Protecting Incumbents Can Negatively Affect Productivity, Innovation, and Growth

Far from promoting economywide growth, productivity, and innovation, government regulation protecting firms from competition is likely to stifle it. If companies put their efforts into seeking government protection from competition (foreign or domestic) they will have less ability and incentive to innovate. Schwab and Werker (2014) look at profits expressed as markups and find that countries grew more slowly where the manufacturing sector presented higher markups. The effect can be strong enough to overcome the "catch-up" advantages of low-income countries, suggesting that, when these countries adopt more open and pro-competition frameworks that govern their industries, there is scope for even faster economic growth. By estimating a knowledge production function on OECD industries through a stochastic frontier analysis, Franco, Pieri, and Venturini (2016) find that restrictive service regulation reduces research and development (R&D) efficiency in the manufacturing sector.

Sectoral studies confirm that this effect on productivity and firm competitiveness also applies to the Japanese and Korean experiences of economic growth, despite the widespread belief that these countries followed a different development model involving protection from competition (Sakakibara and Porter 2001; Baek, Kim, and Kwon 2009).

In particular, Sakakibara and Porter have convincingly demonstrated that it was those sectors in Japan that were the most exposed to competition, including from abroad, and that were the least protected from imports that were the most successful competitors on world markets, while the protected sectors (such as aircraft manufacturing) failed.

A further strand of the literature explores the issue of discriminatory policy treatment of firms and cronyism that dampen competition and their effects on firm performance. For example, Rijkers, Freund, and Nucifora (2014), using firm-level data from Tunisia for 1994–2010, found that entry restrictions enshrined in the Investment Incentives Code favored politically connected firms to the detriment of productivity and consumers. Politically connected firms were larger than their nonconnected competitors in terms of employment and output and were more profitable, but presented lower labor productivity growth. The effect of political connectedness was greater in sectors that were subject to stringent entry regulation. Similarly, as previously discussed, Schiffbauer et al. (2015) focus on the advantages enjoyed by politically connected firms in Egypt as a result of explicit government decisions to grant them policy privileges not received by other firms. They find that connected firms are larger and more profitable solely as a result of these privileges. Importantly, they also show that the entry of connected firms into previously unconnected sectors not only slows aggregate employment growth but also skews the distribution of employment toward less productive firms.

### 2.2.6 Firm Entry Fosters Productivity and Innovation

In the case of low-income economies, there is a small body of empirical analysis revealing a strong positive effect between greater competition from entry of foreign firms, productivity, and firm-level innovation. Aghion et al. (2004, 2009) exploit data on microlevel productivity growth for the United Kingdom and the wave of reforms that in the 1980s introduced greater competition in the economy and find that entry from foreign firms has led to greater innovation and faster TFP growth of domestic incumbents, and thus to faster aggregate productivity growth. Bloom, Draca, and Van Reenen (2011) examine more than a half million firms in 12 European countries between 1996 and 2007 and the impact of Chinese import competition. They find that every 10 percentage point rise in Chinese imports in a firm's industry in Europe was associated with an increase in patenting, information technology (IT) spending, R&D spending, and TFP. These findings hold also when China's entry in the World Trade Organization (WTO) in December 2001 is taken into account. Using data on firms in 27 emerging economies, Gorodnichenko, Svejnar, and Terrell (2010) provide robust evidence of a positive relationship between foreign competition and innovation. The authors use a relevant definition of innovation for emerging economies: development of a major new product line, upgrading of an existing product line, acquisition of a new production technology, and obtaining a new quality accreditation.

### 2.2.7 Competition Law Enforcement May Enhance Productivity, Innovation, and Growth

An effective competition law is an important pillar to promote competition in the marketplace and boost productivity. Evidence on the link between competition, productivity, and growth in developing countries is less prevalent, although there are some studies that provide a foundation for further research. For instance, using a dataset on 97 countries, Voigt (2009) estimates the effect of the quality of competition law and its enforcing institutions on productivity. Voigt finds that there is a positive relationship, though not very strong, between the two variables, and that the result remains valid even if developing countries are analyzed separately. Symeonidis (2008) shows that firms affected by the introduction of competition law outlawing cartels experienced increases in labor productivity. Buccirossi et al. (2013) estimated the impact of competition policy on TFP growth for 22 industries in 12 OECD countries over the period 1995–2005 and identified a positive and significant relationship between the two variables.

This report provides additional evidence on these effects. Büthe and Cheng (chapter 7 of this report) find that the effect of a country having a substantively meaningful competition law[45] on innovation (measured by the number of patent applications) is strongly statistically significant and positive in cross-sectional and panel analyses for OECD and developing countries. For example, Dierx et al. (chapter 6 of this report) propose a novel methodology applying markup shocks to a general equilibrium model to assess the distributional macroeconomic effects of important merger and cartel decisions made by the European Commission between 2012 and 2014. The markup shocks, estimated on the basis of the microeconomic customer savings from these decisions, reduce prices, which in turn results in higher demand and an increase in GDP of 0.4 percent after five years and 0.7 percent in the long term. The simulation also finds that liquidity-constrained households (low-skilled and consuming all their resources in each period) increase their proportionate consumption four times more than non-liquidity-constrained households (high-skilled savers) after five years.

### 2.2.8 Sector Regulations That Enable Competition and Competition Law Enhance Productivity and Growth

Studies on regulatory reform events have also been used to prove that more pro-competitive regulation can foster productivity and efficiency and, as a consequence, growth. This is the case for example for trade liberalization (Pavcnik 2002), deregulation of the telecommunications sector (Olley and Pakes 1996), and deregulation of the electricity sector (Fabrizio, Rose, and Wolfram 2007). Alesina et al. (2005), using data for the transport, communications, and utilities sectors in OECD countries, find evidence that entry liberalization has had a particularly substantial positive impact on capital accumulation—and therefore on growth—when compared to other forms of regulatory reform. For professional services, Pellizzari and Pica (2011) show that the removal of price floors and other restrictions on legal services in Italy is positively associated with greater productivity. In the case of retail, Amin (2007) analyzes a database of 1,948 retail stores in India and concludes that pro-competition regulatory reforms increase labor productivity by 87 percent. For the EU, Griffith, Harrison, and Simpson (2006) find positive productivity and innovation effects from the implementation of the EU's Single Market Program that incorporates competition principles.

Well-functioning product markets that provide essential inputs for other industries can generate broader spillover effects across the economy. However, many developing and emerging economies tend to have heavily regulated sectors, not least in the utilities and network sectors. Box 2.5 gives an overview of the role of ex ante sector regulation in safeguarding competition. The potential impact of upstream regulatory improvements on growth in downstream industries that use those services intensively has recently been estimated in a number of developing countries. These simulations draw on previous evidence of a positive effect of a reduction in the restrictiveness[46] of upstream services (professional services, energy, transport, and telecommunications) on growth in downstream industries (see Barone and Cingano 2011). In South Africa, reducing restrictiveness of professional services regulations would, other things being equal, spur growth in value added in industries that use professional services intensively by between US$1.4 billion

---

**BOX 2.5**

### Role of Ex Ante Sector Regulation in Safeguarding Competition

In sectors characterized by market failures—such as those that occur in the presence of natural monopolies or network effects—competition law enforcement usually needs to be complemented by ex ante sector regulation. The principal policy goal of sector regulation is the removal or amelioration of market failure in a particular sector before harm occurs, that is, ex ante. It requires the sectoral regulator to take a forward-looking view of potentially anticompetitive firm conduct and put in place measures—on a sectorwide basis—to prevent that conduct. For example, one key area of ex ante regulatory policy includes setting terms for providing access to competitors to an essential facility[a] on a fair and nondiscriminatory basis. This should allow for greater entry and thus improve price and access outcomes for consumers.

However, inappropriate sector regulations (or a lack of suitable regulation) can also stifle competition by adding undue compliance burdens, discouraging entrepreneurship, or rewarding monopolies. It is therefore key to ensure the right balance in setting regulation. In particular, whether ex ante regulation is a suitable measure for a particular market depends on whether entry barriers are (i) sufficiently high that the market in question is unlikely to be characterized by effective competition in the absence of ex ante regulation and (ii) of the kind that cannot effectively be addressed through alternative means, such as direct action to reduce or to remove them, or through the application of competition rules in specific cases.

a. Essential services are generally an infrastructure or resource that cannot be reasonably duplicated, and without which competitors cannot reasonably provide goods or services to their customers.

and US\$ 1.6 billion—equivalent to an additional 0.4–0.5 percentage points of GDP growth (World Bank 2016). In Peru, this figure would be about US\$250 million, 0.2 percentage points (World Bank 2015), while in Brazil the effect would be an additional 0.1–0.5 percentage points of GDP growth (World Bank, forthcoming [a]). In Kenya, reducing regulatory restrictiveness across service sectors such as electricity and professional services would generate an additional US\$218 million of GDP, equivalent to 0.39 percentage points of GDP growth (Competition Authority of Kenya 2015). Meanwhile, conservative estimates from Turkey indicate that reducing regulatory and competition constraints on professional and transport services would result in benefits of about US\$557 million in additional value added to the economy per year (World Bank 2013c).

Product market reform has very significant potential to raise GDP in many economies, some by as much as 30 percent (OECD 2013). There is evidence that well-implemented, pro-competition product market regulations can result in increased growth. Nicoletti and Scarpetta (2003) provide evidence on this for OECD countries. Arnold, Nicoletti, and Scarpetta (2011), again for the OECD, demonstrate a statistically significant negative correlation between the level of product market regulation and multifactor productivity. In the case of Croatia, De Rosa et al. (2009) find that eliminating anticompetitive regulation in energy, telecommunications, and transport would increase GDP per capita by 1.35–2.77 percent. For India, Conway and Herd (2008) and Conway, Herd, and Chalaux (2008) find that differences in the stringency of the regulatory environment across states, as measured by the Product Market Regulation indicators, have a significant impact on labor and TFP and therefore on economic growth (figure 2.2).

**FIGURE 2.2**  **Product Market Regulation and Productivity Acceleration in India, by State**

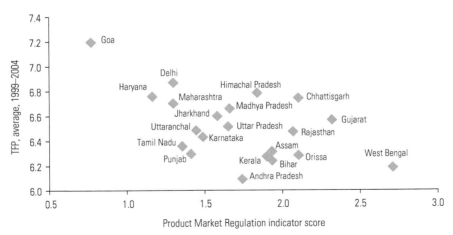

Sources: OECD and Indian National Account Statistics, reproduced from Conway and Herd 2008.
Note: TFP = total factor productivity.

In any case, increasing competition may lead to some short-term trade-offs due to labor mobility costs, but in many cases this will be offset by longer-term gains. Labor mobility costs for developing country workers are more than twice as high as for those in developed economies (World Bank 2014b). Concerns over these costs are influenced by many complex factors, including labor market regulations, sector characteristics, the degree to which the increase in competition triggers innovation or technological change, the skill level and educational attainment of the population, and any cost-mitigating policies, such as retraining programs or wage subsidies. However, some evidence suggests that after an adjustment period, opening markets has a positive effect. As an example, World Bank (2014b) shows, via a simulation, that liberalization of the food and beverage sectors in 47 countries would (in all but four countries) lead to higher real wages in that sector—and higher employment in other sectors—after an adjustment period, averaging around five years for developing countries.

In summary, empirical literature reveals that competition and pro-competitive regulations generate positive impacts on productivity and innovation and general growth; however, there is limited research on the distributional impact of these dynamic effects. There is overwhelming evidence on the links between competition and productivity and the firm, sector, and economy level. Available studies also back up the usefulness of competition policy to encourage innovation and product upgrading. Research based on Product Market Regulation indicators as well as event studies show that the elimination of regulations that restrict competition leads to higher productivity and better performance. Areas where literature is scant, particularly for developing economies, comprise the impact of specific pro-competitive reforms on productivity, output, and employment; the relationship between competition, managerial skills, and innovation; and the analysis of the effects of discriminatory regulations or favoritism—as an obstacle to competition—on firm and sector performance.

## 2.3  Further Research for a Policy Agenda

This review has brought to light several subjects which could provide topics for further research:

- **Research would be valuable on the distributional effects of policies and government decisions that encourage competition.** More analysis on how low-income households benefit from competition when their intersecting roles as consumers, producers, and employees are taken into account would be valuable. As part of this, complementing partial equilibrium models with general equilibrium analysis could help to more accurately predict the expected effects of increased competition in an economy and identify potential winners and losers in the short term. For example, there is room to broaden the analysis to take into account the demand response of households to price changes and the position of households as producers of the goods or services in question, as well as potential second-order wage effects. In general, empirical research on the effects of competition on jobs is fairly limited.

- **It would be enlightening to extend the analysis of consumer benefits of competition to a broader range of sectors than currently exists, and to nonprice dimensions.** For example, there is a dearth of research on the distributional impact of limited competition across services sectors such as telecommunications, energy, retail, and transportation, which make up an important proportion of the consumption basket. The financial sector, and particularly the availability and pricing of credit, is also key for the ability of low-income individuals to start and develop small businesses. Further research on whether regulatory constraints on competition or market power limit access and affordability to credit would be valuable. In some markets, competition goals interact with other policy objectives such as safety, congestion, and stability in the case of health, local passenger transportation, and banking, respectively. In these cases, it would be useful to understand how the various policy goals can be achieved and how embedding competition principles can facilitate the achievement of common sectoral goals such as access and better deals for users.

- **Even in the case of food products and other basic goods, research in low-income economies is lacking.** The subject would benefit from greater theoretical understanding and increased empirical evidence on consumer welfare gains from competition in nonprice dimensions, such as increased variety and quality and, where possible, the distributional effects of this. This may include individual case studies of individual products or further research on whether those goods and services that are disproportionately consumed by the poor, including food, are particularly susceptible either to anticompetitive practices or anticompetitive regulation. It would also be interesting to understand whether low physical mobility exposes the poor disproportionately to geographically local monopoly power, for example in remote settlements with sparse markets.

- **Extending the use of robust methodologies to estimate the effects of specific pro-competition reform events could make a valuable contribution to the literature.** Where data are available it may also be possible to use specific reform events—such as the granting of local monopolies or the opening up of markets that were previously monopolies, or exogenous changes in competition triggered by historical episodes of changes in the competitive environment—to assess the impact of such reforms on the welfare of lower-income households. Geographic variation in the adoption or actual implementation of reforms across districts or states in federal countries can also provide more information on the effects of such pro-competition reforms.

- **In the case of competition law enforcement, further research can provide evidence for competition authorities on how enforcement efforts can be more in**

**line with shared prosperity goals.** Research gaps include the effect of anticartel enforcement, exclusionary behavior, and merger control across income categories, as well as more rigorous estimates of price overcharges and loss in terms of quality and product variety, particularly in middle-income and low-income economies. Given that an important number of anticompetitive practices and mergers involve intermediate products, more work could be done to understand pass-through rates of cartel overcharges to the final consumer. This would also help to identify markets or supply chains in which the rate of pass-through is higher to understand where anticartel enforcement would have a higher beneficial impact on final consumers. Now that more countries are enacting and implementing competition laws, it would be a good opportunity to update and extend previous cross-sectional analysis of the effects of competition law enforcement.

- **Furthermore, there is currently very little work on the links between competition and innovation and entrepreneurship in developing economies.** Innovation in developing economies may be more common at the level of upgrades in the services offering product design and adaptations of existing technologies; the majority of existing empirical research typically captures the effect on R&D and patents, but not these innovations. Additional studies considering a broader definition of innovation would be relevant as well. In addition, exploring the links between developing countries' competition policies, rates of firm entry and exit, and expansion rates for small firms, particularly where these elements interact with industrial policies, would add constructively to the literature.

- **Finally, a new area for research is the link between limited competition due to cronyism or favoritism and its effects on firm performance and consumer welfare.** This topic is particularly relevant for low- and middle-income economies and small economies where politically connected firms are more prevalent. Information on preferential taxes or benefits provided to firms and firm-level data on ownership and performance could allow for this kind of evidence. This topic is relevant not only for promoting competition but also to ensure fiscal sustainability and opportunities for private sector investment.

Research will be useful to inform the design of programs that aim at combating poverty and boosting shared prosperity.

- **More research on the impact of introducing competition in the design of social programs can also be valuable.** For example, testing further how competition among retailers or other service providers can help to increase the effectiveness of cash transfers; testing how competition at the agrodealer level or at the production and import level of agriculture inputs can affect the functioning of voucher systems for agriculture subsidies; or testing how fostering new entry or reducing information asymmetry on quality of service can contribute to better functioning health, education, and professional services markets.

Incorporating these hypotheses into randomized controlled trials to generate more experimental evidence on these issues would help illuminate the merits of such market-based interventions.

■ **Moreover, further research can be conducted on incorporating competition principles in programs that aim at supporting small and medium enterprises (SMEs) and farmers.** Research on the impact and design of contracting arrangements in vertical supply chains can provide evidential support for policy makers involved in regulating or supporting such arrangements. For instance, contract farming arrangements and contracts to link producers to retail chains are common across developing country agricultural markets. In particular, it would be valuable to build evidence of the distributional effects considering gains for producers and efficiency gains for purchasers, in light of varying contract terms and technological features.

Increased availability of higher frequency and detailed data across markets provides the possibility of conducting more robust analysis of the effects of competition and pro-competition reforms.

■ **More firm-level and transaction-level data in developing economies can also facilitate analysis of competition, industry performance, and benefits for consumers.** The increasing use of information technology to record various transactions provides the possibility of exploiting databases generated in retail chains, customs declaration systems (such as ASYCUDA World), telecommunications networks, payment systems networks, banking services, and public procurement systems, among others. Providing access to tax return and customs data as well as firm-level economic variables would allow researchers, development partners, and policy makers to generate more accurate evidence for policy makers.

■ **Exploiting geographic variation of competition conditions and population characteristics can also provide information to estimate distributional effects.** Making use of household survey data in various geographies to analyze the distributional impact of market power in other areas—particularly in other developing economies—can help to build the evidence base on this topic and expose similarities across geographies and products.

## Notes

1. See, for instance, Kitzmuller and Martinez Licetti 2012 for a literature review.
2. Modest exercise is taken here as the equivalent market power in a five-firm symmetric Cournot equilibrium.
3. Nevertheless they also find that the empirical approach taken does not greatly affect the ranking of the welfare loss across food industries (Peterson and Connor 1995).
4. Welfare loss is estimated as the static loss of consumer surplus, net of the profits made by the oligopolistic firms.

5. Dutt (1984) derives this result using a Kaleckian/Post-Keynesian mode. The result holds for economies with excess capacity and market imperfection.

6. In an economy where consumers have homogenous labor productivities and different levels of profit shares of the oligopolistic rents, Rodríguez-Castelán shows that the negative price effect of higher market concentration is always greater than the positive income effect of firm ownership. However, when consumers have heterogeneous productivities, if the profit share of the low-productivity consumers is large enough and there is a significant productivity gap between the low- and high-skilled consumers, then poverty reduction is possible under conditions of increased market concentration.

7. Connor and Helmers (2006) find that for their sample of 283 private international cartels discovered between 1990 and the end of 2005, most cartelized goods are industrial intermediate inputs (62 percent). The leading cartelized industries are in manufacturing (79 percent of sales), especially chemicals, nonmetallic minerals, paper, and electronic devices. Next are services (21 percent), and the least important are raw materials.

8. World Bank Group, Markets and Competition Policy Assessment Tool (MCPAT). See also the OECD's Competition Assessment Toolkit (2010).

9. Studies show that increases of food prices generally contribute to higher poverty, although higher labor income associated to the higher prices works in the opposite direction (World Bank 2011).
   It should be noted that unskilled wages also rise in response to an increase in commodity prices. It is therefore important to distinguish between short-run and long-run effects on poverty, since the elasticity of the wage rate to food prices is higher in the long run (see Ravallion 1990). However, overall, the evidence suggests that the effect of higher consumption prices due to lack of competition are generally not offset by the induced increases in wages (see Rashid 2002; Ivanic and Martin 2008; De Hoyos and Medvedev 2009).

10. Although they also note that this cost must be offset against any benefits that arise, for example, due to reduced congestion.

11. Measured by the compensating variation.

12. Additional assessments of competition enforcement can be found in OECD, forthcoming.

13. OFT Positive Impact 2013/14, http://webarchive.nationalarchives.gov.uk/20140402142426 /http://www.oft.gov.uk/shared_oft/reports/Evaluating-OFTs-work/OFT1532.pdf.

14. FY 2015 Congressional Budget Justification, https://www.ftc.gov/system/files/documents/reports /fy-2015-congressional-budget-justification/2015-cbj.pdf.

15. OFT Positive Impact 2013/14, http://webarchive.nationalarchives.gov.uk/20140402142426 /http://www.oft.gov.uk/shared_oft/reports/Evaluating-OFTs-work/OFT1532.pdf.

16. However, the author also found that agencies have generally been successful in distinguishing cases deserving of approval from those raising the most serious competitive concerns.

17. See NMa decision, Case 2286 Nuon/Reliant Energy Europe, December 8, 2003.

18. http://www.econstor.eu/bitstream/10419/27590/1/dp08107.pdf.

19. OFT Positive Impact 2013/14, http://webarchive.nationalarchives.gov.uk/20140402142426 /http://www.oft.gov.uk/shared_oft/reports/Evaluating-OFTs-work/OFT1532.pdf.

20. FY 2015 Congressional Budget Justification, https://www.ftc.gov/system/files/documents/reports /fy-2015-congressional-budget-justification/2015-cbj.pdf.

21. https://escholarship.org/uc/item/92z491ck#page-3.

22. World Bank 2013b.

23. Policy note available at http://www.cc.gov.pk/images/Downloads/policy_notes/basa%20policy %20note%20%2018%20may%202010.pdf.

24. The Competition Policy Advocacy Awards, Changing Mindsets to Transform Markets, The World Bank, 2014. https://www.wbginvestmentclimate.org/publications/upload/Competition-Policy -Advocacy-Awards.pdf.

25. http://www.sciencedirect.com/science/article/pii/S0308596106000772.

26. Including coffee, cotton, cocoa, and tobacco.

27. Benin, Burkina Faso, Côte d'Ivoire, Ghana, Malawi, Rwanda, Uganda, and Zambia.

28. However, this average masks high variability, with high gains for cotton farmers and low gains instead for coffee smallholders.

29. In the long term, the depressed producer prices may disincentivize producers from entering the market and from innovating, which could lead to higher prices, lower quality, and less choice for consumers in the long run if buyer power persists.

30. Canpotex is a Canada-based state-sanctioned potash export cartel, whose membership consists of three companies (PotashCorp, Mosaic, and Agrium). It controls around 40 percent of global trade in potash.

31. The database used contains information on both policy and private rate-fixing arrangements affecting maritime trade with the United States.

32. The National Competition Policy aimed to achieve an efficient provision of publicly provided goods and services through reforms designed to minimize restrictions on competition and promote competitive neutrality. It also required structural reform of public monopolies and required owners of monopoly facilities to negotiate third-party access agreements with other users.

33. Note that the positive effect in the long run found by Blanchard and Giavazzi (2003) assumes a reduction in entry costs. Without this, there would be no effect in the long run.

34. The applicability of these results outside the OECD is not clear: one might expect the effects of product market regulation to be more modest in developing countries, for example, due to higher levels of informality and a lower capacity for supervision.

35. This is drawn from the OECD income distribution database, which uses the OECD's poverty threshold for each country (that is, 50 percent of the median income) based on the equivalent income figures for each country.

36. Unless specified, the term productivity refers to total factor productivity.

37. Much of the available evidence about the effects of competition is set out in an OECD Factsheet on how competition policy affects macro-economic outcomes (OECD 2014b) and a World Bank Group note on competition policy (Kitzmuller and Martinez Licetti 2012).

38. More empirical evidence of this effect is provided by Harris and Li 2008; Disney, Haskel, and Heden 2003; Hahn 2000; Fukao and Kwon 2006; and Hsieh and Klenow 2009 and 2012.

39. See Backus (2012) for a study of the ready-mix cement industry finding that in this case the within-firm effects (which he terms X-inefficiency) seemed to dominate.

40. See for example Polder and Veldhuizen 2010; Grünewald 2009; and Carlin, Schaffer, and Seabright 2004.

41. Taylor (2002, 2007) finds a 10 percent reduction in output due to NIRA, and notes in Wright and Zeiler (2014), "What would have happened had the NIRA never been passed? The economy would almost certainly have recovered more quickly. Once the banking crisis had permanently ended and [Franklin D.] Roosevelt devalued the dollar, [...], the recovery appeared to be self-sustaining. Had the NIRA not interfered with this progression, the term 'Great Depression' might not have come into existence."

42. Michael M. Weinstein in Brunner (1981).

43. In a subsequent study of differential competition policy responses to the crisis, Cole and Ohanian (2013) also find that pro-cartel policies in fascist European economies delayed recovery.

44. See criticisms by, for example, Krugman (2011).

45. To be considered a "substantively meaningful competition law," the legislation under review had to (i) have, at least inter alia, the declared purpose of fostering or safeguarding market competition

in the national economy and (ii) contain, at a minimum, a prohibition of cartels or cartel-like forms of collusion (that is, disallow price-fixing agreements or coordinated reductions in production, market-sharing agreements, etc.).

46. A reduction in regulatory restrictiveness equivalent to moving from the 75th percentile of regulatory restrictiveness to the 25th percentile of regulatory restrictiveness in terms of a country's Product Market Regulation indicator.

## Bibliography

Abate, M. A. 2013. "Economic Effects of Air Transport Liberalization in Africa." Paper presented at the African Economic Conference, Johannesburg, South Africa, October 28–30.

Aghion, P., N. Bloom, R. Blundell, R. Griffith, and P. Howitt. 2005. "Competition and Innovation: An Inverted-U Relationship." *Quarterly Journal of Economics* 120 (2): 701–28.

———. 2009. "The Effects of Entry on Incumbent Innovation and Productivity." *Review of Economics and Statistics* 91 (1): 20–32.

Aghion, P., R. Blundell, R. Griffith, P. Howitt, and S. Prantl. 2004. "Entry and Productivity Growth: Evidence from Microlevel Panel Data." *Journal of the European Economic Association* 2: 265–76.

Aghion, P., M. Braun, and J. Fedderke. 2008. "Competition and Productivity Growth in South Africa." *Economics of Transition* 16 (4): 741–68.

Aghion, P., J. Cai, M. Dewatripont, L. Du, A. Harrison, and P. Legros. 2015. "Industrial Policy and Competition." *American Economic Journal: Macroeconomics* 7 (4): 1–32.

Ahn, S. 2002. "Competition, Innovation, and Productivity Growth: A Review of Theory and Evidence." OECD Economics Working Paper 317, Organisation for Economic Co-operation and Development, Paris.

Alesina, A., S. Ardagna, G. Nicoletti, and F. Schiantarelli. 2005. "Regulation and Investment." NBER Working Paper 9560, National Bureau of Economic Research, Cambridge, MA.

Amin, M. 2007. "Labor Regulation and Employment in India's Retail Stores." Policy Research Working Paper 4314, World Bank, Washington, DC.

Amin, M., and A. Islam. 2014. "Are There More Female Managers in the Retail Sector? Evidence from Survey Data in Developing Countries." *Journal of Applied Economics* 17 (2): 213–28.

Anderson, Robert D. 2008. "China's Accession to the WTO Agreement on Government Procurement: Procedural Considerations, Potential Benefits and Challenges, and Implications of the Ongoing Re-negotiation of the Agreement." *Public Procurement Law Review* 17: 161.

Andrabi, Tahir, Jishnu Das, and Asim Ijaz Khwaja. 2015. "Report Cards: The Impact of Providing School and Child Test Scores on Educational Markets." Policy Research Working Paper 7226, World Bank, Washington, DC.

Argent, J., and T. Begazo. 2015. "Competition in Kenyan Markets and Its Impact on Income and Poverty: A Case Study on Sugar and Maize." Policy Research Working Paper 7179, World Bank, Washington, DC.

Arkolakis, C., A. Costinot, and A. Rodríguez-Clare. 2012. "New Trade Models, Same Old Gains?" *American Economic Review 2012* 102 (1): 94–130.

Arnold, J. M., G. Nicoletti, and S. Scarpetta. 2011. "Regulation, Resource Reallocation and Productivity Growth." *European Investment Bank Papers* 16 (1): 90–115.

Arvis, J.-F., G. Raballand, and J. Marteau. 2010. "Total Logistics Cost on a Transit Corridor." In *Connecting Landlocked Developing Countries to Markets*, edited by J.-F. Arvis, R. Carruthers, G. Smith, and C. Willoughby. Washington, DC: World Bank.

Assous, M., and A. K. Dutt. 2013. "Growth and Income Distribution with the Dynamics of Power in Labour and Goods Markets." *Cambridge Journal of Economics* 37 (6): 1407–30.

Atkin, D., and D. Donaldson. 2014. "Who's Getting Globalized? The Size and Implications of Intranational Trade Costs." https://bfi.uchicago.edu/sites/default/files/research/Atkin_Donaldson _WGG_paper.pdf.

Atkin, D., B. Faber, and M. Gonzalez-Navarro. 2015. "Retail Globalization and Household Welfare: Evidence from Mexico." NBER Working Paper 21176, National Bureau of Economic Research, Cambridge, MA.

Backus, M. 2012. "Why Is Productivity Correlated with Competition?" Cornell University and eBay Research, October.

Badinger, Harald. 2007. "Market Size, Trade, Competition, and Productivity: Evidence from OECD Manufacturing Industries." *Applied Economics* 39 (17): 2143–57.

Baek, C., Y. Kim, and H. Kwon. 2009. "Productivity Growth and Competition across the Asian Financial Crisis: Evidence from Korean Manufacturing Firms." Center for Economic Institutions Working Paper Series, No. 2009–12.

Baker, J., and S. Salop. 2015. "Antitrust, Competition Policy, and Inequality." Working Paper 41. http:// digitalcommons.wcl.american.edu/fac_works_papers/41.

Banerji, A., and J. Meenakshi. 2004. "Buyer Collusion and Efficiency of Government Intervention in Wheat Markets in Northern India: An Asymmetric Structural Auctions Analysis." *American Journal of Agricultural Economics* 86 (1): 236–53.

Bardasi, E., S. Sabarwal, and K. Terrell. 2011. "How Do Female Entrepreneurs Perform? Evidence from Three Developing Regions." *Small Business Economics* 37 (4): 417–41.

Barone, G., and F. Cingano. 2011. "Service Regulation and Growth: Evidence from OECD Countries." *Economic Journal* 121 (555): 931–57.

Barrett, B., and A. Dorosh. 1996. "Farmers' Welfare and Changing Food Prices: Nonparametric Evidence from Rice in Madagascar." *American Journal of Agricultural Economics* 78 (3): 656–69.

Bassanini, A., and R. Duval. 2009. "Unemployment, Institutions, and Reform Complementarities: Re-assessing the Aggregate Evidence for OECD Countries." *Oxford Review of Economic Policy* 25 (1): 40–59.

Bellows, N. M., B. W. Bellows, and C. Warren. 2011. "Systematic Review: The Use of Vouchers for Reproductive Health Services in Developing Countries." *Tropical Medicine and International Health* 16 (1): 84–96. doi: 10.1111/j.1365-3156.2010.02667.x.

Benham, L. 1972. "The Effect of Advertising on the Price of Eyeglasses." *Journal of Law and Economics* 15 (2): 337–52.

Bertrand, M., and F. Kramarz. 2002. "Does Entry Regulation Hinder Job Creation? Evidence from the French Retail Industry." *Quarterly Journal of Economics* 117 (4): 1369–1413.

Bhatia, M. R., and A. C. Gorter. 2007. "Improving Access to Reproductive and Child Health Services in Developing Countries: Are Competitive Voucher Schemes an Option?" *Journal of International Development* 19 (7): 975–81.

Blanchard, O., and F. Giavazzi. 2003. "Macroeconomic Effects of Regulation and Deregulation in Goods and Labor Markets." *Quarterly Journal of Economics* 118 (3): 879–907.

Bloom, N., M. Draca, and J. Van Reenen. 2011. "Trade Induced Technical Change? The Impact of Chinese Imports on Innovation, IT and Productivity." NBER Working Paper 16717, National Bureau of Economic Research, Cambridge, MA.

Bloom, N., T. Kretschmer, and J. Van Reenen. 2009. "Work-Life Balance, Management Practices, and Productivity." In *International Differences in the Business Practices and Productivity of Firms,* edited by R. B. Freeman and K. L. Shaw, 15–54. Chicago: University of Chicago Press.

Bloom, N., C. Propper, S. Seiler, and J. Van Reenen. 2015. "The Impact of Competition on Management Quality: Evidence from Public Hospitals." *Review of Economic Studies* 82 (2): 457–89.

Bloom, N., and J. Van Reenen. 2007. "Measuring and Explaining Management Practices across Firms and Countries." *Quarterly Journal of Economics* 122 (4): 1351–1408.

Blundell, R., R. Griffith, and J. Van Reenen. 1999. "Market Share, Market Value, and Innovation in a Panel of British Manufacturing Firms." *Review of Economic Studies* 66 (3): 529–54.

Bokhari, S., and G. Fournier. 2013. "Entry in the ADHD Drugs Market: Welfare Impact of Generics and Me-Too's." *Journal of Industrial Economics* 61 (2): 339–92.

Bolotova, Y. 2009. "Cartel Overcharges: An Empirical Analysis." *Journal of Economic Behavior and Organization* 70: 321–41.

Bolotova, Y., M. Connor, and D. Miller. 2009. "Factors Influencing the Magnitude of Cartel Overcharges: An Empirical Analysis of the US Market." *Journal of Competition Law and Economics* 5: 361–81.

Borjas, G. J., and V. A. Ramey. 1995. "Foreign Competition, Market Power, and Wage Inequality." *Quarterly Journal of Economics* 10 (November): 1075–1110.

Bouis, R., O. Causa, L. Demmou, R. Duval, and A. Zdzienicka. 2012. "The Short-Term Effects of Structural Reforms: An Empirical Analysis." OECD Economics Department Working Papers 949, OECD Publishing, Paris.

Boulhol, Herve. 2010. "Pro-competitive Effect of Trade and Non-decreasing Price-Cost Margins." *Oxford Bulletin of Economics and Statistics* 72 (3): 326–56.

Boyer, M., and R. Kotchoni. 2014. "How Much Do Cartels Overcharge?" TSE Working Paper 14–462, Toulouse School of Economics (TSE).

Braconier, H., and J. Ruiz-Valenzuela. 2014. "Gross Earning Inequalities in OECD Countries and Major Non-member Economies: Determinants and Future Scenarios." OECD Economics Department Working Paper 1139, OECD Publishing, Paris.

Brunner, K., ed. 1981. *The Great Depression Revisited.* Boston/The Hague/London: Kluwer-Nijhoff Publishing.

Bryant, G., and E. Eckard. 1991. "Price Fixing: The Probability of Getting Caught." *Review of Economics and Statistics* 73 (3): 531–36.

Brynjolfsson, E., and Michael D. Smith. 2003. "Consumer Surplus in the Digital Economy: Estimating the Value of Increased Product Variety at Online Booksellers." *Management Science* 49 (11): 1580–96.

Buccirossi, P., L. Ciari, T. Duso, G. Spagnolo, and C. Vitale. 2013. "Competition Policy and Productivity Growth: An Empirical Assessment." *Review of Economics and Statistics* 95 (4): 1324–36.

Burda, M., and P. Weil. 2005. "Blue Laws." Unpublished working paper. http://www.philippeweil.com/research/blue2.pdf.

Busso, M., and S. Galiani. 2014. "The Causal Effect of Competition on Prices and Quality: Evidence from a Field Experiment." NBER Working Paper 20054, National Bureau of Economic Research, Cambridge, MA.

Cacciatore, M., R. Duval, and G. Fiori. 2012. "Short-Term Gain or Pain? A DSGE Model-Based Analysis of the Short-Term Effects of Structural Reforms in Labour and Product Markets." OECD Economics Department Working Paper 948, OECD Publishing, Paris.

Cadot, O., L. Dutoit, and J. de Melo. 2009. "The Elimination of Madagascar's Vanilla Marketing Board 10 Years On." *Journal of African Economies* 18 (3): 388–430.

Capobianco, A., J. Davies, and S. Ennis. 2014. "Implication of Globalisation for Competition Policy: The Need for International Co-operation in Merger and Cartel Enforcement." http://papers.ssrn.com/sol3/papers.cfm?abstract_id=2450137.

Card, D., and A. Krueger. 1994. "Minimum Wages and Employment: A Case Study of the Fast-Food Industry in New Jersey and Pennsylvania." *American Economic Review* 84 (4): 772–93.

Carlin, W., M. Schaffer, and P. Seabright. 2004. "A Minimum of Rivalry: Evidence from Transition Economies on the Importance of Competition for Innovation and Growth." *Contributions in Economic Analysis and Policy* 3 (1).

Causa, Orsetta, Alain de Serres, and Nicolas Ruiz. 2014. "Can Growth-Enhancing Policies Lift All Boats? An Analysis Based on Household Disposable Incomes." OECD Economics Department Working Papers, OECD Publishing, Paris.

Chaudhuri, S., P. K. Goldberg, and P. Jia. 2006. "Estimating the Effects of Global Patent Protection in Pharmaceuticals: A Case Study of Quinolones in India." *American Economic Review* 96 (5): 1477–1514.

Christiaensen, L., and L. Demery. 2007. "The Role of Agriculture in Poverty Reduction: An Empirical Perspective." Policy Research Working Paper 4013, World Bank, Washington, DC.

Clarke, J. L., and S. J. Evenett. 2003. "A Multilateral Framework for Competition Policy?" In *The Singapore Issues and the World Trading System*, edited by J. L. Clarke and S. J. Evenett. Bern: State Secretariat for Economic Affairs.

Cole, H. L., and L. E. Ohanian. 2004. "New Deal Policies and the Persistence of the Great Depression: A General Equilibrium Analysis." *Journal of Political Economy* 112 (4): 779–816.

————. 2013. "The Impact of Cartelization, Money, and Productivity Shocks on the International Great Depression." NBER Working Paper 18823, National Bureau of Economic Research, Cambridge, MA.

Comanor, W. S., and R. H. Smiley. 1975. "Monopoly and the Distribution of Wealth." *Quarterly Journal of Economics* 89 (2): 177–94.

Combe, E., C. Monnier, and R. Legal. 2008. "Cartels: The Probability of Getting Caught in the European Union." Bruges European Economic Research Papers no. 12.

ComMark Trust. 2006. "Clear Skies over Southern Africa: The Importance of Air Transport Liberalisation for Economic Growth." ComMark Trust, Woodmead, South Africa.

Competition Authority of Kenya. 2015. "Unlocking Growth Potential in Kenya: Dismantling Regulatory Obstacles to Competition." Competition Authority of Kenya.

Connor, J. 2014. "Price-Fixing Overcharges." Social Science Research Network, Purdue University; American Antitrust Institute (AAI).

Connor, J., and G. Helmers. 2006. "Statistics on Modern Private International Cartels, 1990–2005." Working Paper 06–11, Purdue University, College of Agriculture, Department of Agricultural Economics, West Lafayette, IN.

Connor, J. M., and Y. Bolotova. 2006. "Cartel Overcharges: Survey and Meta-analysis." *International Journal of Industrial Organization* 24 (6): 1109–37.

Connor, J. M., and R. Lande. 2008. "Cartel Overcharges and Optimal Cartel Fines." In Vol. 3 of *Issues in Competition Law and Policy*, edited by S. W. Waller, 2203–18. ABA Section of Antitrust Law, American Bar Association.

Conway, P., and R. Herd. 2008. "Improving Product Market Regulation in India: An International and Cross-State Comparison." Economics Department Working Paper 599, OECD Publishing, Paris.

Conway, P., R. Herd, and T. Chalaux. 2008. "Product Market Regulation and Economic Performance across Indian States." OECD Economics Department Working Papers no. 600, OECD Publishing, Paris.

Correa, J. A. 2012. "Innovation and Competition: An Unstable Relationship." *Journal of Applied Econometrics* 27 (1): 160–66.

Cowling, K., and M. Waterson. 1976. "Price-Cost Margins and Market Structure." *Economica* 43 (177): 267–74.

Creedy, J., and R. Dixon. 1998. "The Relative Burden of Monopoly on Households with Different Incomes." *Economica* 65 (258): 285–93.

Creedy, J., and R. Dixon. 2000. "Relative Welfare Losses and Imperfect Competition in New Zealand." *New Zealand Economic Papers* 34 (2): 269–86.

Davies, S., and P. Ormosi. 2014. "The Deterrent Effect of Anti-cartel Enforcement: A Tale of Two Tails." CCP Working Paper 14-6, ESRC Centre for Competition Policy, University of East Anglia.

De Hoyos, R., and D. Medvedev. 2009. "Poverty Effects of Higher Food Prices: A Global Perspective." Policy Research Working Paper 4887, World Bank, Washington, DC.

De Loecker, J., P. K. Goldberg, A. K. Khandelwal, and N. Pavcnik. 2016. "Prices, Markups, and Trade Reform." *Econometrica* 84 (2): 445–510.

De Rosa, D., S. Madzarevic, A. Boromisa, and V. Sonje. 2009. "Barriers to Competition in Croatia: The Role of Government Regulation." Policy Research Working Paper, World Bank, Washington, DC.

Disney, R., J. Haskel, and Y. Heden. 2003. "Restructuring and Productivity Growth in UK Manufacturing." *Economic Journal* 113 (489): 666–94.

Dunn, A. 2012. "Drug Innovations and Welfare Measures Computed from Market Demand: The Case of Anti-cholesterol Drugs." *American Economic Journal: Applied Economics* 4 (3): 167–89.

Dutt, A. 1984. "Rent, Income Distribution and Growth in an Underdeveloped Agrarian Economy." *Journal of Development Economics* 15 (1–3): 185–211.

———. 2013. "Government Spending, Aggregate Demand and Economic Growth." *Review of Keynesian Economics* 1 (1): 105–19.

Duval, R., J. Elmeskov, and L. Vogel. 2007. "Structural Policies and Economic Resilience to Shocks." OECD Economics Department Working Paper 567, OECD Publishing, Paris.

Edmond, C., V. Midrigan, and D. Yi Xu. 2011. "Competition, Markups, and the Gains from International Trade." Federal Reserve Bank of Minneapolis.

Ellis, K., and R. Singh. 2010. *Assessing the Economic Impact of Competition.* London: Overseas Development Institute.

EL.STAT. 2011. Labour Force Survey (database).

Engelberg, Alfred B. 2014. "Have Prescription Drug Brand Names Become Generic?" *American Journal of Managed Care* 20 (11): 867–69.

Epifani, P., and G. Gancia. 2011. "Trade, Markup Heterogeneity and Misallocations." *Journal of International Economics* 83 (1): 1–13.

European Commission. 2015. "European Competition Policy: Facts, Figures and Priorities." http://ec.europa.eu/competition/publications/facts_figures_2015.pdf.

Fabrizio, K. R., N. L. Rose, and C. D. Wolfram. 2007. "Do Markets Reduce Costs? Assessing the Impact of Regulatory Restructuring on US Electric Generation Efficiency." *American Economic Review* 97 (4): 1250.

Feldmann, H. 2012. "Product Market Regulation and Labor Market Performance around the World." *Labour* 26 (3): 369–91.

Fink, C., A Mattoo, and C. Neagu. 2002. "Trade in International Maritime Services: How Much Does Policy Matter?" *World Bank Economic Review* 16 (1): 81–108.

Fiori, G., G. Nicoletti, S. Scarpetta, and F. Schiantarelli. 2012. "Employment Effects of Product and Labour Market Reforms: Are There Synergies?" *Economic Journal* 122 (558): F79–F104. doi: 10.1111/j.1468-0297.2011.02494.

Franco, C., F. Pieri, and F. Venturini. 2016. "Product Market Regulation and Innovation Efficiency." *Journal of Productivity Analysis* 45 (3): 299–315.

Francois, J., and I. Wooton. 2010. "Market Structure and Market Access." *World Economy* 33 (7): 873–93. doi: 10.1111/j.1467-9701.2010.01234.x.

Fukao, K., and H. U. Kwon. 2006. "Why Did Japan's TFP Growth Slow Down in the Lost Decade? An Empirical Analysis Based on Firm-Level Data of Manufacturing Firms." *Japanese Economic Review* 57 (2): 195–228.

Gebreab, F. A. 2002. "Getting Connected: Competition and Diffusion in African Mobile Telecommunications Markets." Policy Research Working Paper 2863, World Bank, Washington, DC.

Genakos, C., and S. Danchev. 2014. "Evaluating the Impact of Sunday Trading Devaluation." OECD Competition Working Paper. www.oecd.org/officialdocuments/publicdisplaydocumentpdf/?cote=DAF/COMP/WP2(2014)1&docLanguage=En.

Goolsbee, A., and C. Syverson. 2008. "How Do Incumbents Respond to the Threat of Entry? Evidence from the Major Airlines." *Quarterly Journal of Economics* 123 (4): 1611–33.

Gorodnichenko, Y., J. Svejnar, and K. Terrell. 2010. "Globalization and Innovation in Emerging Markets." *American Economic Journal: Macroeconomics* 2 (2): 194–226.

Gorter, A., P. Sandiford, Z. Rojas, and M. Salvetto. 2003. "Competitive Voucher Schemes for Health." Background paper, World Bank, Central American Health Institute, Washington, DC.

Govinda, H., J. Khumalo, and S. Mkhwanazi. 2014. "On Measuring the Economic Impact: Savings to the Consumer Post Cement Cartel Bust." Paper submitted for the Competition Commission and Tribunal 8th Annual Conference on Competition Law, Economics and Policy, September 4–5.

Griffith, R., and H. Harmgart. 2012. "Supermarkets Competition in England and Planning Regulation." *International Review of Retail, Distribution and Consumer Research* 22 (1): 1–25.

Griffith, R., R. Harrison, and G. Macartney. 2007. "Product Market Reforms, Labour Market Institutions and Unemployment." *Economic Journal* 117 (159): C142–C166. doi: 10.1111/j.1468-0297.2007.02039.

Griffith, R., R. Harrison, and H. Simpson. 2006. "The Link between Product Market Reform, Innovation and EU Macroeconomic Performance." European Economy Economic Paper 243, European Commission.

Grünewald, O. 2009. "Market Incentives to Business Innovation in Sweden." *Yearbook on Productivity 2009.* Statistics Sweden, Stockholm.

Guadalupe, M. 2007. "Product Market Competition, Returns to Skill, and Wage Inequality." *Journal of Labor Economics* 25 (3): 439–74.

Gupta, A. 2013. "Estimating Direct Gains in Consumer Welfare in Telecommunications Sector." *Journal of Consumer Policy* 36 (2): 119–38.

Hahn, C. H. 2000. "Entry, Exit, and Aggregate Productivity Growth: Microevidence on Korean Manufacturing." Working Paper 272, OECD Economics Department.

Harris, R., and Q. C. Li. 2008. "Evaluating the Contribution of Exporting to UK Productivity Growth: Some Microeconomic Evidence." *World Economy* 31 (2): 212–35.

Hausman, Jerry A. 1997a. "Valuation of New Goods under Perfect and Imperfect Competition." In *The Economics of New Goods,* edited by Timothy F. Bresnahan and Robert J. Gordon. Chicago: University of Chicago Press.

———. 1997b. "Valuing the Effect of Regulation on New Services in Telecommunications." *Brookings Papers on Economic Activity: Microeconomics* 28: 1–54.

Hausman, Jerry A., and Ephraim Leibtag. 2007. "Consumer Benefits from Increased Competition in Shopping Outlets: Measuring the Effect of Wal-Mart." *Journal of Applied Econometrics* 22 (7): 1157–77.

Hausman, Jerry A., and Gregory K. Leonard. 2002. "The Competitive Effects of a New Product Introduction: A Case Study." *Journal of Industrial Economics* 50 (3): 237–63.

Hoekman, B., and B. Javorcik. 2004. "Policies Facilitating Firm Adjustment to Globalization." Policy Research Working Paper 3441, World Bank and CEPR, Washington, DC.

Hsieh, C. T., and P. J. Klenow. 2009. "Misallocation and Manufacturing TFP in China and India." *Quarterly Journal of Economics* 124 (4): 1403–48.

———. 2012. "The Life Cycle of Plants in India and Mexico." NBER Working Paper 18133, National Bureau of Economic Research, Cambridge, MA.

Hüschelrath, K. 2008. "Detection of Anticompetitive Horizontal Mergers." ZEW Discussion Paper 08–106, Zentrum für Europäische Wirtschaftsforschung/Centre for European Economic Research, Mannheim, Germany.

IMS Institute for Healthcare Informatics. 2013. *Declining Medicine Use and Costs: For Better or for Worse? A Review of the Use of Medicines in the United States in 2012.* Parsippany, NJ: IMS Institute.

Inchauste, Gabriela, João Pedro Azevedo, B. Essama-Nssah, Sergio Olivieri, Trang Van Nguyen, Jaime Saavedra-Chanduvi, and Hernan Winkler. 2014. *Understanding Changes in Poverty.* Directions in Development Series. Washington, DC: World Bank.

Ivanic, M., and W. Martin. 2008. "Implications of Higher Global Food Prices for Poverty in Low-Income Countries." *Agricultural Economics* 39 (s1): 405–16.

Januszewski, S. I., J. Köke, and J. K. Winter. 2002. "Product Market Competition, Corporate Governance and Firm Performance: An Empirical Analysis for Germany." *Research in Economics* 56 (3): 299–332.

Jayne, T. S., and G. Argwings-Kodhek. 1997. "Consumer Response to Maize Market Liberalization in Urban Kenya." *Food Policy* 22 (5): 447–58.

Jayne, T. S., D. Mather, N. Mason, and J. Ricker-Gilbert. 2013. "How Do Fertilizer Subsidy Programs Affect Total Fertilizer Use in Sub-Saharan Africa? Crowding Out, Diversion, and Benefit/Cost Assessments." *Agricultural Economics* 44 (6): 687–703.

Jenny, F. 2012. "Export Cartels in Primary Products: The Potash Case in Perspective." *Trade, Competition, and the Pricing of Commodities* (January): 99–132.

Kerdrain, C., I. Koske, and I. Wanner. 2010. "The Impact of Structural Policies on Saving, Investment and Current Accounts." OECD Economics Department Working Paper 815, OECD Publishing, Paris.

Khumalo, J., J. Mashiane, and S. Roberts. 2014. "Harm and Overcharge in the South African Precast Concrete Products Cartel." *Journal of Competition Law and Economics* 10 (3): 621–46.

Kim, D. 2004. "Estimation of the Effects of New Brands on Incumbents' Profits and Consumer Welfare: The U.S. Processed Cheese Market Case." *Review of Industrial Organization* 25 (3): 275–93.

Kirton, Raymond Mark. 2013. "Gender, Trade and Public Procurement Policy: Kenya, India, Australia, Jamaica." Commonwealth Secretariat, London. http://thecommonwealth.org/sites /default/files/news-items/documents/Gender,%20Trade%20and%20Public%20 Procurement%20Policy.pdf.

Kitzmuller, M., and M. Martinez Licetti. 2012. "Competition Policy: Encouraging Thriving Markets for Development." Viewpoint: Public Policy for the Private Sector, Note 331 (August), World Bank Group, Washington, DC.

Komninos, A., W. Beckert, E. van Damme, M. Dewatripont, J. Franks, A. ten Kate, and P. Legros. 2009. "Quantifying Antitrust Damages." Study prepared for the European Commission.

Krugman, Paul. 2011. "Bad Faith Economic History." *New York Times*, September 27.

Kunaka, C. 2011. *Logistics in Lagging Regions: Overcoming Local Barriers to Global Connectivity.* Washington, DC: World Bank.

Kwoka, Jr., John E. 2013. "Does Merger Control Work? A Retrospective on U.S. Enforcement Actions and Merger Outcomes." *Antitrust Law Journal* 78 (3): 619–50.

Lee, D. H., and D. H. Lee. 2006. "Estimating Consumer Surplus in the Mobile Telecommunications Market: The Case of Korea." *Telecommunications Policy* 30 (10): 605–21.

Lopez, R. A., and E. Lopez. 2003. "The Impacts of Imports on Price-Cost Margins: An Empirical Illustration." *Empirical Economics* 28: 403–416.

Maillebiau, Eric, and Mark Hansen. 1995. "Demand and Consumer Welfare Impacts of International Airline Liberalisation: The Case of the North Atlantic." *Journal of Transport Economics and Policy* 29 (2): 115–36.

———. 2008. "Demand and Consumer Welfare Impacts of International Airline Liberalization: The Case of the North Atlantic Downloads." University of California Transportation Center, Berkeley.

Marinov, Rosen. 2010. "Competitive Pressure in Transition: A Role for Trade and Competition Policies?" *Journal of Industry, Competition and Trade* 10 (1): 1–31.

Masson, Alison, and Robert L. Steiner. 1985. *Generic Substitution and Prescription Drug Prices: Economic Effects of State Drug Product Selection Law.* Washington, DC: U.S. Federal Trade Commission.

Mbongwe, Thabiso, Benson O. Nyagol, Taimi Amunkete, Dr. Michael Humavindu, Junior Khumalo, George Nguruse, and Emmanuel Chokwe. 2014. "Understanding Competition at the Regional Level: An Assessment of Competitive Dynamics in the Cement Industry across Botswana, Kenya, Namibia, South Africa, Tanzania, and Zambia." Draft paper for presentation at pre-ICN Forum, African Competition Forum, Marrakech, April 22.

McCorriston, S. 2006. "Imperfect Competition and International Agricultural Commodity Markets." In *Agricultural Commodity Markets and Trade: New Approaches to Analyzing Market Structure and Instability,* edited by A. Sarris and D. Hallam, 134–62. FAO and Edward Elgar.

Mehta, P. S., N. Nayak, and A. Aggarwal. 2012. "Global Welfare Consequences of Cartelisation in Primary Commodities: Cases of Natural Rubber and Banana." In *Global Welfare Consequences of Cartelisation in Primary Commodities,* 81–98. London: Centre for Economic Policy Research.

Miniaci, R., C. Scarpa, and P. Valbonesi. 2008. "Distributional Effects of Price Reforms in the Italian Utility Markets." *Fiscal Studies* 29: 135–63. doi: 10.1111/j.1475-5890.2008.00071.x.

Mncube, L. 2013. "Strategic Entry Deterrence: Pioneer Foods and the Bread Cartel." *Journal of Competition Law and Economics* 9 (3): 637–54.

Nalebuff, B., and E. Stiglitz. 1983. "Information, Competition, and Markets." *American Economic Review* 73 (2): 278–83. http://www.jstor.org/stable/1816855.

Nevo, A. 2001. "Measuring Market Power in the Ready-to-Eat Cereal Industry." *Econometrica* 69 (2): 307–42.

———. 2003. "New Products, Quality Changes, and Welfare Measures Computed from Estimated Demand Systems." *Review of Economics and Statistics* 85 (2): 266–75.

Nickell, S. 1996. "Competition and Corporate Performance." *Journal of Political Economy* 104 (4): 724–46.

Nicoletti, G., and S. Scarpetta. 2003. "Regulation, Productivity and Growth: OECD Evidence." *Economic Policy* 18 (36): 9–72.

———. 2005. "Product Market Reforms and Employment in OECD Countries." OECD Economics Department Working Paper 472, OECD Publishing, Paris. doi: 10.1787/463767160680.

OECD (Organisation for Economic Co-operation and Development). 2003. "Transparency in Government Procurement: The Benefits of Efficient Governance." TD/TC/WP/(2002)31 /Rev2/14. OECD, Paris, April.

———. 2007. "Taxi Services: Competition and Regulation." OECD Competition Committee Roundtable. http://www.oecd.org/daf/competition/sectors/41472612.pdf.

———. 2009. "Guidelines for Fighting Bid Rigging in Public Procurement." OECD, Paris. Available at http://www.oecd.org/daf/competition/cartels/42851044.pdf.

OECD (Organisation for Economic Co-operation and Development). 2010. Competition Assessment Toolkit. http://www.oecd.org/competition/assessment-toolkit.htm.

———. 2011. "OECD Review of Telecommunication Policy and Regulation in Mexico." http://www.oecd.org/sti/broadband/50550219.pdf.

———. 2012. "Competition and Commodity Price Volatility." OECD Policy Roundtable. http://www.oecd.org/daf/competition/CompetitionAndCommodityPriceVolatility2012.pdf.

———. 2013. *Supporting Investment in Knowledge Capital, Growth and Innovation.* Paris: OECD Publishing. doi: 10.1787/9789264193307-en.

———. 2014a. *Competition Assessment Reviews: Greece.* Paris: OECD Publishing. doi: http://dx.doi.org/10.1787/9789264206090-en.

———. 2014b. "Factsheet on How Competition Policy Affects Macro-economic Outcomes." http://www.oecd.org/competition/factsheet-macroeconomics-competition.htm.

———. 2014c. "Focus on Inequality and Growth." http://www.oecd.org/els/soc/Focus-Inequality-and-Growth-2014.pdf.

———. 2015. "Does Competition Create or Kill Jobs? Background Note by the Secretariat." DAF/COMP/GF(2015)9, October.

———. Forthcoming. *Reference Guide on Ex-post Evaluation of Competition Authorities' Enforcement Decisions.*

OECD (Organisation for Economic Co-operation and Development) and Comisión Federal de Competencia, México. 2010. "A Competition Policy Assessment of the Domestic Airline Sector in Mexico and Recommendations to Improve Competition." Available at http://www.oecd.org/daf/competition/45049588.pdf.

———. 2012. "Eliminación de restricciones a la participación extranjera en México — Evaluación de los beneficios potenciales en algunas industrias." Available at http://www.oecd.org/daf/competition/IEDreporteOCDECFC.pdf.

OFGEM (Office of Gas and Electricity Markets). 2008. "Energy Supply Probe: Initial Findings Report." OFGEM Consultation Document, OFGEM, London, October 6.

———. 2011. "The Retail Market Review: Findings and Initial Proposals." Consultation document. Ref. 34/11. OFGEM, London.

Olley, G. S., and A. Pakes. 1996. "The Dynamics of Productivity in the Telecommunications Equipment Industry." *Econometrica* 64 (6): 1263–97.

Pavcnik, N. 2002. "Trade Liberalization, Exit, and Productivity Improvements: Evidence from Chilean Plants." *Review of Economic Studies* 69 (1): 245–76.

Pellizzari, M., and G. Pica. 2011. "Liberalizing Professional Services: Evidence from Italian Lawyers," Working Paper 372, IGIER, Innocenzo Gasparini Institute for Economic Research, Bocconi University, Milan.

Peterson, E. B., and J. M. Connor. 1995. "A Comparison of Oligopoly Welfare Loss Estimates for U.S. Food Manufacturing." *American Journal of Agricultural Economics* 77 (2): 300–08.

Petrin, A. 2002. "Quantifying the Benefits of New Products: The Case of the Minivan." NBER Working Paper 8227, National Bureau of Economic Research, Cambridge, MA.

Polder, M., and E. Veldhuizen. 2010. "Innovation and Competition in the Netherlands: Testing the Inverted-U for Industries and Firms." Discussion Paper 201021, Statistics Netherlands, The Hague.

Porto, G. G., N. D. Chauvin, and M. Olarreaga. 2011. *Supply Chains in Export Agriculture, Competition, and Poverty in Sub-Saharan Africa.* Centre for Economic Policy Research.

Posner, R. A. 1974. "Theories of Economic Regulation." *Bell Journal of Economics and Management Science* 5: 335–58.

Postema, B., M. Goppelsroeder, and P. Bergeijk. 2006. "Cost and Benefits of Merger Control: An Applied Game Theoretic Perspective." *Kyklos* 59 (1): 85–98.

Price, C. W. 2005. "The Effect of Liberalizing UK Retail Energy Markets on Consumers." *Oxford Review of Economic Policy* 21 (1): 128–44. doi:10.1093/oxrep/gri007.

Productivity Commission. 1999. "Impact of Competition Policy Reforms on Rural and Regional Australia." Report no. 8, Productivity Commission, Australian Government.

Rashid, S. 2002. "Dynamics of Agricultural Wage and Rice Price in Bangladesh." MSSD Discussion Paper No. 44, International Food Policy Research Institute (IFPRI), Washington, DC.

Ravallion, M. 1990. "Welfare Impacts of Food Price Changes under Induced Wage Responses: Theory and Evidence from Bangladesh." *Oxford Economic Papers* 42: 574–85.

Rijkers, B., C. L. Freund, and A. Nucifora. 2014. "All in the Family: State Capture in Tunisia." Policy Research Working Paper 6810, World Bank, Washington, DC.

Rodríguez-Castelán, C. 2011. "Poverty Effects of Market Concentration." Policy Research Working Paper 7515, World Bank, Washington, DC.

Rognlie, M. 2015. "Deciphering the Fall and Rise in the Net Capital Share." Brookings Papers on Economic Activity, Brookings BPEA Conference, March.

Romer, C. D. 1999. "Why Did Prices Rise in the 1930s?" *Journal of Economic History* 59 (1): 167–99.

Ros, A. 2010. "A Competition Policy Assessment of the Domestic Airline Sector in Mexico and Recommendations to Improve Competition." Work Commissioned by the Organisation for Economic Co-operation and Development and Executive Branch of the Mexican Government under the Program *Proceso para el foralecimiento del marco regulatorio para la competitividad en México*. http://www.oecd.org/daf/competition/45049588.pdf.

———. 2011. "The Determinants of Pricing in the Mexican Domestic Airlines Sector." *Review of Industrial Organization* 38 (1): 43–60.

Sakakibara, M., and M. E. Porter. 2001. "Competing at Home to Win Abroad: Evidence from Japanese Industry." *Review of Economics and Statistics* 83 (2): 310–22.

Scherer, F. M. 1967. "Market Structure and the Employment of Scientists and Engineers." *American Economic Review* 57 (3): 524–31.

Schiffbauer, M., A. Sy, S. Hussain, H. Sahnoun, and P. Keefer. 2015. *Jobs or Privileges: Unleashing the Employment Potential of the Middle East and North Africa*. Washington, DC: World Bank.

Schivardi, F., and E. Viviano. 2011. "Entry Barriers in Retail Trade." *Economic Journal, Royal Economic Society* 121 (551): 145–70.

Schmidt, K. M. 1997. "Managerial Incentives and Product Market Competition." *Review of Economic Studies* 64 (2): 191–213. http://restud.oxfordjournals.org/content/64/2/191.short.

Schwab, D., and E. Werker. 2014. "Profits and Economic Development." Harvard Business School BGIE Unit Working Paper 14-087.

Sekkat, K. 2009. "Does Competition Improve Productivity in Developing Countries?" *Journal of Economic Policy Reform* 12 (2): 145–62.

Sexton, R. J., and M. Zhang. 2006. "An Assessment of the Impact of Food-Industry Market Power on U.S. Consumers." In *New Empirical Industrial Organization and the Food System*, edited by H. Kaiser and N. Suzuki, 155–94. Peter Lang Publishing Group in association with GSE Research.

Sithebe, T., K. Barzeva, and L. Mncube. 2014. "Is Breast the Best? Evaluating the Price Effects of the Nestlé/Pfizer Merger in the South African Infant Milk Formula Market." Competition Commission of South Africa. http://www.compcom.co.za/wp-content/uploads/2014/09/Is-breast-the-best-Evaluating-the-price-effects-of-the-NestlPfizer-merger-in-the-South-African-infant-milk-formula-market.pdf.

Spector, D. 2004. "Competition and the Capital-Labor Conflict." *European Economic Review* 48 (1): 25–38.

Steiner, F. 2001. "Regulation, Industry Structure and Performance in the Electricity Supply Industry." *OECD Economics Studies* 32 (2001/I): 143–82.

Steinman, M. A., M. M. Chren, and C. S. Landefeld. 2007. "What's in a Name? Use of Brand versus Generic Drug Names in United States Outpatient Practices." *Journal of General Internal Medicine* 22 (5): 645–48.

Stern, N., and A. Dixit. 1982. "Oligopoly and Welfare: A Unified Presentation with Applications to Trade and Development." *European Economic Review* 19 (1): 123–43.

Stigler, G. 1964. "A Theory of Oligopoly." *Journal of Political Economy* 72.

Stryszowska, M. 2012. "Estimation of Loss in Consumer Surplus Resulting from Excessive Pricing of Telecommunication Services in Mexico." OECD Publishing, Paris.

Sutherland, D., and P. Hoeller. 2013. "Growth-Promoting Policies and Macroeconomic Stability." OECD Economics Department Working Paper 1091, OECD Publishing, Paris.

Swinnen, J. F. M., and A. Vandeplas. 2006. "Contracting, Competition and Rent Distribution in Commodity Value Chains." LICOS, Centre for Transition Economics and Department of Economics, K. U. Leuven, Belgium.

Symeonidis, G. 2008. "The Effect of Competition and Wages and Productivity: Evidence from the United Kingdom." *Review of Economics and Statistics* 90 (1): 134–46.

Syverson, C. 2004a. "Product Substitutability and Productivity Dispersion." *Review of Economics and Statistics* 86 (2): 534–55.

———. 2004b. "Market Structure and Productivity: A Concrete Example." *Journal of Political Economy* 112 (6): 1181–1222.

Taylor, J. E. 2002. "The Output Effects of Government Sponsored Cartels during the New Deal." *Journal of Industrial Economics* 50 (1): 1–10.

———. 2007. "Cartel Code Attributes and Cartel Performance: An Industry-Level Analysis of the National Industrial Recovery Act." *Journal of Law and Economics* 50 (3): 597–624.

Tenn, S., and B. W. Wendling. 2014. "Entry Threats and Pricing in the Generic Drug Industry." *Review of Economics and Statistics* 96 (2): 214–28.

Teravaninthorn, S., and G. Raballand. 2009. "Transport Prices and Costs in Africa: A Review of the International Corridors." World Bank, Washington, DC.

Treichel, V., M. Hoppe, O. Cadot, and J. Gourdon. 2012. "Import Bans in Nigeria Increase Poverty." Africa Trade Policy Note 28, World Bank, Washington, DC.

Urzúa, C. M. 2008. "Evaluación de los efectos distributivos y espaciales de las empresas con poder de mercado en México." Mexican Federal Competition Commission. http://www.oecd.org/daf/competition/45047597.pdf.

———. 2013. "Distributive and Regional Effects of Monopoly Power." *Economia Mexicana NUEVA EPOCA* 22 (2): 279–95.

Van Reenen, J. 2011. "Does Competition Raise Productivity through Improving Management Quality?" *International Journal of Industrial Organization* 29 (3): 306–16.

Viviano, E. 2008. "Entry Regulations and Labour Market Outcomes: Evidence from the Italian Retail Trade Sector." *Labour Economics* 15 (6): 1200–22.

Voigt, S. 2009. "The Effects of Competition Policy on Development: Cross-Country Evidence Using Four New Indicators." *Journal of Development Studies* 45 (8): 1225–48.

Warr, P. 2005. "Food Policy and Poverty in Indonesia: A General Equilibrium Analysis." *Australian Journal of Agricultural and Resource Economics* 49 (4): 429–51.

Wodon, Q., C. Tsimpo, P. Backiny-Yetna, G. Joseph, F. Adoho, and H. Coulombe. 2008. "Potential Impact of Higher Food Prices on Poverty: Summary Estimates for a Dozen West and Central

African Countries." Policy Research Working Paper WPS4745, Vol. 1, World Bank, Washington, DC.

Wodon, Q., and H. Zaman. 2010. "Higher Food Prices in Sub-Saharan Africa: Poverty Impact and Policy Responses." *World Bank Research Observer* 25 (1): 157–76.

World Bank. 2011. *On the Edge of Uncertainty: Poverty Reduction in Latin America and the Caribbean during the Great Recession and Beyond.* Washington, DC: World Bank. https://openknowledge .worldbank.org/handle/10986/17196.

———. 2012a. *World Development Report 2012: Gender Equality and Development.* Washington, DC: World Bank. https://openknowledge.worldbank.org/handle/10986/4391.

———. 2012b. "Toward a More Competitive Business Environment." Mexico Policy Note 2, World Bank Group, Washington, DC.

———. 2013a. *IFC Jobs Study: Assessing Private Sector Contributions to Job Creation and Poverty Reduction.* Washington, DC: World Bank.

———. 2013b. *Republic of Armenia: Accumulation, Competition, and Connectivity.* Washington, DC: World Bank. https://openknowledge.worldbank.org/bitstream/handle/10986/16781/811370revi sion0Box0379837B00PUBLIC0.pdf?sequence=1.

———. 2013c. *Republic of Turkey Reform for Competitiveness Technical Assistance: Fostering Open and Efficient Markets through Effective Competition Policies.* Washington, DC: World Bank.

———. 2014a. *The Unfinished Revolution: Bringing Opportunity, Good Jobs, and Greater Wealth to All Tunisians.* Washington, DC: World Bank.

———. 2014b. *Sticky Feet: How Labor Market Frictions Shape the Impact of International Trade on Jobs and Wages.* Washington, DC: World Bank.

———. 2015. "Peru: Building on Success: Boosting Productivity for Faster Growth." Working Paper 99400, Vol. 1, World Bank, Washington, DC.

———. 2016. *South Africa Economic Update: Promoting Faster Growth and Poverty Alleviation through Competition.* South Africa Economic Update, issue no. 8. Washington, DC: World Bank Group.

———. Forthcoming (a). "Competition-Related Regulatory Restrictions to Engineering Services in Brazil." February 2016 draft.

———. Forthcoming (b). "A Short Review of Competition-Related Regulatory Restrictions in Legal, Accountancy and Architecture Services Based on the OECD Product Market Regulation." February 2016 draft.

World Bank and African Competition Forum. Forthcoming. "Boosting Competition in Africa."

Wright, R. E., and T. W. Zeiler, eds. 2014. *Guide to U.S. Economic Policy.* Washington, DC: CQ Press.

Xiao, W. 2008. "The Competitive and Welfare Effects of New Product Introduction: The Case of Crystal Pepsi." Food Marketing Policy Center Research Report 149938, University of Connecticut.

Zhang, Yin-Fang, David Parker, and Colin Kirkpatrick. 2008. "Electricity Sector Reform in Developing Countries: An Econometric Assessment of the Effects of Privatisation, Competition and Regulation." *Journal of Regulatory Economics* 33 (2): 159–78.

# PART II

# New Research on Competition Policies and Their Welfare-Enhancing Effects

# 3. Cartel Damages to the Economy: An Assessment for Developing Countries

**Marc Ivaldi** (Toulouse School of Economics, France, and CEPR, UK), **Frédéric Jenny** (ESSEC Business School, France), and **Aleksandra Khimich** (Toulouse School of Economics, France)

Competition policy implementation and enforcement, including cartel deterrence and detection, require substantial investments. Therefore, it is important to understand to what extent these investments are compensated in terms of prevented damages to consumers. The answer to this question is especially important for developing countries for which the decision to create or reinforce an antitrust authority largely depends on associated costs, while a sufficient and robust quantitative evaluation of potential benefits is still missing. The present chapter aims at providing the missing evidence by assessing the aggregate economic harm caused by cartels in developing countries. The authors find that the economic damage of cartels already detected in developing countries is substantial—in terms of affected sales related to gross domestic product (GDP), the maximum rate reaches up to 6.38 percent, while excess profits resulting from unjustified price overcharges reach up to 1 percent when related to GDP. Furthermore, if one wants to take into account cartels that were not detected, the total damage appears to be at least four times larger.

## 3.1 Introduction

Detecting and punishing cartels come first on the agenda of antitrust authorities in developed countries because of their potential harm to consumers' welfare and the economy as a whole. Cartels are considered damaging per se because colluding firms have strong incentives to overcharge customers for products or services, without adapting quality, or to block the entry of new rivals. From a sample of international cartels

e-mails: marc.ivaldi@tse-fr.eu; frederic.jenny@gmail.com; khimich.sasha@gmail.com. This research project is funded by the CEPR PEDL (Centre for Economic Policy Research Private Enterprise Development in Low-Income Countries) program. It is also recognized by the UNCTAD RPP (United Nations Conference on Trade and Development Research Partnership Platform) initiative. Any opinions expressed here are those of the authors and not those of the CEPR or the UNCTAD.

operating since 1990 in primary product markets, Connor (2011a) draws a conclusion that cartels' prices have been at least 25 percent higher than their competitive benchmark.

Because implementation of the antitrust enforcement requires substantial investments, it can be questioned to what extent those costs are outweighed by consumer gains. This is especially relevant for developing competition authorities that often experience tough budget constraints, but struggle to find the supportive evidence that could advocate their efforts. The research on these questions in developing countries is scarce and has mainly followed a qualitative approach. Among the few relevant studies—for example, those of Jenny (2006); Connor (2011a); and Levenstein, Suslow, and Oswald (2003)—only the latter offers a relatively comprehensive quantitative assessment of the aggregate economic impact of cartel agreements. Based on international trade flow data and a list of 42 detected international cartels operating in developing markets and prosecuted in the United States and the European Union (EU) in the 1990s, the authors estimated that imports affected by cartel agreements constitute 3.4–8.4 percent of total imports to developing countries—an amount equivalent to 0.6–1.7 percent of the GDP in these countries. The authors suggested that the actual impact is more significant due to the hidden nature of cartels and various methodological problems that did not allow taking all the observations in the dataset into account.

This chapter takes into account both international and local cartels that were prosecuted in more than 20 developing countries from 1995 to 2013 and measures the aggregated cartel excess profits resulting from price overcharges. It, therefore, provides a better understanding of the actual damage suffered by consumers in developing countries. Competition authorities in developing countries may have a practical interest in the respective results for the advocacy of their efforts.

The chapter will conform to the following outline. Section 3.2 comprises a description of the data mining process and a discussion of the descriptive statistics of the collected sample of cartels. In section 3.3 we present our original methodology that was developed to estimate the price overcharges resulting from cartel agreements and that we applied on some cases from our database. While quite simple and intuitive, this methodology can be implemented with a very limited set of data. Competition authorities may wish to take advantage of the proposed methodology for their own cartel investigations because it will reduce the data required to estimate the damages in terms of price overcharge. Overall, the collected data do not have any strong evidence for the widespread idea that cartel price overcharges in developing countries are more significant than those in developed countries. We show, however, that the impact on prices is at least of a similar scale, which calls for adequate antitrust measures.

In section 3.4 we focus on several indicators aggregated on a country level. First, as in Levenstein, Suslow, and Oswald (2003), we calculate aggregate sales affected by collusive practices. Second, and more innovatively, we calculate aggregated cartels' excess profits that result from unjustified price overcharges. Both measures are then related to GDP to take into account different scales of the considered economies. We supplement the discussion with a simplified cost-benefit-like analysis of the antitrust enforcement by relating aggregated cartels' excess profits to the budget of the corresponding competition authority. We find that in terms of affected sales related to GDP the rate reaches up to 6.38 percent. The direct harm to consumers in terms of cartels' excess profits related to GDP is also significant, reaching almost 1 percent. The results also demonstrate that, in a majority of considered countries, excessive profits significantly exceed competition authority budget expenses aimed at preventing them.

Our estimates reflect the minimum bound for the economic harm caused by cartels. One of the major reasons is that quantitative information on detected cartels in developing countries is very limited, but also because a potentially large number of cartels remain undetected. In section 3.5 we assess the extent to which our aggregated estimates of harm are underestimated due to the hidden nature of cartels. Specifically, we adopt the methodology proposed in Combe, Monnier, and Legal (2008) to estimate the annual probability of a cartel to be uncovered. We find that at least three out of four existing cartels remain undetected, implying that the actual damage is at least four times larger than suggested by our estimations. Section 3.6 concludes the chapter.

## 3.2 Collected Data: Cartels' Profiles in Developing Countries

### 3.2.1 Data Collection Process

Given the complexity of possible reasons for collusive behavior among firms and consequent welfare effects, we focus only on so-called "hard-core" cartels, that is, cartels with participants who aim at increasing their profits by the means of collective price or market share fixing. These agreements between firms are assumed to be harmful for consumers per se and, therefore, are illegal in the majority of antitrust jurisdictions. Hence, the database does not include buyers' cartels, collective predatory pricing cases, or collusive agreements that were given an exemption by competition authorities.[1]

Our analysis is based on the original dataset containing information on 249 major hard-core cartels that were prosecuted in more than 20 developing countries from 1995 to 2013. In annex 3A we provide a reduced version of this dataset, containing the list of countries, identified cartels, and their respective periods of existence. We restrict our attention to the period from 1995 to 2013 because many developing countries have established their competition authorities just recently, if at all; hence no data, or only very poor data, could be collected for earlier years. Nevertheless, we find the 1995–2013 time period to be sufficiently long to obtain a representative sample of cartels.

The list of countries chosen to participate in the study was created according to whether the country is officially classified as developing and whether its competition authority (i) exists, (ii) is active, and (iii) has sufficient experience in terms of cartel detection.[2] This selection process excluded many of the developing countries from consideration. However, they can still profit from the current study to advocate for the introduction of antitrust law or its enforcement.

For every defined hard-core cartel, we aimed at collecting quite substantial descriptive data, including:

a. *Relevant market(s)*. When a cartel operated in several markets, we considered those as separate cartel cases whenever the available data allowed doing so;
b. *Number of colluding firms;*
c. *Cartel duration.* When no exact dates but only year of creation or breakdown of a cartel was known, we assumed that the cartel's duration comprised the complete year from January to December, similar for months;
d. *Cartel sales.* Cartel sales were calculated as revenues of all colluding firms during the considered period in the relevant market only;
e. *Applied penalties.* Collected data on penalties include all applied fines (both for companies and responsible executives) as well as finalized settlements; and
f. *Estimated price overcharges.* Given the lack of information on losses in output or consumers' welfare, we have chosen price overcharge as a measure of the economic harm caused by cartels.

To perform the cost-benefit analysis we also collected data on budgets of the selected competition authorities.

When provided in different currencies, a cartel's sales were converted into U.S. dollars by using average exchange rates corresponding to the period of a cartel's operations, while for penalties we used the exchange rate that corresponded to the period when the final decision on the case was made.

The collected pieces of data were obtained from numerous sources such as competition authorities' websites, companies' annual reports, reports of international organizations such as the Organisation for Economic Co-operation and Development (OECD), the United Nations Conference on Trade and Development (UNCTAD), and so on. A significant piece of information came from the existing database on international cartels.[3] However, our sample would not be so rich without cooperation from local competition authorities.[4] For this purpose, they were asked to fill out a special questionnaire (see annex 3B). In addition to the above-mentioned target data, this questionnaire requested some additional inputs required for our methodology, developed to estimate price overcharges. These include prices, market shares, and sales of colluding companies at least for one period during the cartel's existence. All the other cartel-specific information requested in the questionnaire is not mandatory to implement the methodology, but helps to better calibrate market parameters and, eventually, improve the estimation results. We explain the methodology in more detail and report obtained estimates in section 3.3.

Our database makes a substantial contribution in summarizing and, most important, enriching the existing knowledge on price overcharges caused by cartels. It comprises not only international cartels (as, for instance, in Levenstein, Suslow, and Oswald 2003) but also cartels formed locally. Cartels' industrial profile in our sample is similar to the one described extensively by Jenny (2006); therefore we do not go deeper into this aspect, but instead focus on the quantitative assessment of cartels' activities.

### 3.2.2 Descriptive Statistics of the Sample

We provide some descriptive statistics of the collected data in table 3.1.

In our sample, the median number of colluding firms is equal to 5, while the median duration of a cartel is 27 months.[5] Analogous calculations for a sample of cartels in developed economies (see Connor 2011b) indicate similar results for the number of cartel participants but, surprisingly, a higher level of median cartel duration—around 50 months in North America and 70 months in the EU. These results may seem to be in conflict with the popular opinion that collusion is sustainable for longer periods in developing countries because of stronger market imperfections and weaker antitrust enforcements. However, they are in line with theoretical results in Motta (2004), demonstrating that in unstable but growing markets—which developing markets are—cartel life can be shorter than in stable markets as deviations from the collusive agreement can indeed be very attractive.

We do not provide descriptive statistics for the absolute values of cartels' sales and penalties because the considered countries, their economies, and, eventually, cartels are much diversified in scale. Instead, we find it important to report descriptive statistics of some relative measures, such as the ratio between penalties and excess profits, as well as

**TABLE 3.1    Descriptive Statistics of the Collected Sample of Cartels**

| Variable | Number of observations | Mean | Median | Standard deviation | Minimum | Maximum |
|---|---|---|---|---|---|---|
| Duration (months) | 185 | 46 | 27 | 50 | 1 | 420 |
| Number of cartel members | 200 | 15 | 5 | 37 | 2 | 300 |
| Price overcharge (%) | 83 | 23.1 | 20.0 | 14.6 | 2.4 | 75.0 |
| Penalties/excess profits ratio (%) | 72 | 51.8 | 19.0 | 118.2 | 0.0 | 950.5 |

*Note:* We measure the price overcharge as a percentage of the cartel price. When minimum and maximum bounds for the price overcharge were both known, we used the average between the two.

the price overcharge ratio that we measure with respect to the cartel price. We define a cartel's excess profits as the extra margin resulting from sales at unreasonably higher prices, taking cartel unit sales as a basis.[6]

As table 3.2 shows, the median price overcharge rate in our sample is of the same range as the one estimated for the EU countries (20 percent versus 19.50–22.48 percent) and is only slightly higher than the 16.7–19.0 percent estimated for the United States and Canada.

We also observe that the ratio between penalties and excess profits in our sample has quite extreme ends—it varies from 0 to 950 percent. The lower end can be explained by the fact that not all of the detected cartels were subject to the fine. The reason for the extremely high upper end is that, depending on jurisdiction, penalties can be calculated as a percentage of the total sales of cartel members instead of sales in the relevant market only. Nevertheless, the average for developing countries' ratio remains very low compared to the U.S. level (19 percent against 57 percent) and is just slightly below the EU level of 26 percent (see figure 3.1).

A cartel's stability depends on its ability to prevent deviation by firms, while the benefits of deviation depend, in part, on fines to be imposed in case of detection. Remarkably, on average neither developing nor developed competition authorities recoup excess profits gained by cartel members. According to Hammond (2005) and

**TABLE 3.2   Comparison of Cartel Price Overcharges from Existing Studies**

| Country/group and respective period | Number of observations | Mean (%) | Median (%) |
|---|---|---|---|
| Developing countries (our sample), 1995–2013 | 83 | 23.10 | 20.00 |
| Developing countries (Connor 2010b), up to 2009 | 33 | — | — |
| China | 2 | 17.42 | 17.42 |
| Egypt, Arab Rep. | 4 | 20.26 | 19.61 |
| India | 1 | 16.67 | 16.67 |
| Korea, Rep. | 22 | 24.01 | 14.89 |
| Mexico | 1 | 15.25 | 15.25 |
| Pakistan | 1 | 42.53 | 42.53 |
| Turkey | 2 | 53.49 | 53.49 |
| European Union (Connor 2011b), 1990–2010 | 105 | — | 19.50 |
| European Union (Connor 2010b), 2000–09 | 11 | 28.16 | 22.48 |
| United States (Connor 2011b), 1990–2010 | 97 | — | 19.00 |
| United States and Canada (Connor 2010b), 2000–09 | 29 | 39.61 | 16.67 |

*Note:* Estimates from Connor 2010b were originally provided with respect to "but-for" prices, that is, prices that would be observed in the absence of the cartel. These were recalculated with respect to the cartel price to be comparable with the other data in the table.
— = not available.

A Step Ahead

## FIGURE 3.1 Comparison of Penalty-Excess Profits Ratios

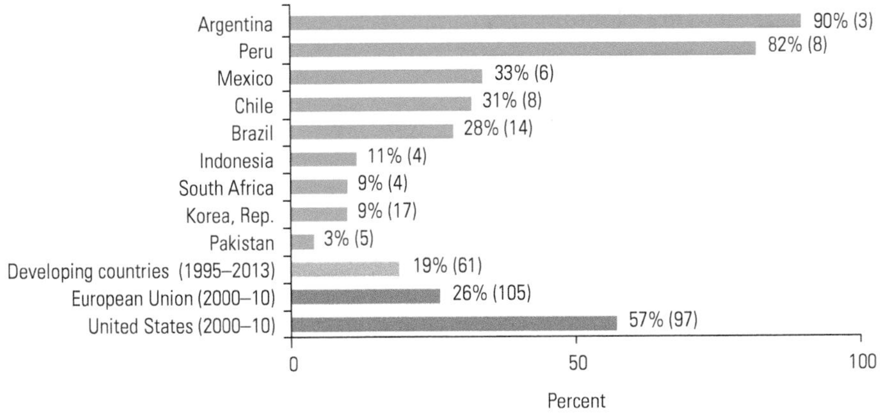

*Source:* Data on the European Union and the United States are obtained from Connor 2011b.

*Note:* In parentheses we provide the number of cartel cases used to calculate each ratio. Country-level data are given only when the number of observations is more than 2.

Connor (2011a), such a situation should be characterized as "under-punishment" because optimal deterrence of cartel formation requires penalties to be higher than the extra profits resulting from collusive arrangements. At the same time, Allain et al. (2011) argue that the majority of fines imposed by the European Commission can nevertheless be considered as "optimal." The authors' understanding of the optimal deterrence relies on the idea that, for a given probability of detection, the fine should be high enough to wipe out any *expected* profit from the infringement, even if the eventual ratio between the fine and *realized* excessive profits is well below one.

The optimality of a penalty rule that does not require a 100 percent recoupment of the excess cartel profits can be also supported by the following reasoning: on the one hand, by imposing fines, competition authorities try to deter formation of cartels or make it more risky for existing collusion to continue, expecting that a more severe penalty rule will result in a stronger deterrent effect. On the other hand, a penalty that is too high can undermine the firm's ability to be an efficient market player, cutting against the initial goal of restoring fair competition. If a cartel was operating on the market for many years, it might be impossible for the firms to pay back all the extra profits that they have obtained by overcharging.

This chapter does not aim at assessing whether penalty rules in developing countries are optimal or not, nor does it claim that they should follow the example of developed antitrust jurisdictions. What we want to highlight here is that factors that define the optimal antitrust deterrence policy are quite numerous, starting from the very definition of the optimality. Therefore, effective penalty rules indeed can (and, most probably, should) be country specific.

## 3.3 Estimation of Price Overcharges

### 3.3.1 Description of the Methodology

The study data on price overcharges constitute a departure point toward the measure of the aggregated economic harm induced by cartelization. We acknowledge that, in the context of developing countries, estimations of price overcharges appear to be very scarce. One of the reasons is that this kind of estimation is usually demanding in terms of time and expertise—this represents a serious constraint for a young competition authority. Besides, to condemn a cartel, antitrust authorities rely mostly on the evidence of coordination activities (such as phone calls, meeting notes, and so on) rather than on economic indications (such as parallel pricing or constant market shares, and the like). To address this issue and to estimate some of the missing price overcharges, we have developed an original methodology that is simple enough to implement in a context of limited data, while having a solid economic basis.

The methodology employs the following approach, applied on a case-by-case basis. Based on the collected cartel data, one first performs the calibration of the supply and demand parameters that are specific to the relevant market. If the cartel operates on several markets, calibration should be performed for each of them separately, given that collected data allow doing so. Having the calibrated demand and supply parameters at hand, one then proceeds with the simulation of hypothetical (counterfactual) competitive equilibrium, that is, market absent cartelization. Finally, by comparing realized and counterfactual (competitive) states, one is able to assess the effect of each particular cartel in terms of price overcharges, volume losses, or even consumers' welfare. Below we explain each of these steps in more detail.

We consider a model that describes the observed equilibrium outcomes (that is, prices and volumes) on the differentiated product market, where firms compete in prices. Differentiating product characteristics—such as, for example, quality—do not depend on prices or volumes and are assumed to be fixed.

Specifically, market demand is derived from a general class of discrete choice models of consumer behavior. The logit specification that we have chosen is simple and flexible enough to obtain the desirable structure of demand. We assume that there are $N$ potential consumers in the relevant market, each of them considering buying one unit of the product from one of $J$ firms that form a cartel. Consumers can also choose the so-called "outside option," which can represent a substitute offered by firms not participating in the cartel, or a decision not to buy at all. We denote the "outside option" with index "0."

The utility of consumer $i$ buying product $j$ is defined as $U_{ij} = \delta_j - \alpha p_j + v_{ij}$, where $\delta_j, j = \overline{1, J}$ are parameters of product differentiation (for example, quality or postsales services) that are specific to each product, and $p_j$ is the price of product $j$. $\alpha$ is the marginal utility of money, common for all products and consumers, that reflects the sensitivity of consumers to the price relative to how they value quality. Higher $\alpha$ would mean that consumers put a higher weight to the price, rather than the quality characteristic of the product. $v_{ij}$ is the consumer $i$'s idiosyncratic utility component that is specific to product $j$. It is assumed to be identically and independently distributed across consumers and products.

Consumer $i$ chooses product $j$ if it maximizes her expected utility, such that $U_{ij} > U_{ij'} \forall j' \neq j$. According to Berry (1994), demand for product $j$ can, therefore, be represented by the following equation:

$$\ln(s_j(p)) = \ln(s_0(p)) + \delta_j - \alpha p_j \qquad (3.1)$$

where $s_j$ is a market share of the firm $j$, $s_0$ is the share of the outside option, and $p = (p_1, p_2, \ldots, p_J)$ is the price vector.

Or, eventually, by

$$s_j(p) = \frac{\exp(\delta_j - \alpha p_j)}{1 + \sum_{i=1}^{J} \exp(\delta_i - \alpha p_i)}, \; \forall j = \overline{1, J} \qquad (3.2)$$

where the utility of the outside option is normalized to zero $(U_{i0} = 0, \forall i = \overline{1, N})$.

Note that, since the size of the market is fixed to $N$, market shares can be easily interpreted in terms of sold quantities and vice versa.

In such a framework, the profit of each firm $j$ is defined by the function $\pi_j(p) = (p_j - c_j)^* s_j(p)^* N$, where $c_j$ are marginal costs that are assumed to be constant.

Further, we employ several hypotheses that help to simplify the model and recover unknown demand and supply functions' parameters. We first presume that cartel participants act in perfect collusion, choosing prices that maximize the joint profit of the cartel. Second, we assume that cartel members agree to fix their gross margins to a certain value that is constant for all firms, such that $(p_j - c_j) = const, \forall j = \overline{1, J}$. Under these assumptions, from the cartel's joint profit maximization problem, it is easy to obtain the following equilibrium condition for the cartelized market:

$$(p_j - c_j) = \frac{1}{\alpha s_0}, \forall j = \overline{1, J}. \qquad (3.3)$$

The system of equations that includes (3.1) and (3.3), therefore, fully describes the cartelized market equilibrium $(p_j^{cartel}, s_j^{cartel}), \forall j = \overline{1, J}$. Cartel prices are those observed on the market during the period of cartelization. However, market shares that are employed in the model (denoted further as $s_j^{cartel}$) are not the same as those observed from the market data (denoted as $\bar{s}_j^{cartel}$). The latter stand for the market shares within the cartel, while the former take into account the presence of the outside option, such that

$$\bar{s}_j^{cartel} = \frac{s_j^{cartel}}{(1-s_0)} \text{ and } \sum_{j=1}^{J} \bar{s}_j^{cartel} = 1. \tag{3.4}$$

To be able to solve the system of equations composed of (3.1) and (3.3), and by doing so recover unknown parameters, we set two of them exogenously.[7] First, we fix the average cartel margin $AM \equiv \sum_{j=1}^{J} \bar{s}_j^{cartel} \dfrac{(p_j^{cartel} - c_j)}{p_j^{cartel}}$. Note, that this is equivalent to fixing the level of gross individual cartel margins $(p_j^{cartel} - c_j), \forall j = \overline{1,J}$.[8] The second input that we set exogenously is the market share of the "outside option," denoted as $s_0$.

Cartel members' gross margins could be extracted from the companies' annual reports, even if often only approximately (due to complexities associated with calculation of marginal costs). Estimation of the market share of the outside option appears more problematic. There is no standard procedure to define the potential market size, and methodologies might differ significantly depending on the product and the market considered. However, independently of the methodology that is chosen, the sum of all market shares, including the one of the outside option, must be always equal to one, that is, $\sum_{j=1}^{J} s_j^{cartel} + s_0 = 1.$

Having set exogenously average cartel margin and the share of the outside option, we first recover parameter $\alpha$ from equation (3.3):

$$\alpha = \frac{1}{s_0(p_j^{cartel} - c_j)} = \frac{\sum_{j=1}^{J} \dfrac{\bar{s}_j^{cartel}}{p_j^{cartel}}}{AM \times s_0}. \tag{3.5}$$

By substituting all known and calculated variables in equation (3.1), one is able to calculate the parameters of differentiation $\delta_j$.

In the list of inputs set exogenously one can choose to replace the cartel's margin or the share of the outside option with marginal costs if they are known. In this case equation (3.5) will remain valid, and further steps of the methodology will not be affected.

While choosing values of exogenous parameters, one needs to make sure that obtained values of marginal costs and parameter of sensitivity to the price ($\alpha$) are non-negative.[9] There are no sign restrictions to the values of $\delta_j$.

At this point, from demand equations (3.1) or (3.2), one is able to calculate the set of own- and cross-price elasticities (respectively):

$$\varepsilon_{jj} = -\alpha p_j^{cartel}(1 - s_j^{cartel}), \forall j = \overline{1,J} \tag{3.6}$$

$$\varepsilon_{ji} = \alpha s_i^{cartel} p_i^{cartel}, \forall j, i = \overline{1,J}, i \neq j. \tag{3.7}$$

Obtained estimates for demand price elasticities can be compared against the existing ones from the other sources. This may be seen as an additional cross-validation for the values of exogenous parameters and may result in corresponding corrections.

At the end of the calibration procedure, all missing demand and supply parameters $(\alpha, \delta_j$ and $c_j, \forall j = \overline{1,J})$ are recovered. They are assumed to remain the same whether the market is cartelized or not. In what follows we explain in more detail the second step of our methodology—simulation of the counterfactual (competitive) state of the market.

In the absence of collusion, each firm would independently set a price to maximize its profits, taking into account its own marginal costs and expected pricing strategy of competitors. A standard solution for each firm's profit maximization problem would be:

$$p_j - c_j = \frac{1}{\alpha(1 - s_j)}, \forall j = \overline{1,J}. \tag{3.8}$$

Note, that demand equation (3.2) remains valid.

As a solution of the system of equations that describes the competitive market—that is, equations (3.8) and (3.2)—we obtain counterfactual (competitive) prices $p_j^c, j = \overline{1,J}$ and corresponding market shares $s_j^c, j = \overline{1,J}$. By comparing the cartel's prices with competitive prices, we can calculate price overcharge for every cartel member as well as the cartel's average price overcharge:

$$\Delta P\% = \sum_{j=1}^{J} \bar{s}_j^{cartel} \frac{(p_j^{cartel} - p_j^c)}{p_j^{cartel}} \times 100. \tag{3.9}$$

The formula in equation (3.9) gives a price overcharge estimate in percentage, but it can easily be transformed into excessive profits expressed in money terms by multiplying firm-specific price overcharges on the corresponding cartel member's revenues.

The chosen demand function allows calculating also the consumers' welfare in terms of consumers' surplus (see Anderson, de Palma, and Thisse [1992]):

$$CS = \frac{1}{\alpha} \ln\left(1 + \sum_{j=1}^{J} \exp(\delta_j - \alpha p_j)\right). \tag{3.10}$$

Consumers' welfare losses due to price overcharge could, therefore, be calculated as the following:

$$Welfare\,losses\,(\%) = \frac{\left( \ln\left( 1 + \sum_{j=1}^{J} \exp(\delta_j - \alpha p_j^c) \right) - \ln\left( 1 + \sum_{j=1}^{J} \exp(\delta_j - \alpha p_j^{cartel}) \right) \right)}{\ln\left( 1 + \sum_{j=1}^{J} \exp(\delta_j - \alpha p_j^c) \right)} \cdot 100.$$

(3.11)

An obvious advantage of our methodology is that it requires very limited data: it can be employed with only information on prices and market shares of colluding companies observed at least for one point in time during the cartel's existence. On the other hand, the methodology is based on a relatively simple economic model and uses a few assumptions that result in certain limitations. We discuss them below.

First, the demand function is based on a simple logit model, which is quite flexible but has a specific property of Independence of Irrelevant Alternatives. In a nutshell, this property transforms in a particular consumer behavior: motivated by a price increase, consumers would switch to the product with the maximum market share, but not the one with the closest quality characteristics. Indeed, it may not be a true behavioral pattern in reality.

On top of this, calibrated demand and supply parameters can be very sensitive to the level of inputs that are set exogenously. Considering reasonable ranges for these inputs rather than exact values will help in assessing the robustness of obtained calibration outcomes. Additional market expertise, when available, could also help to narrow down the range of calibrated market parameters and, eventually, obtain more precise estimations of price overcharges and consumers' welfare losses.

### 3.3.2 Application of the Methodology on Selected Cartel Cases

It is unfortunate to acknowledge that competition authorities in developing countries often do not possess even the minimum economic data required to employ the methodology. Or, even if they do, it is often considered confidential. For this reason, it was possible to perform estimations using our methodology only in 11 cartel cases. Results are provided in table 3.3. Annex 3C illustrates the application of the proposed methodology on the price-fixing cartel between civil airlines in Brazil.

The obtained average and median price overcharge rate of 24.02 percent and 18.60 percent, respectively, are of the same magnitude as for the rest of the sample (23.1 percent and 20.0 percent, respectively; see table 3.1). We acknowledge, however, that the difference between the estimated maximum and minimum bounds of price

TABLE 3.3

**TABLE 3.3** **Estimates of Price Overcharges and Output Losses Obtained with the Use of the Developed Methodology**

| Industry (country) | Period of existence | Price overcharges | | Output losses | |
|---|---|---|---|---|---|
| | | Minimum D$p$ (%) | Maximum D$p$ (%) | Minimum D$q$ (%) | Maximum D$q$ (%) |
| Civil airlines (Brazil) | Jan'99–Mar'03 | 3.20 | 33.90 | 10.00 | 24.20 |
| Crushed rock (Brazil) | Dec'99–Jun'03 | 3.40 | 11.25 | 15.69 | 25.80 |
| Security guard services (Brazil) | 1990–2003 | 4.80 | 27.84 | 14.93 | 23.15 |
| Industrial gas (Brazil) | 1998–Mar'04 | 4.12 | 29.96 | 5.00 | 22.77 |
| Steel bars (Brazil) | 1998–Nov'99 | 5.49 | 37.84 | 10.99 | 27.81 |
| Steel (Brazil) | 1994–Dec'99 | 13.55 | 40.13 | 5.00 | 29.22 |
| Medical gases (Chile) | 2001–04 | 37.50 | 49.40 | 2.00 | 14.93 |
| Petroleum products (Chile) | Feb'01–Sep'02 | 4.57 | 9.90 | 10.43 | 23.35 |
| Construction materials (Chile) | Oct 20, '06 | 47.78 | 83.48 | 7.24 | 22.95 |
| Petroleum products II (Chile) | Mar'08–Dec'08 | 1.78 | 11.13 | 9.63 | 18.99 |
| Cement (Egypt, Arab Rep.) | Jan'03–Dec'06 | 28.20 | 39.30 | 5.00 | 10.00 |
| **Average for the category** | | **14.04** | **34.01** | **8.68** | **21.94** |
| **Average** | | **24.02** | | **15.41** | |
| **Median** | | **18.60** | | **16.90** | |

*Note:* Price overcharges are measured with respect to the cartelized price, while losses in output are measured with respect to the counterfactual (competitive) state. Minimum and maximum estimated output losses can appear rounded. This is a result of employing rounded values for exogenous inputs.

overcharges and output losses is often large. A competition authority that wants to implement the proposed methodology would certainly obtain greater precision provided it uses the best information on the input parameters.

Analysis of aggregated cartels' impact in the next section includes these additional estimations.

## 3.4 Aggregated Cartels' Effects

As we illustrated in the previous section, the descriptive statistics of the collected data demonstrate that the anticompetitive impact in terms of price overcharges is at least similar to that in developed countries, which calls for adequate antitrust measures. Young competition authorities, which often lack resources to efficiently fight against collusive practices, are having difficulty in lobbying for a greater budget and, therefore, are constantly looking for strong and motivating evidence of the benefits that their existence brings. We believe that this evidence could be provided by looking at the aggregate measures of cartelization harm that we provide in this section. The approach that we use consists in summing up the obtained cartel case-specific impact estimates in money terms and assessing their significance on the macro-economic level.

Specifically, in our analysis we focus on three aggregate indicators. First, inspired by Levenstein, Suslow, and Oswald (2003), we find it appropriate to consider aggregated sales that were affected by collusive behavior, that is, total revenues received by cartel members. More innovatively, we also assess the direct aggregate cartel damage to consumers in terms of excess profits. Both measures are summed up for all cartels in each particular country and related to the respective GDP. We supplement the discussion with a sort of "cost-benefit" analysis of the antitrust enforcement by relating the aggregated excess profits to the budget of the corresponding competition authority ("CA budget").

In order to obtain more comprehensive aggregated estimates, we fill in the remaining data gaps by applying an additional treatment to the original collected data.

First, for those countries where the competition authority sets the maximum penalty as a percentage of a cartel's sales (for instance, in Brazil, the Republic of Korea, South Africa, Ukraine, and so on), we approximate the missing cartel sales as the respective penalty in money terms divided by the maximum penalty rate.[10] Note that this approach provides an estimate of the minimum value of the cartel's sales. The penalty in those cases is set based on the sales recorded in the year preceding the one in which the court decision on the case was made. Therefore, the minimum approximated cartel sales need to be further multiplied by cartel duration in years.

Second, when the price overcharge was unknown and it was not possible to employ the proposed methodology to estimate it, we roughly approximated the cartel's excess profits by multiplying the sample median overcharge rate and cartel sales. In case cartel sales were missing, we assumed the cartel's excess profits as equal to applied penalties. Recall that, according to table 3.1, applied penalties do not, on average, compensate for the excess profits gained by cartel members. Therefore, this approximation provides a minimum level of a cartel's excess profits. Knowing the minimum level of a cartel's excess profits allowed, in turn, recovering the missing cartel sales by applying the median price overcharge rate.

Finally, to make the nominal values such as sales, excess profits, penalties, and CA budgets comparable among different years, we apply relevant denominators to take into account money depreciation.

The above data treatment was applied for cartels in countries with relatively sufficient data—namely Brazil, Chile, Colombia, Indonesia, Korea, Mexico, Pakistan, Peru, the Russian Federation, South Africa, Ukraine, and Zambia. The selection criterion is basically the availability of quantified impacts of cartels that represent a significant part of all detected cases in the country, except for Zambia, whose only quantified cartel had a tremendous economic impact.

For the countries in table 3.4 we provide the breakdown of recorded cartel cases, indicating the number of those for which the impact was quantified. Information in

**TABLE 3.4  Availability of Quantified Impacts of Detected Cartels**

| Country (period) | Number of cartels recorded | Number of cartels with data on sales | Number of cartels with data on overcharges | Number of "allocated" cartels |
|---|---|---|---|---|
| Brazil (1995–2005) | 18 | 17 (1) | 17 (3) | 17 |
| Chile (2001–09) | 17 | 16 (6) | 16 (7) | 16 |
| Colombia (1997–2012) | 18 | 17 (17) | 17 (17) | 17 |
| Indonesia (2000–09) | 12 | 8 (0) | 8 (1) | 7 |
| Korea, Rep. (1998–2006) | 26 | 26 (0) | 26 (8) | 26 |
| Mexico (2002–11) | 17 | 17 (9) | 17 (11) | 17 |
| Pakistan (2003–11) | 14 | 14 (6) | 14 (9) | 14 |
| Peru (1995–2009) | 11 | 10 (2) | 10 (2) | 10 |
| Russian Federation (2005–13) | 15 | 11 (10) | 11 (11) | 11 |
| South Africa (2000–09) | 37 | 23 (7) | 23 (18) | 23 |
| Ukraine (2003–12) | 7 | 7 (6) | 7 (7) | 3 |
| Zambia (2007–12) | 7 | 1 (0) | 1 (0) | 1 |

*Note:* The numbers in parentheses refer to the number of cases for which corresponding missing inputs were approximated by means of the treatment discussed in the text. An "allocated" cartel is one for which at least beginning or breakdown year was known.

parentheses refers to the number of cases for which corresponding missing inputs were approximated by means of the treatment already discussed. We employ the term "allocated" for those cartels for which we were able to associate sales and excess profits with a certain year, that is, when at least the cartel's beginning or breakdown year was known.

For these twelve countries we calculated the three selected indicators—aggregated excess profits and affected sales, both related to GDP, as well as aggregated excess profits related to the budget of the relevant competition authority.

Looking at the year-to-year dynamics of these indicators would be misleading because both ends of each considered period have a high risk of not being representative—either because of a low activity of the competition authority in the beginning or because the end of the period is often characterized by multiple ongoing cartel investigations that do not make part of our study. For the same reason, average indicators can also be biased. Thus, we find it important also to report, on top of average values, maximum values of each indicator together with the year that it corresponds to. Table 3.5 summarizes obtained results.

The results confirm that cartels' impact in developing economies can indeed be substantial. In terms of affected sales related to GDP, it varies among countries from 0.01 to 3.74 percent on average for the considered periods, whereas its maximum value reaches up to 6.38 percent for South Africa in 2002. Remarkably, calculations for

**TABLE 3.5  Estimates of Aggregated Economic Harm Caused by Cartelization**

| Country (period) | Aggregated excess profits/GDP (%) | | Affected sales/ GDP (%) | | Ratio of aggregated excess profits to CA budget | |
|---|---|---|---|---|---|---|
| | Average | Maximum (year) | Average | Maximum (year) | Average | Maximum (year) |
| Brazil (1995–2005) | 0.21 | 0.43 (1999) | 0.89 | 1.86 (1999) | 308 | 1,232 (1998) |
| Chile (2001–09) | 0.06 | 0.23 (2008) | 0.92 | 2.63 (2008) | 23 | 91 (2008) |
| Colombia (1997–2012) | 0.001 | 0.002 (2011) | 0.01 | 0.01 (2011) | 7 | 36 (2006) |
| Indonesia (2000–09) | 0.04 | 0.09 (2006) | 0.50 | 1.14 (2006) | 29 | 58 (2004) |
| Korea, Rep. (1998–2006) | 0.53 | 0.77 (2004) | 3.00 | 4.38 (2004) | 144 | 214 (2004) |
| Mexico (2002–11) | 0.01 | 0.02 (2011) | 0.05 | 0.11 (2011) | 7 | 19 (2011) |
| Pakistan (2003–11) | 0.22 | 0.56 (2009) | 1.08 | 2.59 (2009) | 245 | 518 (2008) |
| Peru (1995–2009) | 0.002 | 0.01 (2002) | 0.01 | 0.02 (2002) | 6.44 | 25 (2004) |
| Russian Federation (2005–13) | 0.05 | 0.12 (2012) | 0.24 | 0.67 (2012) | 0.58 | 1.45 (2008) |
| South Africa (2000–09) | 0.49 | 0.81 (2002) | 3.74 | 6.38 (2002) | 124 | 214 (2005) |
| Ukraine (2003–12) | 0.03 | 0.03 (2011) | 0.15 | 0.16 (2011) | 0.84 | 0.88 (2011) |
| Zambia (2007–12) | 0.07 | 0.09 (2007) | 0.18 | 0.24 (2007) | 11 | 27 (2007) |
| **Average** | **0.14** | | **0.90** | | **76** | |

*Note:* CA = competition authority.

Zambia are based on only one cartel for which data are available (market of fertilizers, 2007–12); but, even taking this into consideration, the impact is not negligible (0.24 percent of GDP in terms of affected sales). Actual harm to consumers in terms of aggregated cartels' excess profits is also significant, with maximum rates reaching almost 1 percent in terms of GDP for Korea in 2004 and South Africa in 2002.

We also find that aggregated cartel excess profits exceed the CA budgets on average 76 times and can reach up to 1,232 times (see the last two columns in table 3.5).[11] Data on budgets that we have collected include expenses for all activities of a given competition authority, including merger investigations that are traditionally highly demanding in terms of resources. Therefore, the cartel-specific efficiency rate can turn out significantly higher.

These results can be considered as lower-bound estimates for the economic harm caused by collusive infringements in developing countries. This is so for multiple reasons. First of all, not all of the detected cartels were taken into account. Even though some competition authorities agreed to cooperate, the authors have to acknowledge that the list of prosecuted hard-core cartels for every country is still not complete, nor were all the required data obtained for each of the recorded cases. Out of 249 defined cases, only 83 have data on price overcharges and 114 on cartels' sales. As table 3.4 illustrated, many recorded cases were excluded from calculations of the aggregate effects because of missing data. Second—and, perhaps, most important—some of the existing cartels remained uncovered. To assess how far (or how close) we are from understanding the real scale of the damage caused by cartelization, in the next section we estimate the maximum bound for the deterrence rate, that is, the annual probability of a cartel to be detected. To our knowledge this is the first attempt to do so on a sample of cartels detected in developing countries.

## 3.5  Estimation of the Deterrence Rate

To estimate the deterrence rate, we have adopted the approach proposed in Combe, Monnier, and Legal (2008). We did not modify their methodology; therefore, only a brief description of the main idea and results of its application on our database will be provided. In a nutshell, the authors consider a Markovian process with two elements that are related to the cartel's birth and death, the latter being associated with the cartel's detection. Cartels' interarrival time and duration between their birth and detection are both random variables distributed exponentially and independently across cartels.[12] The model allows estimating the instantaneous probability of cartel detection through the maximum likelihood estimation method. Because the sample naturally contains only cartels that were detected, the estimated probability is conditional on the cartel eventually being detected. This value, therefore, represents the maximum bound of the global instantaneous probability of cartel detection (the sought-for deterrence rate).

In our sample, the maximum annual probability of cartel detection is estimated at 24 percent. It is significantly higher than the upper bound of the same probability estimated by Combe, Monnier, and Legal (2008) for the EU cartels prosecuted from 1969 to 2007 (12.9–13.3 percent).[13] A lower deterrence rate for the EU can be explained by inclusion into consideration of earlier years characterized by weaker antitrust enforcement. An additional explanation can be also offered. When cartel members are international corporations, they often enter collusive agreements in several, often neighboring, developing countries. Apart from the famous vitamins cartel, the sample includes, for instance, medical gas distribution cartels prosecuted in Argentina, Brazil, Chile, Colombia, and Mexico in the late 1990s–early 2000s, or cement cartels that have existed over the last 30 years in Argentina, the Arab Republic of Egypt, Korea, Mexico, South Africa, and other developing countries. Evidence of cartel activities provided by competition authorities in other countries may serve as a trigger for local investigations and can facilitate cartel detection, increasing, therefore, the deterrence rate.

A maximum deterrence rate of 24 percent basically means that *at least* three out of four existing cartels remain uncovered. Therefore, we suggest that the actual economic harm caused by hard-core cartels in developing countries exceeds our estimations from the previous section at least fourfold.

## 3.6 Conclusions and Policy Implications

Competition policy implementation and enforcement, including cartel deterrence and detection, require substantial investments. Therefore, it is important to measure to what extent those costs are outweighed by the damages prevented to consumers. This is especially relevant for developing competition authorities, which often experience tough budget constraints.

To provide the required evidence we have collected an original dataset that contains information on 249 major hard-core cartels that were prosecuted in more than 20 developing countries from 1995 to 2013. Descriptive statistics of the collected data do not bring any strong evidence to the widespread idea that developing countries are exposed to higher cartel price overcharges than the developed ones. However, we do show that price overcharges are at least similar, which calls for adequate antitrust measures. We also show that the aggregated economic impact can be substantial. In terms of affected sales related to GDP, the maximum rate reaches up to 6.38 percent (South Africa in 2002). The actual damage in terms of cartels' excess profits is also significant, with maximum rates reaching almost 1 percent of GDP (Korea in 2004 and South Africa in 2002).

A study by Boyer and Kotchoni (2014) demonstrates, based on the sample from Connor (2010b), that data on price overcharges obtained from different methodologies, sources, and contexts are asymmetric and heterogeneous and, therefore, are subject to a significant estimation bias. Nonbiased estimates are, in fact, lower than simple medians calculated from the raw data. For example, bias correction reduces median price overcharge for the EU countries from 22.48 to 14.04 percent and from 16.67 to 13.58 percent for the United States and Canada.[14] Therefore, ideally, our own sample would require similar corrections to be made. We, nevertheless, highlight that our aggregate damage estimates correspond to their very minimum bound. This is so because of at least six reasons.

First, the present study takes into consideration only cartel cases that are already closed. It therefore does not take into account cases that were still under investigation when our study was held.

The second reason is that data on convicted cartels that are used to quantify their economic effects are very poor. This is so because, to condemn a cartel, competition authorities rely mostly on the evidence of coordination activities rather than on the economic indicators. This, coupled with confidentiality issues, resulted in elimination of multiple recorded cases from the calculation of aggregate economic harm.

Third, our study does not take into account the output effects. Collusive practices harm consumers not only in terms of inflationary effects, but also because they limit consumption. Our analysis demonstrates that, on average, a cartel decreases the production level by about 15 percent (see table 3.3). Taking these output effects into account would provide more accuracy for the estimations.

Fourth, on top of this, our estimates do not take into account either price umbrella effects[15] among noncartel members, or possible degradation in quality as a result of reduced competition among cartel members.[16]

The fifth reason is that many of the cartelized industries produce intermediary goods, such as, for instance, cement or gas. Therefore, the consequent price overcharge may proliferate further on other economic sectors, increasing the final impact manifold. By employing the country-level input-output matrices and corresponding industry pass-through rates together with estimated cartel excess profits, one would be able to (i) assess the potential impact of those proliferations, and (ii) define a set of industries that have the highest potential for creating damages and therefore deserve special attention from the competition authority. We find this to be a very promising area for further development.

The final, but probably the most important, reason for our estimates to reflect only the minimum of damages is the hidden nature of cartels. Because we estimate the maximum annual probability of uncovering an existing cartel to be around 24 percent, we suggest that the actual economic damage resulting from collusive practices in developing countries is at least four times bigger than suggested by our estimations.

We have also demonstrated that even this minimum estimated economic harm for the majority of considered countries significantly exceeds the expenditures to maintain the functionality of the relevant antitrust body. This may be seen as sought-for evidence for the competition authorities who wish to justify the requirement for additional money to improve cartel deterrence and detection. More than that, developing competition authorities may wish to take advantage of the proposed methodology for their own cartel investigations because it will reduce the data required to estimate the economic damages. The efficiency of the penalty rule can be then assessed by comparing the imposed fines with cartels' excess profits. Actual penalty-excess profits rates could be compared against relevant benchmarks that are considered as optimal by the competition authority.

The created cartels database may be seen as a reference list containing industries that are potentially vulnerable to collusive behavior. International cartel members often enter into collusive agreements in multiple, often neighboring, economies. Therefore, evidence from other countries can (and should) be employed by competition authorities in local investigations. This may encourage countries to create a worldwide platform that would allow, for instance, sharing and maintaining a common cartel database.

## Annex 3A: Major "Hard-Core" Cartels Prosecuted in Selected Developing Countries, 1995–2013

**TABLE 3A.1**  **Major "Hard-Core" Cartels Prosecuted in Selected Developing Countries, 1995–2013**

| Cartel case | Period of existence |
|---|:---:|
| **Argentina** | |
| Portland cement | 1981–99 |
| Medical gases | n/a–1997 |
| Health care services | n/a |
| Liquid petroleum gas (S.C. Bariloche) | Jan'98–Dec'98 |
| Sand (Paraná city) | Jun'99–Jul'01 |
| Liquid oxygen | Jan'97–Dec'01 |
| Cable TV (Santa Fe city) | Oct'97–Dec'01 |
| Cable TV service (football transmissions) | Jan'96–Dec'98 |
| **Brazil** | |
| Civil airlines | Jan'99–Mar'03 |
| Retail fuel dealers (Goiânia) | Apr'99–May'02 |
| Retail fuel dealers (Florianópolis) | 1999–2002 |
| Retail fuel dealers (Belo Horizonte) | 1999–2002 |
| Retail fuel dealers (Recife) | Apr'99–Feb'02 |
| Generic drugs | Jul'99–Oct'99 |
| Maritime hose | Jun'99–May'07 |
| Crushed rocks | Dec'99–Jun'03 |
| Security guard services | 1990–2003 |
| Hermetic compressors | 2001–09 |
| Industrial gas | 1998–Mar'04 |
| Air cargo | Jul'03–Jul'05 |
| Transportation | Oct'97–Jan'01 |
| Steel bars | 1998–Nov'99 |
| Construction materials (sand) | 1998–Apr'03 |
| Steel | 1994–Dec'99 |
| Blood products | Jan'03–Dec'03 |
| Toy manufacturers (imports from China) | 2006–09 |
| **Chile** | |
| Petroleum products | Feb'01–Sep'02 |
| Medical gases (oxygen) | 2001–04 |
| Medical insurance plans | 2002–04 |
| Medical services | May'05–May'06 |

*(Table continues on the following page.)*

**TABLE 3A.1** **Major "Hard-Core" Cartels Prosecuted in Selected Developing Countries, 1995–2013 *(continued)***

| Cartel case | Period of existence |
|---|---|
| **Chile *(continued)*** | |
| Construction materials (asphalt) | Oct 20, '06 (bid rigging) |
| Public transportation (bus) | 2006; Nov'07–May'08 |
| Petroleum products | Mar'08–Dec'08 |
| Vehicles and spare parts | Aug 11, '06 (bid rigging) |
| Publishing services | Mar'08–Apr'08 |
| Pharmaceuticals (distribution) | Dec'07–Apr'08 |
| Public transportation | Oct'06–Nov'07 |
| Radio transmission | 2007 |
| Tourism (agent services) | 2008 |
| Public transportation (maritime) | 2009 |
| Public transportation (bus) | Feb'07–Mar'09 |
| Flat-panel TV | n/a |
| **Colombia** | |
| Cement | Feb'06–Jan'10 |
| Mobile phone services | Apr'99–Aug'07 |
| Green onions | Feb'07–Jan'09 |
| Pasteurized milk | Jan'97–n/a |
| Green paddy rice | Jan'04–Nov'06 |
| Chocolate and cocoa products | Oct'06–Oct'09 |
| Private security services | Feb'11–Sep'12 |
| Services of grade systematization (Bogotá District schools) | Jun'08–Dec'09 |
| Milk processing | n/a–2008 |
| Health services | Mar'09–Nov'11 |
| Oxygen supply | May'05–Mar'11 |
| Road paving | Aug'10–Jan'12 |
| Sugar cane remuneration rates | Feb'10–Aug'11 |
| Cars' techno-mechanical and gas review | Mar'10–Oct'11 |
| Cars' techno-mechanical and gas review | Mar'10–Dec'11 |
| Feed ration service for prisons | May'11–Sep'12 |
| Cars' techno-mechanical and gas review | Apr'10–Mar'12 |
| TV advertising market | Apr'10–Apr'11 |
| **Egypt, Arab Rep.** | |
| Construction (Egypt Wastewater Plant) | Jun'88–Sep'96 |
| Cement | Jan'03–Dec'06 |

*(Table continues on the following page.)*

**Major "Hard-Core" Cartels Prosecuted in Selected Developing Countries, 1995–2013** *(continued)*

| Cartel case | Period of existence |
|---|:---:|
| **El Salvador** | |
| Petroleum products | n/a–2007 |
| **Indonesia** | |
| Mobile phone services | Mar'03–Nov'05 |
| Short Message Service (SMS) | Jan'04–Apr'08 |
| School books | Jan'99–Dec'00 |
| Cement | n/a–Dec'09 |
| Airlines | Jan'06–Dec'09 |
| Pharmaceuticals | n/a |
| Poultry (day-old chickens) | Jan'00–Dec'00 |
| Sea cargo (Jakarta-Pontianak) | Jun'02–Oct'03 |
| Sea cargo (Surabaya-Makassar) | Jan'03–Sep'03 |
| Public transportation (city bus) | Sep'01–Oct'03 |
| Salt trade (North Sumatra) | Jan'05–Dec'05 |
| Sea cargo (Sorong seaport) | Mar'00–Nov'08 |
| **Kazakhstan** | |
| Petroleum products (brokers) | 2002–05 |
| **Kenya** | |
| Coffee producers | n/a |
| Fertilizers I | n/a–2003 |
| Beer (production) | n/a–2004 |
| Soft drinks | n/a–2004 |
| Transportation | n/a |
| Mechanical engineering services | n/a |
| Insurance (transportation sector) | n/a–2002 |
| Petroleum (retail) | n/a–2004 |
| Fertilizers II | n/a–2011 |
| Tea growers | n/a–2004 |
| Sugar | n/a–2004 |
| Port Customs Department auctions | n/a |
| **Republic of Korea** | |
| Batteries manufacturing (auto) | Jun'03–Sep'04 |
| Beer | Feb'98–May'99 |
| Cement | Jan'02–Mar'03 |
| Construction machinery (excavators) | May'01–Nov'04 |

*(Table continues on the following page.)*

## TABLE 3A.1 Major "Hard-Core" Cartels Prosecuted in Selected Developing Countries, 1995–2013 *(continued)*

| Cartel case | Period of existence |
|---|---|
| **Republic of Korea *(continued)*** | |
| Forklift manufacturing | Dec'99–Nov'04 |
| Petroleum products (military, wholesale) | 1998–2000 |
| Telecom services (local, landline) | Jun'03–May'05 |
| Telecom services (long-distance, landline) | Jun'03–May'05 |
| Telecom services (international, landline) | Jun'03–May'05 |
| Broadband Internet service | Jun'03–May'05 |
| Detergent manufacturing | 1998–2006 |
| Telecommunications (mobile services) I | Jun'04–May'06 |
| Telecommunications (mobile services) II | Jan'00–Jul'06 |
| Gasoline and diesel (refining) | Apr'04–Jun'04 |
| Industrial motors | 1998–2006 |
| Polyethylene (low density) | Apr'94–Apr'05 |
| Polypropylene (high-density polyethylene) | Apr'94–Apr'05 |
| Movie tickets | Mar'07–Jul'07 |
| Trunked radio system devices | Dec'03–Feb'06 |
| Petrochemicals | Sep'00–Jun'05 |
| Copy paper imports | Jan'01–Feb'04 |
| Soft drink bottling | Feb'08–Feb'09 |
| Gas (liquefied petroleum gas) | Jan'03–Dec'09 |
| Elevators and escalators | Apr'96–Apr'06 |
| Toilet roll manufacturing | Mar'97–Jan'98 |
| Coffee | Jul'97–Jan'98 |
| **Malawi** | |
| Cotton farmers | n/a |
| Tea growers | n/a |
| Tobacco growers | n/a |
| Bakeries | n/a |
| Beer | n/a |
| Petroleum sector | n/a |
| **Mauritius** | |
| Travel agency | 2010 |

*(Table continues on the following page.)*

**Major "Hard-Core" Cartels Prosecuted in Selected Developing Countries, 1995–2013** *(continued)*

| Cartel case | Period of existence |
|---|---|
| **Mexico** | |
| Gas (liquid propane) | Jan'96–Feb'96 |
| Chemicals (film development) | Jan'98–Dec'00 |
| Poultry | Mar'10–Mar'10 |
| Boiled corn and corn tortillas | Mar'11–Jul'12 |
| Corn mass and tortillas | May'10–Aug'12 |
| Transportation (touristic sector) | Jul'09–Mar'12 |
| Anesthesiology (services) | May'03–May'09 |
| Auto transportation (cargo) I | Jan'10–Sep'11 |
| Maritime public transportation | Jun'08–Jun'12 |
| Auto transportation (cargo) II | Sep'08–Jun'10 |
| Health care (medical drugs) | 2003–05 |
| Consulting services (real estate) | Jul'03–Apr'09 |
| Restricted TV signal | Oct'02–Dec'08 |
| Food vouchers | Aug'05–Sep'05 |
| Consulting services (real estate) II | May'03–Jul'09 |
| Railway transportation (cargo) | Nov'05–Jun'09 |
| Cable and cable products | Feb'06–Mar'07 |
| **Pakistan** | |
| Bank interest rates | Nov'07–Apr'08 |
| Cement | Mar'08–Aug'09 |
| Gas (liquefied petroleum gas) | n/a–2009 |
| Jute mills | 2003–Jan'11 |
| High- and low-tension prestressed concrete poles | Aug'09–May'11 |
| Poultry and egg industry | 2007–Aug'10 |
| Newspapers | Apr'08–Apr'09 |
| Vessels handling (ships) | 2001–Mar'11 |
| Port construction | May'09–Jul'10 |
| Ghee and cooking oil | Dec'08–Jun'11 |
| Accounting services | Apr'07–Jan'13 |
| Long-distance and international operators | Sep'11–Apr'13 |
| Gulf Cooperation Council–approved medical centers | Jan'11–Jun'12 |
| Banking services (1-Link Guarantee Ltd) | Sep'11–Jun'12 |
| **Peru** | |
| Urban public transportation I | Aug'08–Oct'08 |
| Urban public transportation II | Aug'08–Oct'08 |

*(Table continues on the following page.)*

**Major "Hard-Core" Cartels Prosecuted in Selected Developing Countries, 1995–2013** *(continued)*

| Cartel case | Period of existence |
|---|---|
| **Peru** *(continued)* | |
| Public notaries | n/a |
| Dock work | Sep'08–May'09 |
| Insurance I | Dec'01–Apr'02 |
| Insurance II | Oct'00–Jan'03 |
| Poultry | May'95–Jul'96 |
| Wheat flour | Mar'95–Jul'95 |
| Heaters/boilers, etc., manufacturing | Oct'95–Mar'96 |
| Oxygen distribution (health care) | Jan'99–Jun'04 |
| Freight transport | Nov'04–May'09 |
| **Russian Federation** | |
| Fuel (gasoline and jet) | Apr'08–Jul'08 |
| Laptop computer operating systems | n/a |
| Fuel (petroleum, Krasnodarki Krai) | Jan'05–Jul'05 |
| Fuel (petroleum, Rostov-on-Don) | n/a–2005 |
| Airlines (Nizhnevartovsk-Moscow flights) | n/a–Dec'05 |
| Railway transportation (Kemerovo) | Oct'11–Dec'12 |
| Soda cartel | 2005–12 |
| Polyvinylchloride cartel | 2005–09 |
| Pharmaceutical cartel | 2008–09 |
| Fish cartel (Norway) | Aug'11–Dec'12 |
| Pollock cartel | Apr'06–Dec'12 |
| Fish cartel (Vietnam) | Jun'08–Sep'13 |
| Salt cartel | May'10–May'13 |
| Sausage cartel | Jun'09–Dec'09 |
| Military uniform supply | 2010–Jun'12 |
| **South Africa** | |
| Fertilizers (phosphoric acid) | Jan'03–Dec'07 |
| Airlines (fuel surcharge) | May'04–Mar'05 |
| Airlines (South Africa-Frankfurt routes) | Jan'99–Dec'02 |
| Milk (farm and retail) | n/a–Jul'06 |
| Bread and flour | 1994–2007 |
| Pharmaceuticals (wholesale distribution) | 1998–2007 |
| Tire manufacturing | 1998–2007 |
| Metal (scrap) | Jan'98–Jul'07 |

*(Table continues on the following page.)*

| Cartel case | Period of existence |
|---|---|
| **South Africa *(continued)*** | |
| Steel (flat) | 1999–Jun'08 |
| Cement I | 1996–2009 |
| Plastic pipes | 1998–2009 |
| Concrete, precast pipes, culverts, manholes, and sleepers | 1973–2007 |
| Fishing | n/a–2009 |
| Cement II | Jan'04–Jun'09 |
| Construction | n/a–2009 |
| Steel distribution | n/a–2008 |
| Steel (rebar, rods, and sections) | n/a–2008 |
| Steel (wire, wire products) | 2001–08 |
| Crushed rock | n/a–2008 |
| Bricks | n/a–2008 |
| Steel (tinplate) | Apr'09–Oct'09 |
| Steel (mining roof bolts) | 2002–09 |
| Flour milling | 2009–Mar'10 |
| Bitumen | 2000–09 |
| Poultry | 2005–09 |
| Polypropylene plastic | 1994–2009 |
| Sugar | 2000–n/a |
| Taxi | n/a |
| Auto dealers | 2005–n/a |
| Health care fees | 2002–07 |
| Pharmaceuticals | n/a–2002 |
| Motor vehicle manufacturers/importers | n/a–2006 |
| Freight forwarding | n/a–2007 |
| Energy/switchgear | n/a–2008 |
| Fertilizer (nitrogen) | 2004–06 |
| Steel (reinforcing mesh) | 2001–08 |
| Soda ashes (imports) | 1999–2008 |
| **Tanzania** | |
| Beer | n/a |
| Pipes, culverts, manholes, and prestressed concrete sleepers | n/a–2009 |
| Petroleum sector | n/a–2000 |
| **Turkey** | |
| Daily newspapers | n/a |
| Traffic lights | n/a |

*(Table continues on the following page.)*

**TABLE 3A.1  Major "Hard-Core" Cartels Prosecuted in Selected Developing Countries, 1995–2013 (continued)**

| Cartel case | Period of existence |
|---|---|
| **Turkey (continued)** | |
| Public transportation (buses) | n/a |
| Poultry | n/a |
| Bakeries | n/a |
| Beer | n/a |
| Soft drinks | n/a |
| Maritime transport service | n/a–2004 |
| Mechanical engineers | n/a |
| Insurance | n/a–2003 |
| Telecommunications | n/a–2002 |
| Architectural and engineering services | n/a–2002 |
| Yeast | n/a |
| Cement | n/a |
| Cement (Aegean region) | 2002–04 |
| Accumulators | n/a |
| **Ukraine** | |
| Acquisition of raw timber auctions (furniture) | 2011 |
| Sale of poultry meat | n/a |
| Sale of sugar | n/a |
| Sale of alcohol | n/a |
| Sale of buckwheat | n/a |
| Individual insurance markets | 2003 |
| Sales of arrested property | 2004 |
| **Zambia** | |
| Pipes, culverts, manholes, and prestressed concrete sleepers | n/a |
| Oil marketing | 2001–02 |
| Fertilizer | 2007–13 |
| Grain procurement and marketing (maize-meal) | Mar'04–Jun'04 |
| Public transport | n/a |
| Poultry | 1998–99 |
| Panel beating services | Sep'11–Dec'11 |
| **Zimbabwe** | |
| Bakeries | n/a |

*Note:* n/a = not available.

## Annex 3B: Questionnaire Submitted to Local Competition Authorities

### FIRST PART. General questions.

1. Please provide the annual budget of the competition policy enforcement unit during the period 1995–2013 (in local currency).

### SECOND PART. Identification of cartels.

1. Please provide a list of major "hard-core" cartels for the period 1995–2013.
2. For each identified cartel, provide information on:
   a. Relevant market (product, geography, etc.)
   b. Names of cartel members
   c. Period of existence of the cartel (beginning/termination)
   d. Date of discovery of the cartel
   e. Date of entry of each company in the cartel coalition, if available
   f. Fines applied, if any (in local currency)
   g. Price overcharge by cartel members, if available (percentage with respect to the cartel price or money terms in local currency).

### THIRD PART. Economic data on each cartel identified in the second section of the questionnaire.

1. At least for one period (month/year) of cartel existence indicate the market share/volume sold and price (in local currency) of the product/products for each colluding company.
2. If possible, give an estimation of the average margin for the cartel = (price − marginal costs)/price.
3. Please provide, when available, the estimate of the volume of the relevant market (in local currency), if not:
4. According to the good that is analyzed, please provide an estimation of the total market share of the non-cartel members on the relative market.

## Annex 3C: Example of the Calibration and Estimation Procedure: Civil Airlines in Brazil

Four national airlines in Brazil, namely Varig, TAM, Transbrasil, and VASP, were convicted in collusive price-fixing behavior on the civil air transportation market between Rio de Janeiro (Santos Dumont Airport) and São Paulo (Congonhas Airport) during 1999. We do not go into detail concerning the evidence that the Brazilian competition authority employed to convict the airlines but rather will focus on the estimation of the economic harm to consumers caused by this anticompetitive practice.

Table 3C.1 provides the collected data regarding the observed one-way ticket prices charged by cartel members, as well as their observed market shares (based on number

**Available Input Data, July 1999**

| Airline | Observed market share (%) | Average price of a one-way ticket (reals[a]) |
|---|---|---|
| VARIG | 46.6 | 129.32 |
| TAM | 41.5 | 124.90 |
| Transbrasil | 6.5 | 106.85 |
| VASP | 5.4 | 108.03 |

*Source:* Conselho Administrativo de Defesa Econômica (the competiton authority of Brazil).

a. Real = Brazilian national currency.

of tickets sold). These are the minimum data that are sufficient to implement our methodology and recover the price overcharges.

We recognize that it would be more correct to separate leisure and business segments of the demand, which would obviously have different sensitivities to price (parameter $\alpha$); however available data did not permit us to do so. Given that the share of the business segment in the relevant market reaches up to 70 percent, we believe that recovered market parameters will correspond mostly to this demand category.

As the developed methodology implies, to perform calibration of supply and demand parameters we need to set the share of the outside option $(s_o)$ and average cartel margin exogenously. We use additional data on the case to set the admissible ranges for these parameters.

The considered airports are the only ones situated close to the city centers of Rio de Janeiro and São Paulo, which makes them especially relevant for business passengers. In addition, there are no convenient substitutes, such as sufficiently fast trains or buses. The airlines that formed the cartel performed nearly 100 percent of the flights between the mentioned airports during the considered period. Therefore, one can assume that the share of the outside option for the business segment cannot be too big. However, the presence of the leisure segment and other airports serving the same origin and destination cities suggest that $s_o$ cannot be too low either. We arbitrarily choose the admissible range for the share of the outside option as $s_o \in [10\%, 50\%]$.

As for the second exogenous parameter—average cartel margin—we first make use of the results in Betancor and Nombela (2001), which demonstrate that marginal costs of the U.S. and European airlines are at least equal and at most twice higher than their average costs. We assume further that Brazilian airlines' cost structure is not much different from that in Europe and the United States. Having extracted average costs from the annual reports of the colluding companies, we get 40 percent as a maximum value for the average margin (when marginal costs are equal to average costs). Given that the airlines' activities on the relevant market include also those non-cartelized, we assume that the possible margin on the cartelized market could have an upper bound above 40 percent. After a final check with sign constraints for marginal costs and price sensitivity parameter $\alpha$, we define a permitted range for the average cartel margin as [10%, 45%].

When one changes the level of external parameters, calibrated market parameters also change. Along with the minimum and maximum bounds for exogenous parameters, considering some intermediary values might be also reasonable if an analyst has an idea about their most probable values inside the chosen interval. In table 3C.2 we provide calibrated price sensitivity $\alpha$ depending on the average cartel margin and share of the outside option: for minimum, maximum, and some intermediary values of external parameters. These dependencies are monotonic. We also report corresponding calibrated values of $\delta_j, j = \overline{1,J}$ in table 3C.3.

We observe that calibrated parameter $\alpha$ and $\delta_j, j = \overline{1,J}$ decrease when the share of the outside option increases, margins being fixed. This dependence follows directly from equations (3.1) and (3.5) and can be explained as follows: lower $\alpha$ indicates that preferences of consumers are driven mostly by quality rather than prices. Lower $\delta_j$, therefore, result in a higher number of consumers who preferred the outside option because its utility is normalized and remains fixed. $\alpha$ also decreases with higher cartel margin—when consumers are less sensitive to the price, cartel members have more incentives to charge a higher price.

For the set of calibrated market parameters, we further perform the simulation of the counterfactual (competitive) state.[17] Tables 3C.4 and 3C.5 report the average for the

**TABLE 3C.2  Calibrated Price Sensitivity Parameter (¯)**

| | | Average cartel margin (%) | | | |
|---|---|---|---|---|---|
| | | **10** | **20** | **35** | **45** |
| **Share of the outside option ($S_0$) (%)** | **10** | 0.80 | 0.40 | 0.23 | 0.18 |
| | **20** | 0.40 | 0.20 | 0.11 | 0.09 |
| | **35** | 0.23 | 0.11 | 0.07 | 0.05 |
| | **50** | 0.16 | 0.08 | 0.05 | 0.04 |

*Source:* Authors' simulations

**TABLE 3C.3  Calibrated Parameters of Differentiation ($c_j$)**

| | Average cartel margin (%)/Share of the outside option (%) | | | |
|---|---|---|---|---|
| **Airline** | **10/10** | **45/10** | **10/50** | **45/50** |
| VARIG | 105.22 | 24.42 | 20.02 | 3.86 |
| TAM | 101.66 | 23.62 | 19.19 | 3.58 |
| Transbrasil | 85.30 | 18.54 | 14.43 | 1.08 |
| VASP | 86.06 | 18.56 | 14.44 | 0.94 |

*Source:* Authors' simulations

## TABLE 3C.4    Estimated Price Overcharge
*Percent*

|  |  | Average cartel margin (%) | | | |
| --- | --- | --- | --- | --- | --- |
|  |  | 10 | 20 | 35 | 45 |
| Share of the outside option ($S_0$) (%) | 10 | 7.3 | 14.7 | 26.2 | 33.9 |
|  | 20 | 4.5 | 9.2 | 13.6 | 21.8 |
|  | 35 | 4.8 | 8.7 | 18.2 | 20.8 |
|  | 50 | 3.2 | 6.5 | 14.2 | 18.9 |

*Source:* Authors' simulations

*Note:* Price overcharge is reported for the cartel on average.

## TABLE 3C.5    Estimated Consumer Welfare Losses
*Percent*

|  |  | Average cartel margin (%) | | | |
| --- | --- | --- | --- | --- | --- |
|  |  | 10 | 20 | 35 | 45 |
| Share of the outside option ($S_0$) (%) | 10 | 78.6 | 78.6 | 78.6 | 78.6 |
|  | 20 | 66.1 | 66.1 | 65.8 | 66.2 |
|  | 35 | 50.4 | 48.0 | 52.8 | 49.5 |
|  | 50 | 35.0 | 35.2 | 41.2 | 42.2 |

*Source:* Authors' simulations

cartel price overcharge rates (equation (3.9)), and consumers' welfare losses (equation (3.11)) estimated for a given combination of values of exogenous parameters.

Variations of the obtained estimations of price overcharges and welfare losses according to the level of external parameters are intuitive. On one hand, when the cartel margin is being fixed, a high share of the outside option informs the analyst about a high elasticity of demand. In these conditions, the ability of colluding firms to increase their prices is rather limited. Accordingly, welfare losses are also less significant. On the other hand, keeping the share of the outside option fixed, a higher desired cartel margin naturally transforms into a greater price increase when compared to a competitive state of the market. However, in this case no definite conclusion can be made concerning the relative change in consumers' welfare.[18]

We acknowledge that variations of the estimates in tables 3C.4 and 3C.5 are quite large. Price overcharge varies from 3.2 percent to 33.9 percent, while the welfare loss estimates range from 35.0 percent to 78.6 percent. A greater precision can be gained provided that more precise inputs concerning the relevant market are at hand.

## Notes

1. Collusive behavior could be granted an exemption by the competition authority if it is shown to be beneficial for consumers or necessary for firms' survival in given economic conditions. This was, for instance, the case of the mixed concrete industry cartel in the Republic of Korea in 2009.

2. We have used the list of developing countries from the International Monetary Fund's *World Economic Outlook Report*, April 2010.

3. Private International Cartels database by John M. Connor, Purdue University, West Lafayette, Indiana (March 2009).

4. We wish to thank, for fruitful cooperation, competition authorities from Brazil, Chile, Colombia, Indonesia, the Republic of Korea, Mauritius, Mexico, Pakistan, Peru, the Russian Federation, South Africa, Ukraine, and Zambia, as well as UNCTAD RPP initiative coordinators.

5. Median values are more convenient to consider because the data are skewed and contain a few outliers with number of cartel participants more than 200 and duration of more than 150 months that renders mean values uninformative.

6. We understand that in some cases this can result in a slightly overestimated estimate of excess profits as output effect is not taken into account. Output effect refers to either reduction in sold quantities of the good due to the overall hike in market prices in the presence of a cartel, or deliberate limitation of quantities by cartel members in order to increase prices.

7. The system comprises 2J equations and 2J + 2 unknown parameters.

8. Recall that the margin constant for all cartel participants is one of the basic assumptions of the methodology. Keeping this in mind, when market shares and prices are known, it is easy to recover average cartel margin from the gross individual margins, and vice versa:

$$AM \equiv \sum_{j=1}^{J} \bar{s}_j^{cartel} \frac{\left( p_j^{cartel} - c_j \right)}{p_j^{cartel}} = \underbrace{\left( p_j^{cartel} - c_j \right)}_{constant \; for \; all \; j} \sum_{j=1}^{J} \frac{\bar{s}_j^{cartel}}{p_j^{cartel}}.$$

9. Marginal costs are calculated from margins, either average for the cartel or firm-specific ones.

10. For example, if a cartel was fined US$100 and the maximum penalty rate is 10 percent of the cartel's sales, then the minimum bound for the cartel's sales can be estimated as 100/0.1 = US$1,000. Because the percentage penalty rule is sometimes applied to a company's total sales, we have employed, where needed and where possible, a coefficient that corresponds to the share of sales on the relevant market in total company sales.

11. Note that a high level of excess cartel profits related to the competition authority budget does not necessarily witness for the efficiency of the antitrust enforcement. First, a low level of the ratio in question can result from a high efficiency of the competition authority if the latter focuses on cartel deterrence (education through mass media or higher penalties, and so on) rather than on cartel detection. A low number of detections or lower excess profits can simply reflect the fact that there exist fewer cartels or that they are weaker. Second, competition authorities can free ride on the experience of others. By "free riding" we mean a situation in which a cartel case already went through an examination in one of the competition authorities, and the others use this fact to trigger investigations of their own or even use the already collected evidence. Therefore a competition authority can win the case without investing too much. As the collected sample demonstrates, free riding can indeed take place—the same cartels are often found in a large number of (often neighboring) countries. For example, this is the case of industrial gas distribution cartels in Latin America or cement cartels in Africa. However, free riding can potentially be considered as a sort of efficiency because it is a way of optimizing available resources.

12. To see whether our data fit model assumptions of independency and exponential distribution we performed the same testing as in Bryant and Eckard (1991). Corresponding estimation results and graphs are available upon request.

13. The maximum bound for the annual deterrence rate of 13–17 percent was estimated with a similar methodology for a set of U.S. cartels (see Bryant and Eckard [1991]). However, these results should not be compared with those from our study because the situation in antitrust enforcement has significantly changed since the period that was considered by the authors (1961 to 1988).

14. Estimates from Boyer and Kotchoni (2014) were originally provided with respect to "but-for" prices; therefore, they were recalculated with respect to the cartel price to be comparable with the other estimates in this chapter.

15. Cartels can potentially cause a price umbrella effect because remaining firms could have more incentives to charge higher prices facing a price increase from cartel members.

16. Even though our model does not allow the quality characteristics to change, the degradations in quality can still appear because colluding firms may have less incentives to maintain it.

17. We solve the system of nonlinear equations implied by proposed methodology with the use of SAS (Statistical Analysis System) routines and procedures.

18. An increase in a cartel's margin decreases calibrated values of marginal costs (cartel prices are given), and also decreases calibrated price sensitivity $\alpha$ (see equation (3.3)). The left side of equation (3.1) remains constant; therefore, to compensate the decrease in $\alpha$, $\delta_j$ should decrease, too. In a competitive state we cannot predict whether $\left(\delta_j - \alpha p_j^c\right)$ will increase or decrease for every product, because all three parameters would have lower values. Equation (3.1) indicates that if market shares in a competitive state will be relatively high compared to the share of the outside option, then the welfare level will be higher, and vice versa.

## Bibliography

Allain, Marie-Laure, Marcel Boyer, Rachidi Kotchoni, and Jean-Pierre Ponssard. 2011. "The Determination of Optimal Fines in Cartel Cases: The Myth of Underdeterrence." http://ssrn.com/abstract=1987107 or http://dx.doi.org/10.2139/ssrn.1987107.

Anderson, Simon P., André de Palma, and Jacques-François Thisse. 1992. *Discrete Choice Theory of Product Differentiation*. Cambridge, MA: MIT Press.

Berry, S. T. 1994. "Estimating Discrete-Choice Models of Product Differentiation." *RAND Journal of Economics* 25 (2): 242–62.

Betancor, O., and G. Nombela. 2001. "European Airlines' Marginal Costs." Annex from *Deliverable 6: Supplier Operating Costs*. European Commission (UNITE—Unification of Accounts and Marginal Costs for Transport Efficiency, University of Leeds).

Boyer, M., and R. Kotchoni. 2014. "How Much Do Cartels Overcharge?" TSE Working Papers 14-462, Toulouse School of Economics.

Bryant, P., and E. W. Eckard. 1991. "Price Fixing: The Probability of Getting Caught." *Review of Economics and Statistics* 73 (3): 531–36.

Combe, E., C. Monnier, and R. Legal. 2008. "Cartels: The Probability of Getting Caught in the European Union." Bruges European Economic Research (BEER) Paper 12, Bruges.

Connor, J. M. 2010a. "Recidivism Revealed: Private International Cartels 1991–2009." http://ssrn.com/abstract=1688508 or http://dx.doi.org/10.2139/ssrn.1688508.

———. 2010b. "Price-Fixing Overcharges, 2nd Edition." http://papers.ssrn.com/sol3/papers.cfm?abstract_id=1610262.

———. 2011a. "Price Effects of International Cartels in Markets for Primary Products." In Materials of the Symposium on Trade in Primary Product Markets and Competition Policy at the World Trade Organization, September 22.

———. 2011b. "Cartels Portrayed." Working papers 11–03, 11–04, 11–05, 11–06, and 11–07, American Antitrust Institute, Washington, DC.

Connor, J. M., and Y. Bolotova. 2006. "Cartel Overcharges: Survey and Meta-analysis." *International Journal of Industrial Organization* 24: 1009–37.

Hammond, S. D. 2005. "Optimal Sanctions, Optimal Deterrence." Presented at the ICN Annual Conference, Bonn, Germany, June 6.

Jenny, F. 2006. "Cartels and Collusion in Developing Countries: Lessons from Empirical Evidence." *World Competition* 29 (1): 109–37.

Levenstein, M. C., V. Y. Suslow, and L. J. Oswald. 2003. "Contemporary International Cartels and Developing Countries: Economic Effects and Implications for Competition Policy." Working Paper 03–10, International Agricultural Trade Research Consortium.

Motta, Massimo. 2004. *Competition Policy: Theory and Practice.* Cambridge, U.K.: Cambridge University Press.

# 4. Undermining Inclusive Growth? Effects of Coordination on Fertilizer Prices in Malawi, Tanzania, and Zambia

**Thando Vilakazi** (Centre for Competition, Regulation and Economic Development, University of Johannesburg)

Anticompetitive behavior can have significant negative effects on low-income producers, particularly when it occurs in agricultural input markets, such as fertilizer, seed, pesticide, and transport. In many cases, the market structure may facilitate firms' anticompetitive conduct. This chapter considers the theory of cartels and the history of coordinated conduct in international fertilizer markets, and relates this to competitive dynamics and market outcomes in fertilizer trading markets in Tanzania and Zambia—Malawi is included as a comparator country also. Through assessing the structure of markets, main players, and prices and costs in each country, the chapter evaluates the market conduct of large multinational suppliers of fertilizer in southern and East Africa. The chapter highlights the importance of control over key infrastructure and access to supply markets in reinforcing the market power of incumbent fertilizer suppliers, and shows that the characteristics of fertilizer markets in these countries and in the region align well with theories of anticompetitive coordination. Observed outcomes in Malawi and Tanzania in particular suggest markups above reasonable competitive benchmarks. Key findings are that a reduction in relative prices in Zambia has been driven in part by the prosecution of a cartel in fertilizer trading whereas the benefits of entry in the Tanzanian fertilizer market may have been undermined by the entrenched position of incumbent multinational importers. In Malawi, a lack of

The author is a Senior Researcher at the Centre for Competition, Regulation and Economic Development (CCRED) at the University of Johannesburg (thandov@uj.ac.za). The views expressed in this chapter are those of the author and do not necessarily reflect those of CCRED. This chapter draws from an earlier study conducted by CCRED for the Southern African Development Community (SADC), funded by Deutsche Gesellschaft für Internationale Zusammenarbeit (GIZ). The study was done in close cooperation with the competition authorities in Tanzania and Zambia, with further inputs from the authority in Malawi, for which we are grateful. Comments from each competition authority have been taken into account.

rivalry at various levels of the value chain and regulatory barriers mean prices of fertilizer have been well above those in the other two countries. We estimate the losses to buyers by measuring against competitive benchmarks.

## 4.1 Introduction

Agricultural production remains an important contributor to the economies of developing countries in Sub-Saharan Africa, not least because of its contribution to food security and sustainability. In the cases of Malawi, Tanzania, and Zambia—the subjects of this chapter—agricultural value-add in 2013 accounted for 27 percent, 34 percent, and 10 percent of GDP, respectively.[1] However, agricultural productivity remains low. Low productivity has been linked to limited use of agricultural technology inputs, and fertilizer in particular (Gregory and Bumb 2006; ACB 2014). Fertilizer imports and usage in Africa are generally not expected to grow rapidly relative to East and South Asia and Latin and Central America (Heffer and Prud'homme 2014). Usage is low in Malawi, Tanzania, and Zambia relative to potential demand (IFDC 2013a, 2013b; Benson, Kirama, and Selejio 2012).

Fertilizer consumption is driven by a range of factors, including the experience of farmers regarding the benefits of fertilizer usage and access to supply (Gregory and Bumb 2006). These factors tend to underlie the emphasis by governments in the region on fertilizer support and subsidy programs, which are currently a feature in each of the three focus countries as well.[2] A crucial dimension of access to fertilizer is price, with fertilizer input accounting for approximately 30–50 percent of grain and oil seed producers' costs (GrainSA 2011). It is therefore critical for increased fertilizer usage that markets are competitive and not constrained by abuses of market power. Almost all of the fertilizer consumed in each of the focus countries is imported by private traders from international suppliers. Thus, prices are determined by international freight costs, large international and local traders, local transport and port costs, and regulations governing the sector. The most common sources of fertilizer include the Middle East, increasingly China and the Far East, the United States Gulf of Mexico, and the Black Sea region (for example, Ukraine). Tanzania is the only one of the three countries with nontrivial local production of phosphates by Minjingu Mines and Fertilizer Ltd, although even here, as in the other countries, the majority of demand is met by imports, with some local blending.

The largest international fertilizer producers are Yara International of Norway and Agrium from Canada (ACB 2014). These producers operate in a concentrated global market with a long history of coordinated conduct between international traders and suppliers (see, for example, Taylor and Moss 2013). Fertilizer products are largely homogenous, and the most common types are urea and/or ammonium nitrate compounds. Almost all bulk fertilizer is produced using some balance of nitrogen, phosphorus, and potassium, although some blends include other minerals and nutrient additives. Each of the countries we consider consumes significant quantities of urea and calcium ammonium nitrate (CAN), and we focus on these products.

The structure of fertilizer markets, domestically and globally, is conducive to coordinated conduct because, among other reasons, products are homogenous and markets are highly concentrated. In the focus countries there are generally several players in the market but only two or three large rivals, together accounting for more than half of the market in 2014. In Zambia the two major players are Omnia Fertilisers Zambia Limited and Nyiombo Investments, each with a share of approximately one-third of the market; in Tanzania Yara International holds approximately 40 percent of the market, and the Export Trading Group (ETG) holds an estimated 20–40 percent of the market; in Malawi the picture is less clear, although Yara, Omnia, and ETG are present along with the international group Farmers World, which is a strong player.

This chapter briefly considers the theory of cartels and the history of coordinated conduct in fertilizer markets in the region, and relates this to competitive dynamics and market outcomes in Tanzania and Zambia. Outcomes in Malawi are considered at points throughout the chapter. Although not assessed in great detail here, the Malawian market provides a helpful comparator against which to assess certain outcomes in Zambia in particular, given that both countries are landlocked with limited domestic production, and substantial fertilizer subsidy programs are in place. Through assessing the structure of markets, main players, and prices and costs in each country, a case is developed for closer consideration of market conduct by large multinational suppliers. These suppliers have multimarket contacts in markets for commodities in the region through their control of key infrastructure, sources of supply, and influence on the regulatory environment. In addition, vertical integration and access at different levels of the value chain, such as port offloading, bagging and storage facilities, warehousing, and transportation, create the ability for large players to control margins and prices for the final output throughout the value chain and across geographic markets. These characteristics lend weight to the likelihood of cartel conduct in these markets and the ability of cartelists to keep out or control entrants as we will discuss. This is not to say that there *is* a cartel in fertilizer trading in Tanzania or Malawi where we show that margins are high. Instead, the analysis reinforces the fact that the characteristics of fertilizer markets in these countries and in the region align well with possible theories of coordination, and that observed outcomes suggest markups above reasonable competitive benchmarks.

Our findings are that a reduction in relative prices in Zambia has been driven in part by the prosecution of a cartel in fertilizer trading whereas the benefits of entry in the Tanzanian fertilizer market may have been undermined by the entrenched position of incumbent multinational importers. In Malawi, a lack of rivalry at various levels of the value chain and regulatory barriers mean prices of fertilizer have been well above those in the other two countries. We estimate the losses to buyers by measuring against competitive benchmarks. The study highlights the importance of control over key infrastructure and access to supply markets in reinforcing market power.

## 4.2 Inclusion, Cartels, and Recent Experiences in Fertilizer Markets in the Region

The links we draw between cartel conduct and inclusive growth in this chapter are based on a broad conception of inclusion. Inclusive growth has been defined as being both an outcome and a process that emphasizes participation in the growth process itself, and in the sharing of its benefits (Ramos, Ranieri, and Lammens 2013). Fully considered, this conception should be taken to mean not only participation of people as labor in the process of employment creation but also the ability of new firms to enter and participate in markets. Cartels by their nature need to deter or undermine entry in order to ensure their stability and survival. This effectively means that new firms cannot enter markets, compete, or expand their operations, including by employing more people. Furthermore, where cartels affect key input sectors or important consumer goods, they directly or indirectly affect societal welfare and inclusive growth (see Banda et al. 2015). In the case of fertilizer, which has become a critical input to agricultural production, farmers are harmed by higher input costs, and consumers in turn are harmed by higher prices for food and produce. Understanding this link is, in our view, central to realizing meaningful and dynamic inclusion. In the countries that we consider, governments make significant investments into farmer support schemes to enhance rural development and food security, such that higher prices for agricultural inputs directly affect many of the poorest users and consumers. In this very simple and practical way, inclusion becomes about dealing with anticompetitive arrangements that undermine the competitive process and increase entry barriers. It is in this context that we consider the fertilizer markets in each of the countries.

### 4.2.1 Cartel Mechanisms for Monitoring and Punishment

Collusive practices allow firms to jointly exercise market power in a market through, for example, allocating quotas, prices, customers, or geographic markets. This understanding between firms can be reached through direct (although secretive) communication, or express agreement between firms, or tacitly where there is mutual understanding with no communication between firms at all. The collusive equilibrium is one in which prices are supracompetitive, that is, above the competitive price level. In this equilibrium a firm prices above and/or supplies quantities below those that would maximize its short-run profits. However, it is in the firm's interest to do so because of cartel profits and the likely reaction of other cartelists if it were to undercut them (Harrington 2011; Motta 2004).

It is worth briefly recalling the "plus" factors and characteristics of industries that make collusion easier to maintain and by which collusion can be identified in markets (see Motta 2004; and Harrington 2006). In general, cartel conduct is more likely to occur in markets where there is a high concentration of firms, relatively homogenous products, high barriers to entry, stable demand conditions, firm symmetry, multimarket contact between firms, and cross-ownership, among other facilitating factors, including the sharing of disaggregated information (Bernheim and Whinston 1990; Motta 2004). Evidence on prices, quantities, and discounting behavior over time can be assessed, with collusion being likely when there is low variance in prices over time, and there are high levels of price transparency, strong correlation in prices, high prices without an increase in imports, and highly stable market shares over time for individual firms (Harrington 2006).

Cartels rely on certain mechanisms to ensure that each firm sticks to the agreed outcome and does not give in to the incentive to cheat and capture profits in the short term by undercutting the other members. This would most likely trigger a retaliatory price war or collective predation. To prevent cheating or opportunistic behavior, cartelists develop mechanisms for monitoring and detecting cheating and for punishing deviations, using methods such as exchanging detailed information on sales volumes, and using excess capacity to flood the market and punish a firm that cheats. Similarly, cartel members face the problem of how to deal with new entry in the market, which may undermine the prevailing understanding between them through undercutting to win customers. Again, in this case, being able to exercise collective predation, by, for example, flooding the market at low prices to undermine the entrant, is a powerful mechanism for dealing with entry or creating a reputation sufficient to deter new entry (Khumalo, Mashiane, and Roberts 2014).

These issues are typical of most cartels and also tend to cause the demise of arrangements between firms, that is, the failure to agree on and sustain a mutually beneficial equilibrium outcome (Levenstein and Suslow 2006). Market allocation arrangements are more stable in this regard because, as long as a firm does not sell into the geographic or product market segment allocated to a rival, prices in each area or segment can be changed without disrupting the cartel arrangement (Motta 2004). The Zambian fertilizer cartel, which we discuss, was an example of this.

Similarly, firms will find it easier to sustain a cartel arrangement where there are common, well-known pricing focal points (Motta 2004). For instance, if a regulator regularly sets a maximum price that is permissible in an industry, firms will find it more sustainable to coordinate around this price. The firms will in all likelihood jointly set their prices at this level despite any cost differences between them that would otherwise give them an incentive to set a lower price.

International prices can easily serve as benchmarks around which collusive prices are structured and maintained, as we will discuss. This is akin to what is known as "posted pricing" wherein firms make public announcements of a policy to "set a list price with no discounting off that list price" (Harrington 2011, 4). On the one hand this has the effect of reducing search costs for customers. However, on the other hand, under certain conditions the posted price may serve as a focal point and an invitation for coordination between firms. In fact, Harrington (2011) argues that the adoption of posted pricing is profitable for firms only if they anticipate that other firms will follow, that is, if it results in coordinated pricing. If it does not, other firms may simply view the posted price as an opportunity to discount below it and win customers. In the South African fertilizer cartel, which we describe below, cartelists emphasized the sharing of information on cost parameters and used international pricing benchmarks to agree on prices domestically. In fertilizer supply, international free on board (FOB)[3] prices, as well as the costs of shipping, port charges, port handling, and distribution are generally well known to market participants and therefore constitute a strong platform for monitoring. As in the case of posted prices and information sharing, this creates a degree of transparency in the market, which is conducive to collusive outcomes. If there is also information exchange, particularly of "private, disaggregated and sensitive information shared on a regular basis," market transparency is increased and strategic uncertainty about competitors' actions is reduced (Das Nair and Mncube 2012, 181). In this way, the information can be used to monitor adherence to agreed prices or volumes and thus ensure the durability of the cartel arrangement.

Aspects of the structure of regional markets in southern and East Africa are interesting in the context of the structural markers of cartel conduct. For instance, fertilizer markets in the region are largely concentrated with a tight oligopoly of global players controlling significant shares of the regional market. Furthermore, because fertilizer is largely imported to the region, divisions of multinational firms effectively act as distributors for international manufacturers and suppliers. In most cases, this means that these importers gain competitive advantages through controlling access to supply and the vertical chain of distribution by investments in, for example, port handling facilities, storage and warehousing, and transport networks. Importantly, through making these investments, the importer is able to control margins throughout the value chain and can largely observe the final prices in the market or at the wholesale level. This allows for control of quantities sold downstream that may serve as a monitoring mechanism in a coordinated arrangement. Integration can also serve as a mechanism for punishing other cartelists if they deviate from the agreement, such as smaller members of the arrangement that rely on inputs or infrastructure access from vertically integrated members. Therefore, the presence of vertically integrated players in the market makes reaching a tacit or explicit agreement on collusion easier and/or the enforcement of an agreement easier (Ncube, Roberts, and Vilakazi 2015). In these cases, integration downstream can reinforce the sustainability of a cartel arrangement (Levenstein 1993).

In theories of coordination, vertical exclusion could also have the effect of undermining or deterring entry in markets where firms that are part of the cartel are also involved in other levels of the value chain (Levenstein and Suslow 2006; Levenstein 1993). This is because potential entrants in the market would need to enter at multiple levels of the value chain in order to be able to compete effectively. In regional fertilizer markets, we have seen new players gaining access to supply, but also presence in distribution, which has increased competition. While this does not imply that there are existing cartel arrangements, it does show the benefits of entry where markets have been dominated by a small handful of firms. The profitability of entry further suggests that markets were not contested or contestable in the past, as we show in the case of Zambia.

This interaction between theories of vertical foreclosure and coordination is, in our view, especially relevant in regional fertilizer markets, at least insofar as importers are able to control infrastructure and manipulate access to supply. For example, a hallmark of the Zambian cartel involving the fertilizer subsidy program was the ability to allocate geographic markets on the basis of the relative strengths of the fertilizer importers at the level of distribution as well.

### 4.2.2 Firm Conduct in Regional Fertilizer Markets

The experience of the competition authorities in South Africa and Zambia demonstrates in a practical manner the dynamics of coordinated conduct. In each country, the competition authorities have prosecuted cartels in the fertilizer sector. The characteristics of these arrangements allow us to draw some interesting insights for the analysis of competitive dynamics and outcomes in Malawi, Tanzania, and Zambia.

*South Africa*
The South African fertilizer cartel was characterized by a range of complex information-sharing schemes. The Competition Commission found that fertilizer firms had been involved in allocating markets and fixing prices until around 2006. The arrangement affected prices for fertilizer not only in South Africa but also in several Southern African Development Community (SADC) countries.[4] The collusive agreement was identified following a complaint by Nutri-Flo in 2003.

Sasol Chemical Industries was found to be in a cartel with two other major producers of intermediate fertilizer products, Omnia (a South African producer also present in Zambia, interestingly) and Kynoch Fertilizer (then owned by Yara) (Makhaya and Roberts 2013). Central to this arrangement was the sharing of detailed information between suppliers through various industry structures and bodies. These included the Nitrogen Balance Committee (NBC), the Import Planning Committee (IPC), the Export Club, and the Fertiliser Society of South Africa (FSSA), comprising the primary fertilizer suppliers.[5] The purpose of the NBC was to ensure security of supply where there were shortages of ammonia products. Members submitted information on forecasts and requirements per region, and planned imports for key fertilizer products. This included information on stock availability, capacity, usage, surpluses, and deficits. Information was also disaggregated by nitrogen usage between competing end users and circulated to all members of NBC. The IPC was used to share data relating to imported fertilizer volumes, available shipping capacities, and other logistical costs.

The Export Club was used to share information on sales of fertilizer to be exported, in order to coordinate bids for the supply of products to the southern African region through traders. Finally, the FSSA collated information received from members on market shares based on sales data. This allowed for deviations from agreed market shares to be detected, which could be caused by aggressive discounting by one player in a particular local market.

An important aspect of the coordination was an agreement on how list prices would be determined, through adding on agreed costs to the international benchmark prices to get local prices in different markets. This is consistent with the discussion of price focal points, which can be used as a benchmark on which to maintain a coordinated outcome.

### Zambia

In Zambia, the Competition and Consumer Protection Commission (CCPC) found Omnia Fertilisers Zambia Limited and Nyiombo Investments Limited to have rigged government contracts for fertilizer supply between 2007 and 2011 (CCPC 2013).[6] The two firms were each fined 5 percent of annual turnover for the conduct, which was found to have largely affected the supply of fertilizer to farmers under the government's fertilizer subsidy program.

Historically, Nyiombo and Omnia have dominated the fertilizer program although it appears that they have done so because of tender bidding requirements that favored incumbents and inhibited an open and competitive process. On its website Nyiombo indicates that it won the tender for supplying the Farmer Input Support Programme (FISP) in Zambia (which is focused on fertilizer for maize production) due to its capacity to deliver, and a proven track record from having been involved with the FISP since the program's inception in 2004/05.[7] However, the CCPC of Zambia found collusion between Omnia and Nyiombo in the FISP tender. Omnia and Nyiombo have in recent years also been linked to allegations of fraudulent relations with the government agents in charge of facilitating the tender process in the Zambian Public Procurement Authority and Ministry of Agriculture.[8] The Permanent Secretary of Agriculture had to intervene in the tender process for the 2012/13 period to change clauses of the tender bidding requirements.[9]

Previously, the bidding documents contained requirements that made it extremely difficult for other players in the market to win the government tender.[10] On this basis, Omnia and Nyiombo have dominated supplies to the FISP, although some of the other firms, including Zambian Fertilizers and Greenbelt Fertilizers, have on occasion also supplied the FISP over the years since its inception.[11]

The small size of national markets in the region creates opportunities for rent seeking. Concentrated markets with large international players tend toward coordinated outcomes, as in South Africa and Zambia. Where governments get involved with allocating tenders to specific players or distorting the competitive process for awarding contracts to supply large subsidy programs, entry barriers are increased.

## 4.3 Fertilizer Pricing in Malawi, Tanzania, and Zambia

We consider the monthly pricing of urea and CAN in Malawi, Tanzania, and Zambia from May 2010 to April 2014, which is the period for which data were available. The data for urea and CAN reflect national average retail prices collected from agrodealers and retailers in key agricultural towns in each country (figures 4.1 and 4.2).

The first observation to be made is the significant differences between domestic and international (Eastern Europe) prices for urea, a gap which seems to widen from 2012 to 2014, where the differential is approximately US$400/ton near the end of the period. This difference is not explained by any increase in the costs of sea freight and insurance.[12] Based on the Baltic Freight Index, prices for sea freight seem to have

**FIGURE 4.1  Urea Monthly (National Average Delivered) Prices, 2010–14**

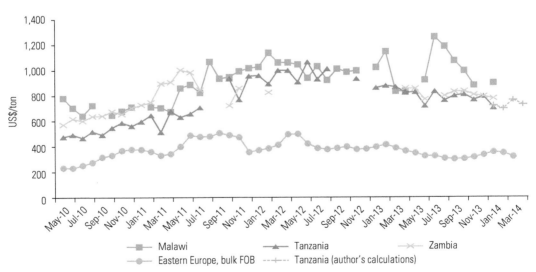

Sources: www.amitsa.org; World Bank (MIDAS).

Note: We have removed outliers in the data where the value is different by more than 50 percent (absolute value) from the value in the previous or next month for which data are available. Malawian urea prices showed an outlier of US$1,179/ton in September 2010, and another outlier of US$355/ton in December 2013. Zambian urea prices showed an outlier of US$1,702/ton in January 2012, and another outlier of US$1,619/ton in June 2012. FOB = free on board.

**FIGURE 4.2   CAN Monthly (National Average Delivered) Prices, 2010–14**

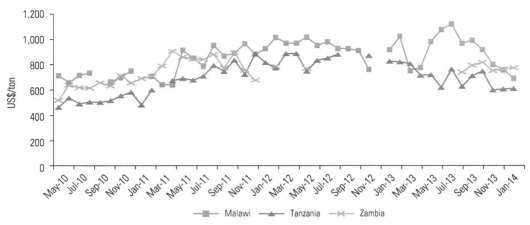

*Source:* www.amitsa.org.

*Note:* We have removed outliers in the data where the value is different by more than 50 percent (absolute value) from the value in the previous or next month for which data are available. Malawian CAN prices showed an outlier of US$1,215/ton in September 2010. Zambian CAN prices showed an outlier of US$1,477/ton in January 2012, and another outlier of US$1,579/ton in June 2012. CAN = calcium ammonium nitrate (formulation 26 0 0).

declined on average over this period, although there were some fluctuations throughout. This suggests a significant accumulation of costs and margins from the time the fertilizer arrives at the port to when it is delivered to end users. Furthermore, given an increase in the volumes of fertilizer sourced by various African countries from sources in the Middle East and China in recent years, where prices at the source and from where shipping costs tend to be lower, it is likely that the gap with international FOB prices is larger than that reflected in figure 4.1.

In both urea and CAN, prices in Malawi are higher than those in the other two countries. This is consistent with the fact that Malawi is a landlocked market such that additional transport and transit costs may add to the price differential. However, prices in Malawi are also significantly above those in neighboring Zambia, which is also landlocked. Fertilizer supply to Malawi and Zambia largely comes through the port of Durban in South Africa, which is approximately 2,457 km and 2,143 km from Lilongwe in Malawi and Lusaka in Zambia, respectively. We note that international fuel prices did increase by a third from 2010 to early 2011, which is significant when considering that the majority of fertilizer imports in the region are transported from the different ports using road freight. This increase in fuel prices may explain, in part, the sharp increases in prices in Malawi and Zambia in early 2011, greater than those in Tanzania, which has shorter transport distances from the port to major agricultural regions such as Mbeya in the southwest of the country, some 828 km from the port of Dar es Salaam. However, this increase in fuel prices does not explain why prices remain high and increase further following this period.

The developments in the Zambian prices of both urea and CAN relative to the other countries are most interesting in the period between 2010/11 and 2013. For both urea and CAN we observe that Zambian prices in 2010 are in line with those in its landlocked neighbor Malawi and substantially above the prices in Tanzania as a coastal country. However, by 2013 the Zambian prices shift to be in line with prices in Tanzania. This is in contrast to the expectation that prices would be higher in Zambia to reflect the additional transport distance and thus cost that is required to take fertilizer from the ports to the Zambian end user. Table 4.1 compares the average annual prices of urea over the full period from 2010, indicating markups (in italics) of Zambian and Malawian price relative to those in Tanzania (as a coastal country) and the Black Sea FOB benchmark (in square brackets). We do not calculate the average prices for Zambia for 2012 given the very small number of data points.

As discussed, the prices for Malawi are a significant margin above those in Tanzania by US$204/ton in 2013. However, those in Zambia, which we expect to be different from those in Tanzania by at least the inland transport rate, are only US$6/ton higher, with margins above the FOB benchmark that are far less than those for Malawi by 2013. This is surprising, considering that overland transport distances from ports in Tanzania and South Africa to Malawi are similar to those in Zambia. The differential of US$6/ton can be compared to US$119/ton in 2010 and US$147/ton in 2011.[13] These findings suggest that there has been a significant change in relative conditions in each of these markets. Certainly, it is curious that fertilizer in the Tanzanian market has become more expensive relative to Zambia, and that changes in Zambia have resulted in fertilizer prices that are significantly reduced.

**TABLE 4.1  Average Annual Fertilizer (Urea) Prices and International FOB Prices, 2010–13**
*US$/ton*

| Year | Malawi | Tanzania | Zambia[a] | Average Black Sea FOB (urea) |
|---|---|---|---|---|
| 2010 (May–Dec)[b] | 696 | 516 | 635 | 296 |
| | *+180* | | *+119* | |
| | [+407] | [+220] | [+339] | |
| 2011 | 873 | 706 | 853 | 421 |
| | *+168* | | *+147* | |
| | [+452] | [+285] | [+432] | |
| 2012 | 1,019 | 965 | | 405 |
| | *+54* | | | |
| | [+613] | [+559] | | |
| 2013 | 1,014 | 810 | 816 | 340 |
| | *+204* | | *+6* | |
| | [+674] | [+470] | [+476] | |

*Sources:* www.amitsa.org; www.africafertilizer.org; World Bank (MIDAS).

*Note:* Slight discrepancies in the markups calculated are due to rounding. Figures in italics indicate markups of Malawian and Zambian prices over those in Tanzania, and square brackets indicate markups of Malawian and Zambian prices over the Black Sea FOB benchmark price. FOB = free on board.

a. There are only two data points for 2012 for Zambia, and so we do not compute an annual average.

b. For 2010 we average data from May to December, which corresponds to the months for which national average fertilizer prices were available.

**TABLE 4.2   Port and Landlocked Country Price Benchmarks, 2013**

| | |
|---|---|
| Competitive port country fertilizer price | US$709/ton (South Africa) |
| Competitive transport rate | US$110/ton (Johannesburg to Lusaka) |
| Competitive landlocked country fertilizer price | US$819/ton (Zambia) |

*Source:* World Bank calculations based on interview data and average pricing data.

**TABLE 4.3   Markups over Benchmark Competitive Prices, by Country, 2013**
*US$/ton*

| Country | Average fertilizer price | Markup over competitive price per ton |
|---|---|---|
| Zambia | 816 | −3 |
| Tanzania (compared to port country) | 810 | 101 |
| Malawi (compared to landlocked country) | 1,014 | 195 |

*Source:* World Bank calculations based on interview data and average pricing data.

To separate out the possible effect of relative transport costs as an explanatory factor, we impute competitive prices for urea in 2013 and compare these to prices in Tanzania and Malawi. To do this we use the average delivered price for South Africa as a relatively competitive price in a country with a major port (like Tanzania) (table 4.2). For a landlocked country we add a competitive transport rate from Johannesburg to Lusaka of US$110/ton.[14] Note that the South African price is an average price for sales to farmers across the country and hence already includes local delivery transport within South Africa, including to Johannesburg. This calculation shows that average Zambian prices were even lower in 2013 than the imputed competitive prices by US$3/ton, suggesting that we have been conservative and the competitive benchmark should be lower by at least this amount (table 4.3). Our exercise suggests that the Tanzanian prices are too high by about US$101/ton (against the South African price) and the Malawi prices are too high by US$195/ton.

This confirms substantial markups in Tanzania and Malawi in particular, over what would be competitive rates in a "similar" port and landlocked country, respectively. Effectively, the calculated markups represent the portion of the difference between the costs of fertilizer in each country that is not (or should not be) accounted for by transport costs.

## 4.4  Changing Dynamics in Fertilizer Markets in Tanzania and Zambia

This section explores possible explanations for the relative changes in prices of fertilizer in Tanzania and Zambia. In so doing, we look to isolate those aspects that can objectively be explained by changes in competitive dynamics in fertilizer trading, and those margins that seem to have accrued along the value chain and appear to be above competitive benchmarks.

It is worth briefly describing key elements of the fertilizer value chain. Once fertilizer arrives at the port, it is first cleared by the port authorities and customs. Importers will typically use a clearing and forwarding company to handle clearance procedures. The bulk quantities are then offloaded (break bulk), separated, and packed into 50 kg bags.[15] At the Dar es Salaam port the Dar es Salaam Corridor Group (DCG) introduced a private initiative to handle and move some fertilizer out of the port area and have it bagged at facilities just outside the port.[16] This initiative, which began in 2004, has made it possible for some importers to offload 3,000 tons per day compared to 1,500 tons when handling is done by the port authority, which has improved efficiency.[17] Once fertilizer is bagged, it is transported to importer warehouses (owned or leased) a short distance from the port at a trucking cost of approximately US$9–US$10/ton.[18] At this point, importers arrange transportation by truck to different parts of the country, or for transit to neighboring countries where fertilizer is either stored once more in the importer's warehouses or sold from warehouses to wholesalers, stockists, and end users.

### 4.4.1  Ending of the Cartel in Zambia in 2011/12

The competition authority in Zambia uncovered and prosecuted the cartel involving the two largest suppliers, Nyiombo and Omnia, in 2011/12. The arrangement between the firms largely affected the FISP supply to farmers, including through the allocation of markets to each player. It was agreed by the players to operate in allocated zones where each has sustainable competitive advantage (CCPC 2013). The trend was that the companies would not tender in areas where the other had indicated intention to supply. The firms were also found to be involved in bid rigging for the FISP and sharing of price information. These contraventions are estimated to have cost the government more than US$20 million over the years of supply, 2007 to 2011. The volume of fertilizer imported by the government accounts for only a limited proportion of the total market size. Estimates in 2013 were that the program, which is based on a tender system whereby private firms are invited to submit bids for the contract to import fertilizer and supply it to the government, provides 200,000 tons of D-Compound and urea fertilizer to farmers (IFDC 2013a). Although there are varying estimates of the total market size in Zambia, we estimate the total fertilizer imports to be around 500,000 tons based on data from the Zambia Revenue Authority. Freeing up the volumes under the subsidy program and the market overall to greater competition allows smaller players to achieve scale economies in their operations and bulk shipping of import consignments, and to make investments in capacity, which can be passed through in the form of lower prices as reflected in the data in the previous section. In this regard, Greenbelt Fertilizers has grown in the market since the cartel's prosecution, and in 2011 the firm launched a fertilizer processing (blending) plant at the Beira port in Mozambique with plans for another plant in the north of Zambia.

The decision to fine the firms was made in April 2013, although cartel findings were made before this. In that year the government also announced that the tender process would be opened up to other companies, which may have been related to the fraud allegations already discussed, in which the suppliers were accused of fraudulent relations with government agents in charge of the tender process. Although the companies have since appealed the decision of the competition authority, it is likely that the investigation and public attention to the issue, which included a dawn raid at the premises of each supplier in October 2012, would have nonetheless disrupted the existing arrangement between the players.

Available information suggests that ETG has been able to grow substantially in Zambia in the past two years, following these findings. By 2013/14 the firm was said to be the market leader in Zambia, having grown from holding approximately 10 percent in earlier years.[19] Indications are that, although ETG and other firms have been in the market for some years, the market became more contestable following the cartel findings, such that ETG has been able to gain share at the expense of Nyiombo in particular, and Omnia to some extent. ETG has also established a bulk blending plant in Zambia, as well as plants at the Beira port (which is half the distance to Lusaka from Durban and Dar es Salaam).

Cartel arrangements, as in the case of monopoly, protect incumbents from direct competition, which reduces firm incentives to invest in remaining competitive and efficient. When competition is introduced and arrangements are destabilized, incumbents can find it difficult to adapt and compete. An important aspect of ETG's approach has been to enter into reciprocal arrangements with farmers to purchase their output for export, while ensuring that farmers receive fertilizer inputs at affordable prices. This is different from the business model of traditional fertilizer companies that specialize in agrochemicals and are unable to diversify their revenues across a variety of operations. An additional advantage for ETG is the fact that it operates its own fleet of trucks, which allows the firm to internalize the transport margin and pass this through in the form of a lower price for fertilizer.[20] Through reaching agreements with farmers, ETG is also able to exploit the increased volume of return loads in transportation, which, other things equal, reduces transport costs.

To the extent that the cartel controlled output and increased prices for fertilizer supply in Zambia, competition law interventions appear to have resulted in gains to consumers of fertilizer. This translates to improved access to inputs for farmers, which would allow them to increase yields and pass cost savings through to customers.

## 4.4.2  Control of Key Infrastructure and Access to Markets and Supply

In markets where the products are largely imported, control over the FOB price lies largely in the hands of large manufacturers and suppliers. In many cases, importers in African markets are price takers in this regard, and do not directly control shipping costs either. For an importer in one of these markets, the ability to control the market domestically lies in being able to control key infrastructure and the influence of regulation once the product lands at the port, and being able to leverage discounts from bulk purchases from international suppliers that smaller players cannot achieve. Smaller importers often cannot purchase directly from manufacturers and rely on dealing with traders. Furthermore, firms such as Yara have the advantage of purchasing products from the group's international manufacturing facilities, although this may also prevent them from purchasing fertilizer from cheaper alternative sources.

In Tanzania, Yara has made investments in its own bulk terminal at the port, which will be strictly for fertilizer imports into the region. Unlike the DCG terminal, which can cater to different importers and other products, the facility is expected to service only Yara and not competitors. This will give some advantages to Yara, which is a significant player in Tanzania and other regional markets. To the extent that the cost savings will be passed on to consumers in the region, the investment can be viewed as a positive development. It is likely, given the increased rivalry from large importers such as ETG in many countries in the region, such as Malawi, Rwanda, Tanzania, and Zambia, that Yara's investments are also in response to greater demand and competition in the different markets.

ETG's own investments in transport infrastructure, warehousing, and bagging facilities just outside the port in Dar es Salaam, have meant that in Tanzania its prices are up to 10 percent cheaper than those of large players such as Yara.[21] This is a significant development in Tanzania and the regional market. It is worth adding that, according to some market participants, ETG has also benefited from assistance from the Tanzania Investment Corporation.[22] These investments allow the firm to better control distribution in the market and undercut incumbent operators. This is likely to have contributed to the decline in market shares of the major players in the regional oligopoly such as Yara, Omnia, and smaller incumbents such as Nyiombo. Nyiombo also has a presence in Malawi, Tanzania, and Zimbabwe. Omnia has regional offices in Angola, Mozambique, South Africa, Zambia, and Zimbabwe, and also services Botswana, the Democratic Republic of Congo, Ethiopia, Kenya, and Namibia largely from its South African office. ETG reports significant growth in the past three years in Malawi, Rwanda, Tanzania, and Zambia, although the firm is present in different forms in more than 30 African countries.

### 4.4.3 Changing Market Dynamics in Tanzania

We assess the composition of fertilizer costs and prices for urea sold in Mbeya in Tanzania in early 2014, based on available data from interviews with two fertilizer companies operating in Tanzania and a study by the Tanzania Fertilizer Regulatory Authority (TFRA) (Ngowi 2013) (table 4.4). Mbeya is an agriculturally active region in southwest Tanzania 828 km from Dar es Salaam where maize, rice, and wheat, among other crops, are grown and fertilizer is in high demand.

The following key observations can be made:

1. Estimates of FOB prices are similar across the three sources, which is to be expected given that domestic suppliers in most African markets are price takers on the international market.

2. Sea freight and related costs are about US$50/ton. Port charges and bagging can add further costs. Firms with their own bagging facilities are expected to have a lower cost. Together these costs (excluding FOB cost) account for about US$130–US$140/ton, including a modest allowance for an importer margin. The TFRA data are for 2013 when there appears to have been slightly higher international prices, although the estimated price of cost, insurance, and freight (CIF) may also include a TFRA margin.

**TABLE 4.4   Urea Price Composition in Mbeya, Tanzania**
*US$/ton*

| Price and cost parameter | Fertilizer Company A, Q1 2014 | Fertilizer Company B, Q1 2014 | TFRA, 2013 | Benchmark |
|---|---|---|---|---|
| FOB | 352 | 350 | — | 350 |
| CIF | 402 | 400 | 420 | 400 |
| Port charges | 50 | 50 | 60 | 50 |
| Bags, bagging, and storage | 18.15 | — | 20 | — |
| Importer margin | 20 | — | — | — |
| Subtotal: export warehouse (bagged) | 490.15 | 450 | 500 | 480 |
| Inland transport costs | 43 | 60 | 50 | 50 |
| Wholesale price | 573 | 545 | 563 | 560 |
| Final retail price | 646.60 | 545 | 688 | 640 |
| Chimala average retail list price (AMITSA) | 882 | 882 | 757 | 882 |
| National average retail list price (AMITSA) | 720 | 720 | 810 | 720 |

*Sources:* Interview data from fertilizer companies; Ngowi 2013.

*Note:* Some of the figures do not necessarily add up to the total retail price in this table due to the unavailability of estimates for some of the components. Mbeya is 828 km from Dar es Salaam. Chimala prices are from available AMITSA disaggregated monthly price data. Chimala is 74 km from Mbeya city (average of prices in January and March 2014). AMITSA = Regional Agricultural Input Market Information and Transparency System; CIF = cost, insurance, and freight; FOB = free on board; TFRA = Tanzania Fertilizer Regulatory Authority; — = not available.

3. The local transport and trading activities add about US$160/ton to get to a final (net) retail price of about US$640/ton at retail level.

4. Note that the transport cost is just US$50/ton, and lower than TFRA's data in some estimates, which may reflect integration into transport operations or strong bargaining relationships with transporters by Fertilizer Company A and Fertilizer Company B.

The final retail price of Fertilizer Company B is significantly below the average prices recorded at Chimala (approximately 74 km from Mbeya) and nationally,[23] reflecting lower costs at transport and handling. This is consistent with the view that rivals in the Tanzanian market have been able to undercut prevailing prices most recently, indicating the possibility for greater competition in the future.

In addition, the difference of US$195/ton between Fertilizer Company B's 2014 final retail price and the FOB price is close to the 2010 difference of US$220/ton over FOB for Tanzania overall. In 2013 the difference was about US$350/ton (based on the TFRA study) and US$470/ton from table 4.1, although the average retail prices are list prices and some discounting may take place. This is some US$150/ton to US$250/ton higher than the cost buildup suggests should be a competitive price. This accords with our assessment of the amount by which Tanzanian prices have been marked up in 2011–13.

These are significant differences and suggest that fertilizer prices in Tanzania are far above what farmers should be paying and that farmers could benefit from more competitive rivalry in Tanzania. The margin by which we find that prices have been too high is split between inefficiencies, regulatory issues, trader margins, and other rents that may be due to competition issues, related to barriers to entry and the level of contestability of the market.

## 4.5 Conclusions and Policy Implications

The estimates provided above suggest that a number of factors have affected outcomes in the fertilizer markets of each country. It is worth bringing these aspects together, which we do in this section using available data and simple calculations of cost savings in Zambia where there have been clear benefits from competition relative to national expenditures on fertilizer.[24]

Total imports of urea to Zambia in 2013 amounted to 188,061 tons, and urea constituted 35 percent of all fertilizer imports to Zambia in 2013. The annual national average delivered price for urea in Zambia in 2013 was US$816/ton (table 4.1). This price is essentially equal to (and slightly lower than) what we computed as the competitive price for a landlocked country, with efficient transport, for 2013 using available benchmarks (see tables 4.2 and 4.3). The Zambian price is assumed to have been above competitive levels in 2010 prior to competition law interventions and other developments already discussed.

Had the market in Zambia not become more competitive in the period leading up to 2013, outcomes might have been very different and total expenditure on fertilizer far greater. The two scenarios below demonstrate the potential savings in expenditure, partly as a result of the market becoming more competitive.

### 4.5.1 Scenario A: Zambian Urea Price Remains About US$119/ton above the Tanzanian Price, as It Was in 2010 (after Accounting for Transport Costs)

If the same markup over Tanzanian urea prices of US$119/ton had applied in 2013, the Zambian price would have been approximately US$929/ton compared to the actual price in 2013 of US$816/ton. On this basis, additional aggregate expenditure in Zambia on urea in 2013, other things equal, would have been about US$21 million.

### 4.5.2 Scenario B: Zambian Urea Prices Followed the Trend of Prices in Malawi and Showed Markups of Approximately US$195/ton above Competitive Levels for an Inland Country Assuming Efficient Transport of US$110/ton in 2013 (based on tables 4.2 and 4.3)

Urea prices in Malawi, a comparable landlocked country, were about US$195/ton above competitive levels benchmarked for an inland country with efficient transport in 2013 (see table 4.3). If the Zambian market had not become more competitive in relative terms it might have had similar markups above competitive levels such that the price of fertilizer would have been approximately US$1,019/ton. At this price, additional aggregate expenditure on urea would have been approximately US$38 million. These estimates represent only the markups and savings on urea, which accounts for 35 percent of imports. This likely means that savings across all fertilizer products would have been even greater.

To the extent that incumbent fertilizer companies have been able to coordinate their market behavior to manipulate fertilizer supplies, as in the Zambian case, there have been significant losses to users of fertilizer. It is also clear that opening up the fertilizer market in Zambia has resulted in gains to consumers, whereas outcomes in Malawi and Tanzania have been far less positive. Although there have not been investigations into the fertilizer sectors in Malawi and Tanzania, indications are that there are significant constraints to achieving more competitive outcomes. High markups in downstream levels of the market in Tanzania are worrisome, indicating that there may be significant inefficiencies or anticompetitive conduct. In Malawi, there may also be issues in transportation given high levels of concentration at this level, although we have not explored this aspect here. The competition authority in Malawi has explored these potential concerns. However, given that transportation is a relatively small contributor to the costs of fertilizer, it would be worth exploring in further detail the possibility of anticompetitive arrangements in fertilizer trading as well.

As discussed in section 4.2, the potential for coordinated outcomes can be enhanced through the market interactions of vertically integrated players in a market. This is not to say that there is a cartel in fertilizer trading in Malawi or Tanzania, for that matter. The analysis in this chapter seeks to show that the characteristics of fertilizer markets in these countries and in the region align well with the theories of coordination, and that observed outcomes suggest markups above reasonable competitive benchmarks. Fertilizer importers, although not always integrated at all levels of the value chain, tend to be present at more than one level through the control of infrastructure in particular. Examples of this are fertilizer terminals and transport networks. Table 4.4 demonstrates the powerful effects of having a presence at various levels of the value chain in fertilizer markets. Entrants in Tanzania have seemingly been able to undercut prevailing market prices through leveraging presence at the bagging and distribution level. This ability to enter markets and compete, in the absence of strategic barriers imposed by incumbent firms, is central to a broader conception of inclusive growth, in our view. The simple calculations just presented demonstrate the strong, welfare-enhancing benefits of this theory.

## Notes

1. World Bank, World Development Indicators (database), http://data.worldbank.org/data-catalog /world-development-indicators.
2. See the Farm Input Subsidy Programme (FISP) in Malawi launched in 2005/06, the National Agricultural Input Voucher Scheme (NAIVS) introduced in 2008 in Tanzania, and the Farmer Input Support Programme (FISP) in Zambia, which is focused on maize production. Each program has an emphasis on increasing fertilizer usage, including among small-scale farmers.
3. Free on board (FOB) terms generally stipulate that the supplier pays for the transportation of the goods to the port of shipment and for loading on board the vessel, and the buyer pays for and bears the risk of additional shipping, port costs at the receiving port, and any further transportation over land once the goods are loaded at the port of shipment.
4. Competition Tribunal Case No. 31/CR/May05.
5. Adapted from Das Nair and Mncube 2012.
6. The firms appealed the penalties issued with the Competition and Consumer Protection Tribunal.
7. Nyiombo Investments website: http://www.nyiombo.co.zm/.
8. See, for example, "Government Broadens FISP Tender Process" (April 18, 2012), at http:// www.postzambia.com/post-read_article.php?articleId=26958; "Corruption Deal Backfires" (December 18, 2013), at http://zambiadailynation.com/2013/12/18/corruption-deal-backfires/; and "PAC Questions Govt over Nyiombo Investments, Omnia's Contracts" (March 25, 2010), at http://www.postzambia.com/Joomla/post-read_article.php?articleId=7395.
9. See "Government Broadens FISP Tender Process" (April 18, 2012), at http://www.postzambia .com/post-read_article.php?articleId=26958.
10. See "Government Broadens FISP Tender Process" (April 18, 2012), at http://www.postzambia .com/post-read_article.php?articleId=26958.

11. "Corruption Deal Backfires" (December 18, 2013), at http://zambiadailynation.com/2013/12/18/corruption-deal-backfires/. Losing bidders will sell under competitive commercial market conditions parallel to the subsidy program.

12. See Baltic Freight Index and National Agricultural Marketing Council Markets and Economic Research Centre, "Input Cost Monitoring: An Update on Selected Items, February 2014," at http://www.namc.co.za/upload/Trends-in-selected-Agricultural-input-prices-February-2014.pdf.

13. Assuming the same FOB prices for all countries.

14. Interview with truck company. This was the rate at which it stated that it could break even on a trip from the Copperbelt to Johannesburg.

15. Generally fertilizer in bulk quantities is shipped in bulk; containers are used mostly for small consignments.

16. The DCG was established in 2004. Yara is also reported to be planning to open a bagging facility that will handle only fertilizer, whereas DCG's platform also handles other dry bulk goods. See http://www.bloomberg.com/news/articles/2014-09-02/yara-plans-2-5-billion-gas-based-fertilizer-plant-in-africa.

17. Interview with fertilizer company.

18. Interview with fertilizer company and freight forwarder.

19. Interview with fertilizer company.

20. Interview with fertilizer company.

21. Interview with fertilizer company.

22. Interview with fertilizer company.

23. Although these are list prices from which discounting may still take place.

24. A detailed estimation of benefits would require disaggregated data on specific volumes of imports, by importer and product type over time, which were not available.

## Bibliography

ACB (African Centre for Biosafety). 2014. *The Political Economy of Africa's Burgeoning Chemical Fertiliser Rush*. Melville, South Africa: ACB.

Banda, Fatsani, Genna Robb, Simon Roberts, and Thando Vilakazi. 2015. "Review Paper One: Key Debates in Competition, Capabilities Development and Related Policies—Drawing the Link between Barriers to Entry and Inclusive Growth." CCRED Working Paper 4/2015, Centre for Competition, Regulation and Economic Development, Johannesburg, South Africa.

Benson, Todd, Stephen L. Kirama, Sr., and Onesmo Selejio. 2012. "The Supply of Inorganic Fertilizers to Smallholder Farmers in Tanzania." IFPRI Discussion Paper No. 01230, International Food Policy Research Institute, Washington, DC.

Bernheim, B. D., and M. D. Whinston. 1990. "Multimarket Contact and Collusive Behaviour." *Rand Journal of Economics* 21 (1): 1–26.

CCPC (Competition and Consumer Protection Commission of Zambia). 2013. *Competition and Consumer Protection News* April–June 2013, Issue No. 6.

Das Nair, R., and L. Mncube. 2012. "The Role of Information Exchange in Facilitating Collusion: Insights from Selected Cases." In *The Development of Competition Law and Economics in South Africa*, edited by K. Moodaliyar and S. Roberts, 181–206. Pretoria: HSRC Press.

GrainSA. 2011. *Grain SA Fertiliser Report 2011*. Praetoria: GrainSA. http://www.grainsa.co.za/upload/report_files/Kunsmisverslag-Volledig.pdf.

Gregory, D. I., and B. L. Bumb. 2006. "Factors Affecting Supply of Fertilizer in Sub-Saharan Africa." Agriculture and Rural Development Discussion Paper 24, World Bank, Washington, DC.

Harrington, J. E. 2006. "Behavioural Screening and the Detection of Cartels." EU Competition Law and Policy Workshop 2006 – Proceedings.

———. 2011. "Posted Pricing as a Plus Factor." *Journal of Competition Law and Economics* 7 (1): 1–35.

Heffer, P., and M. Prud'homme. 2014. *Fertilizer Outlook 2014–2018*. Paris: International Fertilizer Industry Association (IFA).

IFDC (International Fertilizer Development Centre). 2013a. *Zambia Fertilizer Assessment*. Muscle Shoals, AL: IFDC.

———. 2013b. *Malawi Fertilizer Assessment*. Muscle Shoals, AL: IFDC.

Khumalo, J., J. Mashiane, and S. Roberts. 2014. "Harm and Overcharge in the South African Precast Concrete Products Cartel." *Journal of Competition Law and Economics* 10 (3): 621–46.

Levenstein, M. 1993. "Vertical Restraints in the Bromine Cartel: The Role of Distributors in Facilitating Collusion." NBER Working Paper Series, Historical Paper 49, National Bureau of Economic Research, Cambridge, MA.

Levenstein, M., and V. Y. Suslow. 2006. "What Determines Cartel Success?" *Journal of Economic Literature* 44 (1): 43–95.

Makhaya, G., and S. Roberts. 2013. "Expectations and Outcomes: Considering Competition and Corporate Power in South Africa under Democracy." *Review of African Political Economy* 40 (138): 556–71.

Motta, Massimo. 2004. *Competition Policy: Theory and Practice*. Cambridge, U.K.: Cambridge University Press.

Ncube, P., S. Roberts, and T. Vilakazi. 2015. "Study of Competition in the Road Freight Sector in the SADC Region – A Case Study of Fertilizer Transport and Trading in Zambia, Tanzania and Malawi." CCRED Working Paper 3/2015, Centre for Competition, Regulation and Economic Development, Johannesburg, South Africa.

Ngowi, H. P. 2013. "Impacts of Removal of Fertilizer Value Added Tax (VAT) on Fertilizer Use and Productivity in Tanzania." Tanzania Fertilizer Regulatory Authority (TFRA). Presented at the Tanzania Soil Health Policy Action Node Stakeholders Conference, Dar es Salaam, November 28–29.

Ramos, A. R., R. Ranieri, and J. Lammens. 2013. "Mapping Inclusive Growth." IPC-IG Working Paper 105, International Policy Centre for Inclusive Growth, Brasília, Brazil.

Taylor, C. R., and D. L. Moss. 2013. "The Fertilizer Oligopoly: The Case for Global Antitrust Enforcement." AAI Working Paper 13–05, American Antitrust Institute, Washington, DC.

# 5. Market Power and Wealth Distribution

**Sean F. Ennis** and **Yunhee Kim** (OECD)

Lack of competition can drive up prices of goods and services, with substantive negative effects for the poor, whose consumption basket is dominated by first necessity goods and services. Understanding the distributional effects of market power is important for showing the value of policies that reduce monopoly power, which yield positive effects on both growth and wealth distribution. Firms that possess market power can charge supracompetitive prices for their products and earn profits above the competitive rate of return. The impacts of these higher prices can, on net, be beneficial to holders of substantial financial assets because these holders may pay higher prices for their consumption but will receive more than a counterbalancing boost in income from the increased profits arising from their financial holdings. The increased prices will disproportionately harm the poor, who will pay more for goods without receiving a counterbalancing share of increased profits. Using new data, this study calibrates the overall impact of market power, showing a substantial impact on wealth inequality in the eight countries examined. In typical results, the share of wealth of the top 10 percent of households (by wealth) rises by 10 to 24 percent in the presence of market power. Reducing illegal or government-granted market power could reduce inequality.

## 5.1 Introduction

Measuring inequality has been a substantial focus of economic research in recent years, notably with the seminal work of Piketty and Saez (2003) on income inequality in the United States, and their follow-up work, along with their coauthors, to create income and wealth distribution estimates for many countries.[1] Government policies

Organisation for Economic Co-operation and Development (OECD), 2 rue André-Pascal, Paris, CEDEX 75775. Corresponding author: sean.ennis@oecd.org. Special thanks to John Davies, who had the idea to perform this work, and to Esther Danitz, who assembled much of the data used in this study. Thanks for comments on this project and study to Walter Beckert, John Davies, Ana Rodrigues, Ania Thiemann, Cristiana Vitale, other OECD staff, World Bank staff, and participants in the Inaugural World Bank-OECD Conference on Competition Policy, Shared Prosperity and Inclusive Growth. The opinions expressed and arguments employed herein do not necessarily reflect the official views of the OECD or OECD member countries. This chapter is © OECD and available under the Creative Commons Attribution Non-Commercial No Derivatives 3.0 IGO (CC BY-NC-ND 3.0 IGO) public license.

aimed at moderating inequality have been argued to yield potential broad-based economic benefits, with Cingano (2014) estimating that reducing inequality could augment total gross domestic product (GDP) by as much as 20 percent in some countries. In order to design appropriate government policies, though, a better understanding is needed of the potential sources of inequality. This study focuses on one potential source, monopoly power. For the purposes of this study, monopoly power, or market power, is deemed present when there is a return on capital above the competitive rate of return. Based on our model, market power can account for as much as one-quarter of the assets of the wealthiest decile of the population.

Until recently, the potential role of market power has been little considered, except by Baker and Salop (2015), and Rognlie (2015). Recent calibrations of the impact of market power on wealth distributions have not been provided, but are essential for determining whether the magnitude of the effect is substantial. Rognlie disputes Piketty's suggestion that capital share of income is increasing, proposing that increases in the capital share of income come from a residual increase in profits, which the author suggests may arise from cyclical changes in markups and market power. This argument can only enhance the relevance of this chapter's quantitative calibration of the role of market power on wealth.

Extending and updating the main quantitative approach, initially introduced and applied by Comanor and Smiley (1975), this chapter simulates how profits from market power are distributed to shareholders and provides the first calibration since 1975 (to the authors' knowledge) of the potential redistributive effects of market power.[2] This method is extended beyond the United States to include a total of eight countries. These countries were selected to ensure they covered a large share of the world's wealth, in light of data availability.

The existence of corporate market power has a dual effect, not only generating profits for companies that are above the competitive rate of return, but also imposing higher prices on consumers. The increased margins charged to customers as a result of market power will disproportionately harm the poor, who will pay more for goods without receiving a counterbalancing share of increased profits. The wealthy, while also paying more, will at the same time receive higher profits from market power, because of their generally higher ownership of the stream of corporate profits and capital gains. These market power gains are assumed to be distributed in proportion to current total business ownership claims.

Using new data, this study illustrates the overall impact of market power, showing that the disproportionate impact of market power on the poor and the wealthy—while varying from one country to another in magnitude—is substantial across the eight countries examined (Australia, Canada, France, Germany, Japan, the Republic of Korea, the United Kingdom, and the United States). In a typical result, we find that, of the share of wealth of the top 10 percent (richest), about one-tenth to one-quarter comes from market power.

These results do not imply, and should not be taken to suggest, that the origin of wealth is always illegitimate or illegal activity. The sources of market power, for example, clearly vary, with many sources generally considered legitimate, such as pricing power originating from intellectual property and legally protected by patents, trade secrets, or trademarks. Further, policy makers may wish to reward market power that comes from being first to a market and gaining some consequent advantage, in order to ensure that companies retain a substantial incentive to innovate. At the same time, some sources of market power are considered illegitimate, such as market power coming from illegal cartels, exclusionary behavior by dominant companies, and government regulations that imbue market power on select companies, while creating undue barriers to entry for others.[3] The aggregate size of these illegitimate effects is controversial but likely nontrivial.[4] This study concludes that the extent of illegitimate market power, and wealth inequality that arises from it, can be reduced by government actions either to control the illegal origins of market power or to reduce government regulations that create or enhance market power.

The rest of this chapter is organized as follows: section 5.2 explains the model; section 5.3 explains the data; section 5.4 calibrates the impacts of market power on wealth; and section 5.5 concludes.

## 5.2 Model

One basic approach to assessing the impact of market power on inequality is set out in Comanor and Smiley (1975). They calculate how profits from market power transfer income from the poor to the wealth holder. The purpose of this calibration is to indicate the possible order of magnitude of the effect of market power on wealth distributions.

The assumptions underlying the model are significant and merit further discussion. There are four primary assumptions. The first is that the ratio of market power profits to GDP has remained constant over the period of the analysis (1920–2010).[5] Market power profits are those that exceed the market return on capital and arise from the difference between price and marginal cost. The second is that profits from market power have a fixed life span, being created and terminated in a steady state throughout these years. Companies gain market power and then they lose it with time, as appears to happen with technology companies that are leapfrogged by others, or as happens when profits from patents are reduced as a result of patent expiration. The third is that market power gains are distributed in proportion to current total financial wealth distribution. This reflects the observation that corporate income and capital gains are distributed via shareholding, so that those with the largest shareholding will, in proportion, receive the largest share of the profits.[6] The fourth is that higher prices from market power will be distributed in proportion to consumption. Each unit of consumption will be inflated equally by higher prices from market power. This suggests that products for the poor and products for the wealthy will be equally affected by market power, with each unit of consumption paying more regardless of the wealth decile of the consumers.[7]

The model presented in this study yields a formula for the market power gains and the market power losses. The difference between the market power profits and the excess payments for consumption (arising from market power raising prices) for each wealth class gives a figure for the net impact of the market power. These figures are then subtracted from existing wealth positions to determine hypothetical distributions of household wealth in the absence of market power. Other determinants of the distribution remain unchanged.

We assume that total market power profits are a constant share of GDP, $a$, over time, with monopolies created and dying in a steady state, and the life of monopolies being constant $T$ years. This is expressed by equation (5.1):

$$\pi_t = a\text{GDP}_t. \tag{5.1}$$

Profits for wealth class $i$ at time $t$ are spread out over time according to equation (5.2):

$$\pi_{it} = \sum_{n=0}^{T-1} \pi_{it(t_0-n)}. \tag{5.2}$$

In this notation, $\pi_{it}$ represents the flow of aggregate excess returns in year $t$ that come from each vintage of monopoly[8] that is yielding returns and for which the original owners were members of wealth class $i$. $\pi_{it}(t_0-n)$ is the annual flow of excess returns (after corporate tax) in year $t$ due to members of the $i$th wealth class from monopolies created in year $t_0-n$. Monopolies thus generate excess returns over a period of $T$ years from $t_0-n$ to $t_0-n+T-1$.

We assume that the flow of excess returns due to market power is distributed in proportion to the total business ownership claims $(P_i)$ of each wealth class $i$, as in equation (5.3). Stated another way, each unit of claim on business ownership has an equal probability of realizing market power gains.

$$\pi_{it} = P_i\pi_t. \tag{5.3}$$

The calibration proceeds by noting that each individual wealth class $i$ at time $t$ has a wealth gain and a wealth loss of $V_{it}$ and $I_{it}$, respectively.

The wealth gain of wealth class $i$ at time $t$, with interest rate $i$, taxation on capital gains for year $t_0-n$, and the number of years after which gains are realized in which they are taxed ($m$) is given by equation (5.4):[9]

$$V_{it_0} = \sum_{n=0}^{N} \left[ \sum_{t=t_0-n}^{t_0-n+T-1} \frac{\pi_{it}/T}{(1+i)^j} \right] (1-d_i)^n (1+i)^n \left( 1 - \frac{r_{t_0-n+m}}{(1-d_i)^m (1+i)^m} \right) \qquad (5.4)$$

where $j \equiv t-t_0+n$ and $j = 0, 1, 2, \ldots T-1$.

The wealth foregone for wealth class $i$ in the current year (for example, as a result of dissipation of wealth) is given by equation (5.5):

$$I_{it_0} = \sum_{n=0}^{N} \left[ \pi'_{it(t_0-n)} \right] s_i (1-d_i)^n (1+i)^n \qquad (5.5)$$

where $s_i$ is the proportion of income saved by wealth class $i$, and $d_i$ is the dissipation rate of accumulated wealth from the $i$th wealth class.

The net wealth changes combining the wealth gain and the wealth loss of wealth class $i$ at time $t$ is then given by equation (5.6), which will be calibrated separately for each country in the analysis:

$$V_{it_0} - I_{it_0} = \sum_{n=0}^{N} \left[ (1-d_1)^n (1+i)^n \right]$$
$$\left\{ \frac{ap_i}{T} \left( \sum_{t=t_0-n}^{t_0-n+T-1} \frac{GNP_t}{(1+i)^j} \right) \left( 1 - \frac{r_{t_0-n+m}}{(1-d_i)^m (1+i)^m} \right) - ap'_i s_i GNP_{t_0-n} \right\}. \qquad (5.6)$$

## 5.3 Data

A calibration of the impact of wealth distribution is made for eight countries. This section describes the variables used for the model and their underlying sources. To the extent possible, data sources have been used that are common across these countries to ensure comparability. The countries are Australia, Canada, France, Germany, Korea, Japan, the United Kingdom, and the United States. Data sources are listed in tables 5.1 and 5.2.

All figures are converted into US\$ for comparability (billions), using the OECD purchasing power parity (PPP) converters. Extrapolation is made by applying the relative rates of inflation observed in different countries to the base year PPPs. GDP series in national currency and at current prices can be converted with these PPPs to yield volume measures that are comparable across countries. The resulting measures

**TABLE 5.1    Definition and Sources of Variables**

| Variable | Definition and sources |
|---|---|
| Wealth and income | This study relies on two datasets, the Organisation for Economic Co-operation and Development (OECD) Wealth Distribution Database (first released May 21, 2015) and the OECD Income Distribution Database (first released May 21, 2015). The wealth distribution data break out financial assets. |
| Consumption | Consumption expenditures by $i$th class have been derived from a number of sources (see table 5.2). In light of data confidentiality limitations, we assume the $i$th wealth class coincides with the $i$th income class. While there is not a perfect overlap, we consider the overlap is likely relatively stronger at the higher income and wealth classes that are most important for this analysis. |
| Saving rate | The saving rate comes from OECD *National Accounts at a Glance*, equaling net saving divided by net disposable income. We assume the same saving rate for all wealth classes. |
| Interest rate | The interest rate comes from OECD.Stat; OECD Economic Outlook No. 96, with pre-1970 data imputed by analogy with interest rates in the United States. |
| Tax on capital gains | The tax on capital gains comes from OECD supplemented by Wikipedia entries where necessary. The number of years passing before tax is paid is derived from OECD sources. |
| Dissipation rate | The dissipation rate is assumed to be 1.7 percent, consistent with Comanor and Smiley 1975. |
| Average length of monopoly | The average length of monopoly, $T$, cannot easily be derived from data. We calibrate using a 10-year monopoly time span. |
| Share of GDP accounted for by market power | The share of gross domestic product (GDP) accounted for by market power is assumed to be 1 percent or 3 percent, based on calculations such as Baker 2003 and Schwartzman 1959. Considering that listed corporate profits account for 5–9 percent of GDP in countries like the United States, for example, and that market power has many origins, the order of magnitude of this figure is reasonable. |

of GDP comparisons are volume indexes at constant prices and PPPs. The same result would have been achieved by applying volume growth rates of GDP to the comparative GDP levels of the base year. Table 5.2 shows selected variables by country.

## 5.4  Calibration of Impacts

Tables 5.3 to 5.10 each show an overview by country of business ownership, consumption distributions, and wealth distributions (net worth) in the eight countries of analysis. These are descriptive statistics, from previously identified sources or imputed from these sources.

The main results are presented in tables 5.11 to 5.18. Column 3 states the current distribution of wealth share by deciles. This distribution is empirically observed and incorporates the impact of all existing market power. In order to simulate a hypothetical distribution in the absence of any market power, one should remove from the existing distribution the impact of all market power. This is done through the formula described in equation (5.6) with a monopoly life span of 10 years.

In a typical result, the share of wealth of the top 10 percent of households (by wealth) rises by between 10 percent and 24 percent in the presence of market power. For example, in Australia (table 5.11), the wealth of the top 10 percent, assuming monopolies are 10 years, is 43 percent of wealth with no market power and 50 percent actually.

**TABLE 5.2  Selected Variables and Sources, by Country**

| Variable | Australia | France | Germany | Japan | United Kingdom | United States | Canada | Korea, Rep. |
|---|---|---|---|---|---|---|---|---|
| GNP/GDP | OECD datasets: GDP Gross National Income 1950–2013 Gross Domestic Product 1950–2013 in national currency and current prices | | | | | | | |
| Standard year—the year of the Antitrust Act (N) | 2010–1920 | | | | | | | |
| Monopoly profits ratio to GNP/GDP ($a$) – 3%, 2% | Estimation coming from Comanor and Smiley 1975; Scherer 1975, 409 | | | | | | | |
| Interest rate ($l$) | OECD datasets: OECD Economic Outlook No. 96 Long-term interest rate on government bonds 1970–2014 OECD Economic Outlook No. 96 Short-term interest rate 1970–2014 | | | | | | | |
| Wealth distribution ($p_i$) = financial wealth; net worth (Wi) = financial + nonfinancial liabilities | OECD datasets: Wealth distribution data (WDD) by decile from STD/HSPM (OECD 2015) | | | | | | | |
| Consumption expenditures ($p'_i$) | Consumption expenditures of households by income quintile for 2009–10 Source: Australian Bureau of Statistics: Household Expenditure Survey 2009–10 | Consumption expenditures of households by income decile Source: Eurostat | Consumption expenditures of households by income decile Source: Eurostat | Consumption expenditures of households by income decile Source: Eurostat | Average weekly household expenditure by gross income decile group for 2011 and 2013 Source: Office for National Statistics, U.K. | Average annual expenditure by income quintiles Source: U.S. Bureau of Labor Statistics, Consumer Expenditure Survey | Average annual expenditure by income quintiles Source: Statistics Canada; Survey of Household Spending 2012, Table 2 | Average annual expenditure by income quintiles, kostat.go.kr: Korean Statistical Information Service website |
| Saving rates ($si$) | OECD disposable income and net lending–net borrowing dataset | OECD dataset: OECD National Accounts at a Glance 2013 household net saving 1998–2011 | OECD disposable income and net lending–net borrowing dataset | OECD disposable income and net lending–net borrowing dataset | Institute for Fiscal Studies "Wealth and Saving of UK Families 2000–2005," 47 | OECD disposable income and net lending–net borrowing dataset | | |
| Dissipation rate ($d$) | 1.7% | 1.7% | 1.7% | 1.7% | 1.7% | 1.7% | 1.7% | 1.7% |
| Capital gain taxation $rt_g - n + m$ | Source: Harding 2013 | Source: Harding 2013 | Source: Harding 2013 | Source: Harding 2013 | Source: Harding 2013 | Source: Harding 2013 | Source: Harding 2013 | Source: Harding 2013 |

*Note:* GDP = gross domestic product; GNP = gross national product; OECD = Organisation for Economic Co-operation and Development.

139

**Australia: Existing Distributions of Business Ownership, Consumer Expenditures, and Net Worth, by Wealth Decile**

| Wealth decile | Percentage of business ownership claims ($p_j$) | Percentage of consumer expenditures ($p'_j$) | Percentage of net worth ($w_0$) | Number of households (WDD) |
|---|---|---|---|---|
| Poorest | 0.32 | 4.54 | 0.20 | 839,850 |
| 2 | 0.32 | 4.54 | 0.60 | 839,850 |
| 3 | 1.53 | 6.57 | 1.90 | 839,850 |
| 4 | 1.53 | 6.57 | 3.00 | 839,850 |
| 5 | 2.39 | 9.46 | 4.70 | 839,850 |
| 6 | 2.39 | 9.46 | 6.00 | 839,850 |
| 7 | 5.23 | 11.97 | 7.70 | 839,850 |
| 8 | 5.23 | 11.97 | 10.30 | 839,850 |
| 9 | 9.08 | 17.47 | 15.10 | 839,850 |
| Richest | 68.61 | 17.47 | 50.40 | 839,850 |
| **Total** | **97.00** | **100.00** | **100.00** | **8,398,500** |

*Note:* WDD = wealth distribution data.

TABLE 5.4 **Canada: Existing Distributions of Business Ownership, Consumer Expenditures, and Net Worth, by Wealth Decile**

| Wealth decile | Percentage of business ownership claims ($p_j$) | Percentage of consumer expenditures ($p'_j$) | Percentage of net worth ($w_0$) | Number of households (WDD) |
|---|---|---|---|---|
| Poorest | 0.13 | 3.97 | 0.00 | 1,351,401 |
| 2 | 0.13 | 3.97 | 0.30 | 1,351,401 |
| 3 | 0.97 | 5.77 | 0.30 | 1,351,401 |
| 4 | 0.97 | 5.77 | 1.60 | 1,351,401 |
| 5 | 2.66 | 8.49 | 2.60 | 1,351,401 |
| 6 | 2.66 | 8.49 | 4.60 | 1,351,401 |
| 7 | 6.54 | 11.68 | 6.90 | 1,351,401 |
| 8 | 6.54 | 11.68 | 10.30 | 1,351,401 |
| 9 | 14.70 | 20.09 | 15.80 | 1,351,401 |
| Richest | 64.69 | 20.09 | 57.70 | 1,351,401 |
| **Total** | **100.00** | **100.00** | **100.00** | **13,514,009** |

*Note:* WDD = wealth distribution data.

TABLE 5.5 **France: Existing Distributions of Business Ownership, Consumer Expenditures, and Net Worth, by Wealth Decile**

| Wealth decile | Percentage of business ownership claims ($p_i$) | Percentage of consumer expenditures ($p'_i$) | Percentage of net worth ($w_0$) | Number of households (WDD) |
|---|---|---|---|---|
| Poorest | 0.28 | 4.49 | 0.10 | 2,852,400 |
| 2 | 0.28 | 5.40 | 0.30 | 2,852,400 |
| 3 | 1.78 | 6.52 | 0.60 | 2,852,400 |
| 4 | 1.78 | 7.39 | 1.10 | 2,852,400 |
| 5 | 3.60 | 8.53 | 1.80 | 2,852,400 |
| 6 | 3.60 | 9.80 | 3.90 | 2,852,400 |
| 7 | 5.96 | 11.32 | 5.70 | 2,852,400 |
| 8 | 5.96 | 12.54 | 8.90 | 2,852,400 |
| 9 | 12.28 | 14.67 | 14.90 | 2,852,400 |
| Richest | 64.49 | 19.33 | 62.70 | 2,852,400 |
| **Total** | **100.00** | **100.00** | **100.00** | **28,524,000** |

*Note:* WDD = wealth distribution data.

TABLE 5.6 **Germany: Existing Distributions of Business Ownership, Consumer Expenditures, and Net Worth, by Wealth Decile**

| Wealth decile | Percentage of business ownership claims ($p_i$) | Percentage of consumer expenditures ($p'_i$) | Percentage of net worth ($w_0$) | Number of households (WDD) |
|---|---|---|---|---|
| Poorest | 0.32 | 3.80 | 0.00 | 3,864,200 |
| 2 | 0.32 | 4.79 | 0.00 | 3,864,200 |
| 3 | 1.31 | 5.99 | 0.20 | 3,864,200 |
| 4 | 1.31 | 7.07 | 0.70 | 3,864,200 |
| 5 | 4.21 | 8.28 | 1.50 | 3,864,200 |
| 6 | 4.21 | 9.56 | 3.40 | 3,864,200 |
| 7 | 6.75 | 11.09 | 6.40 | 3,864,200 |
| 8 | 6.75 | 12.78 | 11.50 | 3,864,200 |
| 9 | 12.34 | 15.37 | 16.30 | 3,864,200 |
| Richest | 62.57 | 21.28 | 60.70 | 3,864,200 |
| **Total** | **100.00** | **100.00** | **101.00** | **38,642,000** |

*Note:* WDD = wealth distribution data

TABLE 5.7  **Japan: Existing Distributions of Business Ownership, Consumer Expenditures, and Net Worth, by Wealth Decile**

| Wealth decile | Percentage of business ownership claims ($p_i$) | Percentage of consumer expenditures ($p'_i$) | Percentage of net worth ($w_0$) | Number of households (WDD) |
|---|---|---|---|---|
| Poorest | 0.30 | 5.60 | 0.40 | 48,536 |
| 2 | 0.70 | 6.53 | 1.40 | 48,536 |
| 3 | 1.60 | 7.55 | 2.40 | 48,536 |
| 4 | 2.80 | 8.44 | 3.40 | 48,536 |
| 5 | 4.30 | 8.94 | 4.60 | 48,536 |
| 6 | 6.00 | 9.75 | 6.00 | 48,536 |
| 7 | 8.10 | 11.11 | 8.00 | 48,536 |
| 8 | 10.90 | 11.92 | 11.10 | 48,536 |
| 9 | 16.30 | 13.24 | 16.40 | 48,536 |
| Richest | 49.10 | 16.92 | 46.20 | 48,536 |
| **Total** | **100.00** | **100.00** | **100.00** | **485,360** |

*Note:* WDD = wealth distribution data.

**TABLE 5.8**  **Republic of Korea: Distributions of Business Ownership, Consumer Expenditures, and Net Worth, by Wealth Decile**

| Wealth decile | Percentage of business ownership claims ($p_i$) | Percentage of consumer expenditures ($p'_i$) | Percentage of net worth ($w_0$) | Number of households (WDD) |
|---|---|---|---|---|
| Poorest | 0.00 | 4.25 | 0.00 | 1,795,068 |
| 2 | 0.20 | 5.96 | 0.20 | 1,795,068 |
| 3 | 1.20 | 7.26 | 1.20 | 1,795,068 |
| 4 | 2.10 | 8.49 | 2.10 | 1,795,068 |
| 5 | 3.30 | 9.24 | 3.30 | 1,795,068 |
| 6 | 4.50 | 10.38 | 4.50 | 1,795,068 |
| 7 | 6.50 | 10.86 | 6.50 | 1,795,068 |
| 8 | 8.80 | 12.62 | 8.80 | 1,795,068 |
| 9 | 13.00 | 13.80 | 13.00 | 1,795,068 |
| Richest | 60.70 | 17.13 | 60.70 | 1,795,068 |
| **Total** | **100.00** | **100.00** | **100.00** | **17,950,675** |

*Note:* WDD = wealth distribution data.

**TABLE 5.9    United Kingdom: Existing Distributions of Business Ownership, Consumer Expenditures, and Net Worth, by Wealth Decile**

| Wealth decile | Percentage of business ownership claims ($p_i$) | Percentage of consumer expenditures ($p'_i$) | Percentage of net worth ($w_0$) | Number of households (WDD) |
|---|---|---|---|---|
| Poorest | 0.23 | 5.42 | 0.10 | 2,632,300 |
| 2 | 0.23 | 5.47 | 0.30 | 2,632,300 |
| 3 | 1.12 | 6.22 | 1.10 | 2,632,300 |
| 4 | 1.12 | 7.37 | 2.40 | 2,632,300 |
| 5 | 2.40 | 8.52 | 3.90 | 2,632,300 |
| 6 | 2.40 | 9.68 | 5.50 | 2,632,300 |
| 7 | 5.81 | 10.21 | 7.70 | 2,632,300 |
| 8 | 5.81 | 12.37 | 10.40 | 2,632,300 |
| 9 | 12.81 | 14.48 | 15.70 | 2,632,300 |
| Richest | 68.06 | 20.28 | 53.00 | 2,632,300 |
| **Total** | **100.00** | **100.00** | **100.00** | **26,323,000** |

*Note:* WDD = wealth distribution data.

**TABLE 5.10    United States: Existing Distributions of Business Ownership, Consumer Expenditures, and Net Worth, by Wealth Decile**

| Wealth decile | Percentage of business ownership claims ($p_i$) | Percentage of consumer expenditures ($p'_i$) | Percentage of net worth ($w_0$) | Number of households (WDD) |
|---|---|---|---|---|
| Poorest | 0.10 | 4.31 | 0.00 | 12,110,700 |
| 2 | 0.10 | 4.31 | 0.00 | 12,110,700 |
| 3 | 0.16 | 6.34 | 0.20 | 12,110,700 |
| 4 | 0.16 | 6.34 | 0.50 | 12,110,700 |
| 5 | 0.57 | 8.35 | 1.10 | 12,110,700 |
| 6 | 0.57 | 8.35 | 2.00 | 12,110,700 |
| 7 | 2.20 | 11.64 | 3.50 | 12,110,700 |
| 8 | 2.20 | 11.64 | 6.00 | 12,110,700 |
| 9 | 7.24 | 19.36 | 11.70 | 12,110,700 |
| Richest | 86.69 | 19.36 | 76.00 | 12,110,700 |
| **Total** | **100.00** | **100.00** | **101.00** | **121,107,000** |

*Note:* WDD = wealth distribution data.

**TABLE 5.11    Australia: Impacts of Market Power with Varying Monopoly Life Span, by Wealth Decile**

| Wealth decile | Households | Current wealth share (%) ($W_0$) | Wealth share with no market power (%) |
|---|---|---|---|
| Poorest | 839,850 | 0.20 | 0.38 |
| 2 | 839,850 | 0.60 | 0.88 |
| 3 | 839,850 | 1.90 | 2.23 |

*(Table continues on the following page.)*

**TABLE 5.11  Australia: Impacts of Market Power with Varying Monopoly Life Span, by Wealth Decile (continued)**

| Wealth decile | Households | Current wealth share (%) ($W_0$) | Wealth share with no market power (%) |
|---|---|---|---|
| 4 | 839,850 | 3.00 | 3.60 |
| 5 | 839,850 | 4.70 | 5.60 |
| 6 | 839,850 | 6.00 | 7.22 |
| 7 | 839,850 | 7.70 | 8.60 |
| 8 | 839,850 | 10.30 | 11.83 |
| 9 | 839,850 | 15.10 | 16.91 |
| Richest | 839,850 | 50.40 | 42.74 |
| **Total** | **8,398,500** | **100.00** | **100.00** |

**TABLE 5.12  Canada: Impacts of Market Power with Varying Monopoly Life Span, by Wealth Decile**

| Wealth decile | Households | Current wealth share (%) ($W_0$) | Wealth share with no market power (%) |
|---|---|---|---|
| Poorest | 1,351,401 | 0.00 | 0.39 |
| 2 | 1,351,401 | 0.30 | 0.92 |
| 3 | 1,351,401 | 0.30 | 0.40 |
| 4 | 1,351,401 | 1.60 | 2.69 |
| 5 | 1,351,401 | 2.60 | 3.30 |
| 6 | 1,351,401 | 4.60 | 6.83 |
| 7 | 1,351,401 | 6.90 | 7.82 |
| 8 | 1,351,401 | 10.30 | 13.83 |
| 9 | 1,351,401 | 15.80 | 17.31 |
| Richest | 1,351,401 | 57.70 | 46.51 |
| **Total** | **13,514,009** | **100.00** | **100.00** |

**TABLE 5.13  France: Impacts of Market Power with Varying Monopoly Life Span, by Wealth Decile**

| Wealth decile | Households | Current wealth share (%) ($W_0$) | Wealth share with no market power (%) |
|---|---|---|---|
| Poorest | 2,852,400 | 0.10 | 0.45 |
| 2 | 2,852,400 | 0.30 | 0.85 |
| 3 | 2,852,400 | 0.60 | 0.49 |
| 4 | 2,852,400 | 1.10 | 1.34 |
| 5 | 2,852,400 | 1.80 | 1.39 |
| 6 | 2,852,400 | 3.90 | 4.70 |

*(Table continues on the following page.)*

**TABLE 5.13** France: Impacts of Market Power with Varying Monopoly Life Span, by Wealth Decile *(continued)*

| Wealth decile | Households | Current wealth share (%) ($W_0$) | Wealth share with no market power (%) |
|---|---|---|---|
| 7 | 2,852,400 | 5.70 | 6.13 |
| 8 | 2,852,400 | 8.90 | 11.10 |
| 9 | 2,852,400 | 14.90 | 16.50 |
| Richest | 2,852,400 | 62.70 | 57.05 |
| **Total** | **28,524,000** | **100.00** | **100.00** |

**TABLE 5.14** Germany: Impacts of Market Power with Varying Monopoly Life Span, by Wealth Decile

| Wealth decile | Households | Current wealth share (%) ($W_0$) | Wealth share with no market power (%) |
|---|---|---|---|
| Poorest | 3,864,200 | 0.00 | 0.26 |
| 2 | 3,864,200 | 0.00 | 0.40 |
| 3 | 3,864,200 | 0.20 | 0.03 |
| 4 | 3,864,200 | 0.70 | 1.05 |
| 5 | 3,864,200 | 1.50 | 0.03 |
| 6 | 3,864,200 | 3.40 | 3.52 |
| 7 | 3,864,200 | 6.40 | 6.68 |
| 8 | 3,864,200 | 11.50 | 15.81 |
| 9 | 3,864,200 | 16.30 | 19.53 |
| Richest | 3,864,200 | 60.70 | 52.69 |
| **Total** | **38,642,000** | **100.00** | **100.00** |

**TABLE 5.15** Japan: Impacts of Market Power with Varying Monopoly Life Span, by Wealth Decile

| Wealth decile | Households | Current wealth share (%) ($W_0$) | Wealth share with no market power (%) |
|---|---|---|---|
| Poorest | 48,536 | 0.40 | 1.52 |
| 2 | 48,536 | 1.40 | 3.08 |
| 3 | 48,536 | 2.40 | 4.18 |
| 4 | 48,536 | 3.40 | 4.98 |
| 5 | 48,536 | 4.60 | 5.75 |
| 6 | 48,536 | 6.00 | 6.76 |
| 7 | 48,536 | 8.00 | 8.54 |
| 8 | 48,536 | 11.10 | 11.48 |
| 9 | 48,536 | 16.40 | 15.92 |
| Richest | 48,536 | 46.20 | 37.79 |
| **Total** | **485,360** | **100.00** | **100.00** |

TABLE 5.16 **Republic of Korea: Impacts of Market Power with Varying Monopoly Life Span, by Wealth Decile**

| Wealth decile | Households | Current wealth share (%) ($W_0$) | Wealth share with no market power (%) |
|---|---|---|---|
| Poorest | 1,795,068 | 0.00 | 1.09 |
| 2 | 1,795,068 | 0.20 | 1.67 |
| 3 | 1,795,068 | 1.20 | 2.75 |
| 4 | 1,795,068 | 2.10 | 3.73 |
| 5 | 1,795,068 | 3.30 | 4.81 |
| 6 | 1,795,068 | 4.50 | 5.99 |
| 7 | 1,795,068 | 6.50 | 7.60 |
| 8 | 1,795,068 | 8.80 | 9.76 |
| 9 | 1,795,068 | 13.00 | 13.18 |
| Richest | 1,795,068 | 60.70 | 49.42 |
| **Total** | **17,950,675** | **100.00** | **100.00** |

**TABLE 5.17** **United Kingdom: Impacts of Market Power with Varying Monopoly Life Span, by Wealth Decile**

| Wealth decile | Households | Current wealth share (%) ($W_0$) | Wealth share with no market power (%) |
|---|---|---|---|
| Poorest | 2,632,300 | 0.10 | 0.09 |
| 2 | 2,632,300 | 0.30 | 0.41 |
| 3 | 2,632,300 | 1.10 | 1.15 |
| 4 | 2,632,300 | 2.40 | 3.21 |
| 5 | 2,632,300 | 3.90 | 4.83 |
| 6 | 2,632,300 | 5.50 | 7.35 |
| 7 | 2,632,300 | 7.70 | 8.83 |
| 8 | 2,632,300 | 10.40 | 13.09 |
| 9 | 2,632,300 | 15.70 | 17.35 |
| Richest | 2,632,300 | 53.00 | 43.70 |
| **Total** | **26,323,000** | **100.00** | **100.00** |

**TABLE 5.18** **United States: Impacts of Market Power with Varying Monopoly Life Span, by Wealth Decile**

| Wealth decile | Households | Current wealth share (%) ($W_0$) | Wealth share with no market power (%) |
|---|---|---|---|
| Poorest | 12,110,700 | 0.00 | 0.18 |
| 2 | 12,110,700 | 0.00 | 0.18 |
| 3 | 12,110,700 | 0.20 | 0.60 |

*(Table continues on the following page.)*

| Wealth decile | Households | Current wealth share (%) ($W_0$) | Wealth share with no market power (%) |
|---|---|---|---|
| 4 | 12,110,700 | 0.50 | 1.12 |
| 5 | 12,110,700 | 1.10 | 1.95 |
| 6 | 12,110,700 | 2.00 | 3.50 |
| 7 | 12,110,700 | 3.50 | 4.97 |
| 8 | 12,110,700 | 6.00 | 9.28 |
| 9 | 12,110,700 | 11.70 | 15.53 |
| Richest | 12,110,700 | 76.00 | 62.70 |
| **Total** | **121,107,000** | **100.00** | **100.00** |

Wealth classes used in this chapter are deciles because these are most easily reported or imputed from the reported data. Future refinements would include a greater focus on the top 1 percent of the population.

The poorest households start with almost zero in the distribution of wealth. Based on the model, it is possible to estimate how wealth class 1 (the poorest) has lost money (wealth) because of existing market power. The first wealth class receives a very small share of the profits from market power (0.1 percent) because their share in business ownership claims is very low. In addition, since they represent a higher share in consumption expenditures, they transfer much of their income to monopoly owners because of their excess payments (the higher prices for the goods produced by monopolies). At the end, the impact of market power for them is a high negative figure (they lose much more than they win). This is why, in the hypothetical distribution of wealth in the absence of monopolies (column 4 in tables 5.11 to 5.18), instead of zero, they get a positive share of total wealth. Without market power, the bottom of the wealth class would be wealthier. These results are then presented for a 10-year monopoly life span in figures 5.1 to 5.8 in order to show the impact of reducing market power across wealth classes.

According to these calibrations, market power may increase the wealth of the top wealth class by 10–24 percent, depending on the country and monopoly life span. For example, in table 5.11 for Australia, wealth shares of the top decile are 50 percent. Absent market power, the wealth shares would fall to between 42 and 45 percent. As the summary table 5.19 suggests, assuming a 10-year life span of market power, of the countries examined, France has the lowest impact (10 percent) whereas Canada, Japan, Korea, the United Kingdom, and the United States have the largest (ranging between 21 and 24 percent). The differences in the impact of market power arise from the

## FIGURE 5.1    Australia: Illustration of Impact of Monopoly, by Wealth Decile

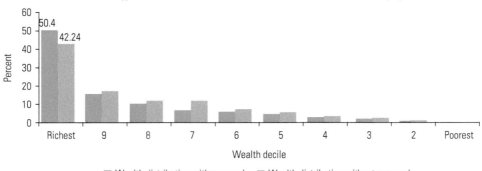

Hypothetical distributions of household wealth with and without monopoly

## FIGURE 5.2    Canada: Illustration of Impact of Monopoly, by Wealth Decile

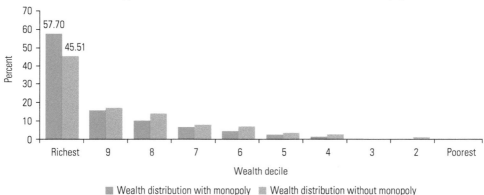

Hypothetical distributions of household wealth with and without monopoly

## FIGURE 5.3    France: Illustration of Impact of Monopoly, by Wealth Decile

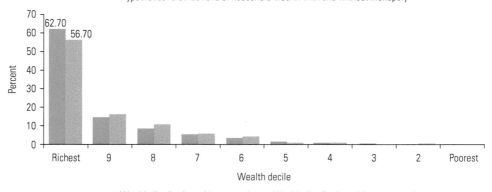

Hypothetical distributions of household wealth with and without monopoly

A Step Ahead

## FIGURE 5.4 Germany: Illustration of Impact of Monopoly, by Wealth Decile

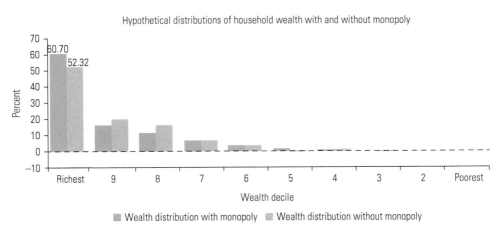

Hypothetical distributions of household wealth with and without monopoly

## FIGURE 5.5 Japan: Illustration of Impact of Monopoly, by Wealth Decile

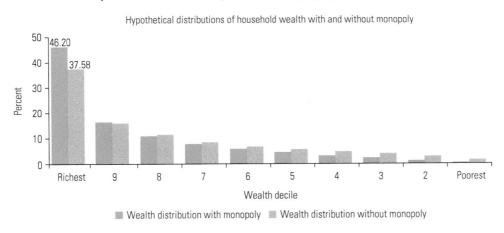

Hypothetical distributions of household wealth with and without monopoly

## FIGURE 5.6 Republic of Korea: Illustration of Impact of Monopoly, by Wealth Decile

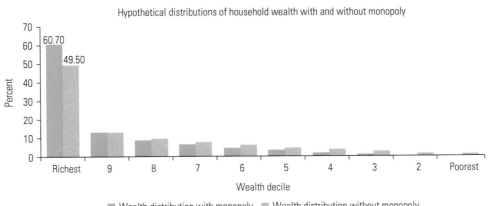

Hypothetical distributions of household wealth with and without monopoly

## FIGURE 5.7　United Kingdom: Illustration of Impact of Monopoly, by Wealth Decile

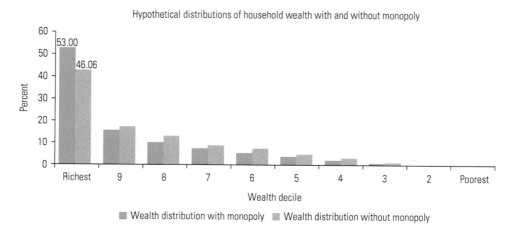

Hypothetical distributions of household wealth with and without monopoly

■ Wealth distribution with monopoly　■ Wealth distribution without monopoly

## FIGURE 5.8　United States: Illustration of Impact of Monopoly, by Wealth Decile

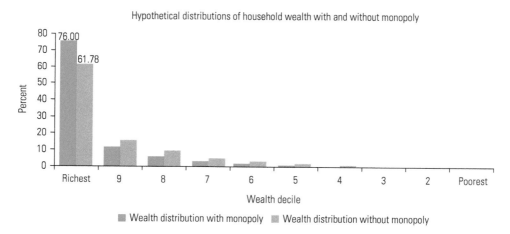

Hypothetical distributions of household wealth with and without monopoly

■ Wealth distribution with monopoly　■ Wealth distribution without monopoly

## TABLE 5.19　Comparative Impacts of Market Power in the Eight Countries of Analysis
*Percent*

| Country | Actual wealth share of top decile (A) | Wealth share of top decile with no market power (B) | Impact of market power (A–B)/B |
|---|---|---|---|
| Australia | 50.4 | 42.7 | 17.9 |
| Canada | 57.7 | 46.5 | 24.1 |
| France | 62.7 | 57.1 | 9.9 |
| Germany | 60.7 | 52.7 | 15.2 |
| Japan | 46.2 | 37.8 | 22.3 |
| Korea, Rep. | 60.7 | 49.4 | 22.8 |
| United Kingdom | 53.0 | 43.7 | 21.3 |
| United States | 76.0 | 62.7 | 21.2 |

combination of interest rates, saving rates, and capital taxation that affect the people earning monopoly profits.

Sensitivity analyses have been conducted to see the impact of reducing the size of economywide impacts from market power. These find that a reduction to 1 percent from 3 percent does not yield a proportionate decrease in the impact of market power.

The assumption of constant market power as a percentage of GDP was used by Comanor and Smiley (1975). In this selection of countries, we recognize that there are reasons to think that the percentage could reasonably have changed in some cases, for example, through creation of a competition law enforcement regime, through changing political regimes, or changing technology. The results should therefore be considered as tentative and suggest the value of future work that would allow market power's share of GDP to change over time.

## 5.5 Conclusions and Policy Implications

Policy makers are interested in learning about actions they can take to enhance wealth equality. In order to create targeted policies for reducing inequality, they need evidence about the origins of the inequality. This chapter extends the existing work on the origins of inequality, specifically focusing on the role of market power.

This chapter has found that, under various parameters, and for a variety of countries, market power may account for a substantial amount of wealth inequality, with market power accounting for between 10 and 24 percent of the wealth of the wealthiest class. The method used has received remarkably little attention since its origin with Comanor and Smiley (1975). While sources of market power vary, and many are generally considered legitimate, such as intellectual property protection for products, processes, or brands, significant sources of market power are violations of competition law or government-created barriers to entry. By reducing market power with such origins, either through enhancing enforcement of competition law or reviewing and revising excessively restrictive government regulations, wealth inequality itself may decline. That is, policy makers can take actions to reduce wealth inequality apart from direct redistributive mechanisms with their distortionary and incentive-blunting impacts.

Future research is needed. First, increasing the extent to which relevant data from developing countries is included in the model would enhance the breadth of results. This should be possible, as the quality of data measuring inequality is rapidly increasing. Second, newer and updated work is needed on different sources of market power, ideally divided into at least three categories: legally obtained without government help, legally obtained with government help (for example, due to competition-restricting regulations), and illegally obtained market power. Such figures would provide an underpinning for one of the key variables for this analysis.

Third, accuracy of certain parameters may be improved through access to survey or tax data. Fourth, increasing the focus on the top 1 percent of the wealth distribution would be informative, given the high concentration of wealth among the top decile that falls under the top 1 percent. Fifth, estimating confidence intervals for these figures would be of substantial value by providing a greater sense of the potential range of reasonable calibrations.

To avoid misinterpretation, it is worth emphasizing that this study does not argue that market power is harmful in and of itself. Many sources of market power yield economic benefits, stimulating innovation and investment. Specific benefits may include intellectual property, first-mover advantages, and network effects.

The results are nonetheless suggestive. Illegitimate market power, which is frequently considered harmful for consumers in the long run, is a substantial contributor to overall market power. Consequently, government action to limit illegitimate market power may enhance equality of wealth distributions.

## Notes

1. For the most unified treatment, see Piketty 2014.
2. Urzúa (2013) estimates the extent to which the poor and rural populations in Mexico may be disproportionately affected if there is market power in certain goods, but does not estimate the link to wealth nor characterize the extent of market power for these goods.
3. See Peltzman 1976.
4. While the scale of this effect is not studied here, initial estimates of the size of commerce affected by international cartels, from 1990 to 2013, are up to US$48.5 trillion (Ennis 2014), suggesting that the illegal market power effects may be nontrivial. Baker (2003) suggests that the beneficial effect of competition law enforcement is conservatively estimated at 1 percent of GDP in line with the work by Crandall (1991).
5. This assumption makes the formulas tractable and provides an approximation intended to suggest the rough level of profits from market power; in practice, the figures may change over time, such as when there are major technological changes or when competition laws are introduced.
6. Market power may potentially be shared with employees, including lesser-paid workers. Notably, if the workers receive a substantial increase in their incomes as a result of market power, the distribution of profits will go not only to those with substantial financial wealth but also to those without, thus weakening the result presented in this study. While this point is important to consider, to the extent that union negotiating power has declined over time, and that top management pay has substantially outpaced inflation, redistribution via labor income, to the extent it occurs, may accrue increasingly to the wealthiest workers (that is, management) in current times.
7. While the population of the top wealth decile and top consumption decile are not perfectly overlapping, the authors believe there is a high correlation between consumption shares of the income for those persons in the xth wealth decile and those in the xth income decile. This approximation is used because data on the consumption shares of the top wealth decile were unavailable to the authors at the time of writing.
8. The term monopoly is here used as shorthand to indicate market power in the context of life span in which companies have market power.
9. Note that this equation does not account for the redistribution of taxes on the wealthy to the poor.

# Bibliography

Baker, J. B. 2003. "The Case for Antitrust Enforcement." *Journal of Economic Perspectives* 17 (4): 27–50.

Baker, J., and S. Salop. 2015. "Antitrust, Competition Policy, and Inequality." Working Paper 41, American University Washington College of Law. http://digitalcommons.wcl.american.edu/fac_works_papers/41.

Cingano, F. 2014. "Trends in Income Inequality and Its Impact on Economic Growth." OECD Social, Employment and Migration Working Papers 163, OECD Publishing, Paris. http://dx.doi.org/10.1787/5jxrjncwxv6j-en.

Comanor, W. S., and R. H. Smiley. 1975. "Monopoly and the Distribution of Wealth." *Quarterly Journal of Economics* 89 (2): 177–94.

Crandall, R. W. 1991. "Efficiency and Productivity." In *After the Breakup: Assessing the New Post-AT&T Divestiture Era*, edited by Barry G. Cole. New York: Columbia University Press.

Ennis, S. 2014. "Commerce Affected by Cross-Border Private Cartels." OECD Working Paper 3, OECD Publishing, Paris.

Harding, Michelle. 2013. "Taxation of Dividend, Interest, and Capital Gain Income." OECD Taxation Working Paper 19, OECD Publishing, Paris.

OECD (Organisation for Economic Co-operation and Development). 2015. "In It Together: Why Less Inequality Benefits All." OECD Publishing, Paris. http://dx.doi.org/10.1787/9789264235120-en.

Peltzman, S. 1976. "Toward a More General Theory of Regulation." *Journal of Law and Economics* 19 (2): 211–40.

Piketty, T. 2014. *Capital in the 21st Century*. Cambridge, MA: Harvard University Press.

Piketty, T., and E. Saez. 2003. "Income Inequality in the United States, 1913–1998." *Quarterly Journal of Economics* 118 (1): 1–39.

Rognlie, M. 2015. "Deciphering the Fall and Rise in the Net Capital Share." Brookings Papers on Economic Activity, Brookings BPEA Conference, March.

Scherer, F. M. 1975. *Industrial Market Structure and Economic Performance*. Rand McNally College Publishing Company.

Schwartzman, D. 1959. "Effect of Monopoly on Price." *Journal of Political Economy* 67 (4): 352–62.

Urzúa, C. M. 2013. "Distributive and Regional Effects of Monopoly Power." *Economía Mexicana Nueva Epoca* 22 (2): 279–95.

# 6. Distributional Macroeconomic Effects of the European Union Competition Policy: A General Equilibrium Analysis

**Adriaan Dierx**, **Fabienne Ilzkovitz**, **Beatrice Pataracchia**, **Marco Ratto**, **Anna Thum-Thysen**, and **Janos Varga** (European Commission)

Evidence on the links between effective competition policies and their distributional effects and on countries' ability to manage negative macroeconomic shocks and associated repercussions on the income of households at the bottom of the income distribution is relatively scarce. This chapter proposes a novel methodology to assess distributional macroeconomic effects of important merger and cartel decisions by the European Commission. A unique database containing microeconomic estimates of customer savings associated with merger and cartel decisions is exploited to run policy simulations using a dynamic stochastic general equilibrium model. The model allows the authors to investigate the effects of European Union (EU) competition policy interventions not only on standard macroeconomic variables such as gross domestic product (GDP) and employment, but also on distributional outcomes across households with different skill levels and across different types of income earners (capital owners, wage earners, and benefit recipients). The policy simulations presented include both direct and indirect (deterrent) effects of competition policy interventions. They show that competition policy has a sizeable impact on GDP growth and important redistributive effect.

Directorate-General for Competition, Mado 3/28, European Commission, 1049 Brussels, Belgium, tel. +32 2 299 33 79, e-mail: fabienne.ilzkovitz@ec.europa.eu (corresponding author). The authors would like to thank Alexander Italianer for his support to this study project. We would also like to acknowledge the comments and suggestions on earlier drafts of this chapter by the participants of the 2015 conference on Competition Policy, Shared Prosperity and Inclusive Growth, organized by the World Bank and the Organisation for Economic Co-operation and Development; and the CRESSE 2015 conference, organized by the Athens University of Economics and Business. We would also like to thank Antonio Bosisio, Luisa Carrer, Jukka Heikkonen, and Ronal Muresano Caceres for their contributions to the preparation of this chapter, and Karin Hunin for her editorial support. The chapter has been written under the sole responsibility of the authors and does not present the views of the European Commission. Please do not cite or quote this chapter without permission from the authors.

## 6.1 Introduction

Competition authorities use estimates of the macroeconomic effects of competition policy to illustrate the benefits of their activities and legitimize competition policy interventions to the larger public. Recently, there has been an increasing interest in this type of analysis, both by competition authorities and academics (Ilzkovitz and Dierx 2014, 2015). This is partly in response to an increased skepticism about the benefits of competition policy, which became evident around the turn of the century (Kovacic 2006). The Great Recession has reinforced the need to assess the effects of competition policy, not only on economic growth but also on inequality.

Less empirical analysis has been done on the macroeconomic impact of competition policy in comparison with that of other EU policies affecting the conditions of competition, such as internal market or trade liberalization policies. Similarly, while it is often argued that the poorest in society are more affected by higher prices, lower quality, and lack of choice resulting from an absence of competition, these effects have been little studied. This chapter attempts to fill this gap and proposes a novel methodology to assess the distributional macroeconomic effects of important merger and cartel decisions made by the European Commission.

The lack of empirical analysis on the distributional macroeconomic impact of competition policy may be explained by the difficulties associated with this type of work. First, finding appropriate competition policy indicators is not a straightforward process. In this chapter, we circumvent this difficulty by using a unique database containing microeconomic estimates of customer savings associated with important merger and cartel decisions. These estimates are calculated by multiplying the foreseen reduction in prices (in comparison with the counterfactual of no competition policy intervention) by the expected duration of such price reduction and the turnover in the market affected by the decision.

Second, it is difficult to empirically establish a causal relationship between competition policy and competition, which is commonly used to make the link with macroeconomic outcomes. The approach taken in this chapter is to use a unique database aimed at calculating microeconomic estimates of customer savings resulting from competition policy interventions to calibrate markup shocks, which are then applied to a dynamic stochastic general equilibrium (DSGE) model, for example, the QUEST model (see Ratto, Roeger, and in 't Veld 2009).

Third, it is harder to track the chain of events that may follow a competition policy intervention in the medium to long term, and to attempt measuring its distributional macroeconomic impact, than to look at the immediate microeconomic impact of a specific decision in a given market. However, a DSGE model that (i) assumes that goods markets are imperfectly competitive; (ii) disaggregates employment into various skills categories; and (iii) considers different types of income earners (capital owners, wage earners, and benefit recipients) is well-suited for this task and can be used to get an indication of the distributional macroeconomic effects of competition policy.

Finally, the methods used to assess the aggregate effects of competition often look only at the direct price effects and ignore the deterrent effects of competition policy. These deterrent effects, which discourage future anticompetitive behavior, are difficult to assess because they are not felt immediately and cannot be measured directly. Nevertheless, there appears to be a consensus in the literature that these effects are considerable. This chapter makes the assumption that, for each important merger and cartel decision made by the European Commission, the avoided price increase covers not only the relevant market directly affected by the decision (direct effects) but also the whole subsector concerned by this decision (deterrent effects). However, the multiplying factor of the deterrent effects over the direct effects of a given decision is subjected to a maximum threshold reflecting results reported in the literature on the size of deterrent effects. In addition to such sectoral spillover effects, the chapter also considers intertemporal deterrence effects, which arise from companies' expectations that the European Commission will continue its competition policy interventions at the same pace into the foreseeable future. The results of the simulations measuring the total (that is, the direct plus the sectoral and intertemporal deterrent effects) of EU competition policy are then compared with those of other competition-friendly structural policies.

The chapter is organized as follows. Section 6.2 presents the integrated framework used in this chapter to move from the microeconomic estimates of customer savings to the macroeconomic effects of competition policy. Section 6.3 describes how customer savings are estimated and presents the results of these estimations. It makes a distinction between the direct and deterrent effects of competition policy enforcement actions and summarizes what can be learned from the literature on deterrent effects. Section 6.4 contains a short description of the QUEST model used to run the simulations and explains how the macroeconomic and distributional effects of competition policy are derived in this model. Section 6.5 describes how the markup shocks have been derived reflecting both the direct and deterrent effects of the competition policy interventions. This section also presents the results of the model simulations. The final section concludes and offers some ideas for further research.

## 6.2 Integrated Framework

Two main approaches may be used to assess the aggregate effect of competition policy: a bottom-up approach measuring the direct benefits of competition policy for consumers (the customer savings approach); and a macro-modeling approach analyzing the impact of competition policy on competition and (directly and indirectly) on GDP growth or other macroeconomic variables. (See Ilzkovitz and Dierx 2015 for a comprehensive survey of this latter literature, which is briefly summarized in box 6.1.)

**Empirical Work Analyzing the Macroeconomic Impact of Competition Policy**

Ilzkovitz and Dierx (2015) make a distinction between (i) studies analyzing the impact of competition policy on the degree of competition; and (ii) studies analyzing the impact of competition policy on economic performance at the national or sectoral level.

- Krakowski (2005), Hylton and Deng (2007), and Samà (2013) come to the conclusion that the strength of competition policy (as perceived by business leaders or as measured by the quality of competition laws and institutions) has a positive impact on the perceived competition intensity. Other variables, such as the size of the economy, the population of the country, its degree of openness, and gross domestic product (GDP) per capita also have a positive impact on competition, suggesting that having wealthy, large, and open markets is as important for competition as good competition laws. However, these results are not always robust, in particular if corrected for endogeneity.

- Papers by Kee and Hoekman (2007), Clougherty (2010), Petersen (2013), and Buccirossi et al. (2013) aim to make a link between the strength of competition policy and various measures of economic growth. Kee and Hoekman, for example, find that the introduction of competition laws has had a high positive and long-lasting effect on the number of firms in a sample of 28 industries in 42 countries. Clougherty uses the annual budget of competition authorities as a measure of a country's commitment of resources to competition policy, and he finds a positive relation between this variable and real per capita GDP growth. Petersen, however, concludes that antitrust law has a significant positive effect only after 10 years, as new institutions take time to run effectively and to have a noticeable effect on the economy as a whole. Buccirossi et al. estimate the impact of competition policy on total factor productivity (TFP) growth for 22 industries in 12 Organisation for Economic Co-operation and Development (OECD) countries over 1995 to 2005. They find a positive and significant relationship between competition policy indexes combining both input and output variables and TFP growth.

The macro-modeling approach analyzing the impact of competition policy is less developed than the body of literature analyzing the impact of competition. Although there is a consensus that competition offers macroeconomic benefits, it is less clear-cut from an empirical perspective that competition *policy* increases economic growth. In this chapter, we propose a framework to integrate the bottom-up customer savings approach with a top-down macro-modeling approach. This framework is described in figure 6.1.

An integrated macro-modeling of the impact of competition policy should first analyze the impact of competition policy on competition and, second, the impact of competition on macroeconomic performance. This requires indicators of competition policy and of competition.

**FIGURE 6.1  An Integrated Framework to Assess the Impact of Competition Policy**

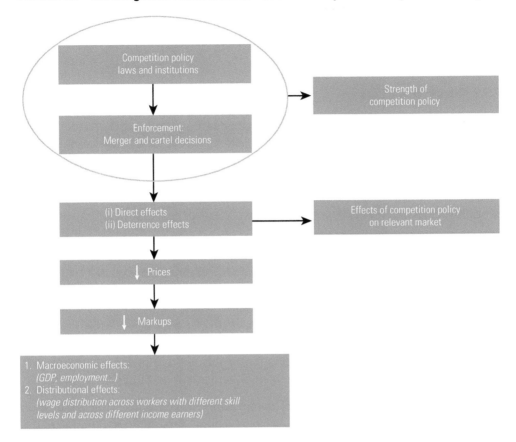

Competition policy is defined here as the enforcement of competition policy legislation covering the prohibition of cartels and the control of mergers. The strength of the European Commission's competition policy is measured by the number and importance of its interventions in these areas. Microeconomic estimates of the customer savings associated with important cartel and merger decisions are used as a proxy for this. Because of data limitations, other aspects of competition policy, such as the prohibition of abuse of dominant position or state aid control are not covered here.

Competition cannot be observed directly and, therefore, indirect measures of competition are commonly used. Here, competition is measured by the markup of prices over marginal costs, an indicator often used in empirical work. The price effect of important merger and cartel decisions by the European Commission and the size of the market affected by such decisions are used to calculate markup shocks reflecting the impact of competition policy interventions. The deterrent effects of these interventions are taken into account as well. The QUEST model simulations are then used to assess the macroeconomic and distributional effects of these shocks.

## 6.3 Measuring the Microeconomic Effects of Important Merger and Cartel Decisions

### 6.3.1 Customer Savings

Some competition authorities (in the EU, Netherlands, United Kingdom, and United States) use a relatively simple method to estimate the customer savings resulting from competition policy interventions, including, in particular, merger decisions and cartel prohibitions. This section starts by presenting the estimation method used by the European Commission and continues with a description and discussion of the results of the estimates obtained.

*Methodology*
The European Commission started to calculate the customer savings associated with important merger and cartel decisions relatively recently (in 2008). These customer savings are obtained by multiplying the estimated reduction in prices resulting from the competition policy enforcement in the market concerned by the estimated duration of the price reduction. A summary of the assumptions made regarding the market concerned, the price effect, and the duration of this effect is presented in table 6.1. These assumptions are based on the relevant literature and are rather conservative.

For cartels, the turnover of the cartel members directly concerned is used as an estimate of the scope of the competition policy intervention. Regarding the duration of the effect, one, three, or six years are considered, reflecting the European Commission's judgment of the future sustainability of the cartel at the date of detection. Cartels are judged to be either "unsustainable," "fairly sustainable," or "very sustainable," depending on a case-by-case analysis of market conditions, the life span of the cartel, and the ease of reaching and renewing the agreements. Finally, a 10 percent price overcharge is generally applied to calculate customer savings from cartel decisions, although a 15 percent overcharge is sometimes used if it can be justified.

TABLE 6.1   **Overview of Assumptions Used by the European Commission**

| Competition policy intervention | Cartel prohibition | Merger decision |
|---|---|---|
| Affected turnover | Turnover of cartel members | Size of relevant market |
| Yearly price effect | 10–15% | 1–3–5% |
| Duration (years) | 1/3/6 depending on the stability of the cartel | 2/3/5 depending on entry barriers |

Mudde (2012) and Davies (2013) made an assessment of these assumptions. Mudde considers that the assumption of a one-year duration of the price overcharge is too conservative because according to his dataset the average lifetime of cartels detected by the European Commission is eight years. For Davies, the European Commission's case-dependent approach is quite persuasive given that there are various determinants of cartel duration, such as the severity of fines and leniency programs, the type of industry, or the ease of entry. However, this approach requires significant judgmental input; and, if sufficient case-specific information is not available, Davies recommends using a single number, somewhere between one and six years. Regarding cartel overcharges, the empirical evidence in the academic literature (see Bolotova and Connor 2006; Smuda 2014) suggests that the median cartel overcharge lies between 17 and 30 percent, which makes the 10 percent assumption conservative.

The merger decisions included in the sample considered for the calculation of customer savings are important decisions, that is, Phase 1 and Phase 2 merger decisions with remedies or Phase 2 merger prohibitions.[1] The affected turnover is defined as that of all firms in the relevant markets, using a broader definition of the affected turnover than in cartels. This is because the price effect of a merger is unlikely to be confined to just the parties involved, as rivals will increase their price in response to an increase in price by the merging parties. This argument can also be made for cartels, indicating that the narrow definition of the affected turnover in cartels may lead to an underestimation of the customer savings. The duration of the price effects is generally three years, but sometimes an assumption of two or five years is made depending on the size of market entry barriers.

For the price effect, a default assumption of 3 percent has been made from 2012 on, but assumptions of a 1 percent and 5 percent price overcharge are also used as sensitivity tests. Before 2012, the European Commission used PCAIDS (Proportionally Calibrated Almost Ideal Demand System) model simulations to calculate the price effects of merger decisions. PCAIDS models are simple representations of the competitive interaction of firms, allowing the prediction of the price effects of merger decisions. The European Commission services decided to simplify the method used because the sophistication of the PCAIDS methodology made the exercise quite costly and, despite its sophistication, this methodology did have limitations (see European Commission 2013). For example, in some cases, model simulations were not feasible, either because the models could not adequately describe the nature of competition or because data required for the model calibration were not available and, therefore, a default assumption of a 1 percent or 3 percent price overcharge was already made. Davies (2013) considers that a 1 percent price overcharge is too low as an assumption and quotes studies using default price overcharges from mergers ranging between 3 and 9 percent. He therefore suggests using a default price overcharge of 3 percent, which is the baseline scenario used by the European Commission.

In this chapter, the price effect, its duration, and the size of the market affected by cartels and mergers are used to calculate markup shocks applied to the QUEST model.

### Results

Table 6.2 presents the latest data on the reported customer savings (expressed as a percentage of GDP $\times 10^{-2}$) from four jurisdictions (that is, the European Union, Netherlands, United Kingdom, and United States) that regularly publish their estimates of customer savings. This table should not be used to compare the performances of the competition authorities in the four jurisdictions but rather to show the order of magnitude of the estimates, which vary widely over time and between jurisdictions. For example, over the period 2008–15, the average yearly customer savings resulting from interventions by competition authorities ranges between $1.2 \times 10^{-2}$ percent of GDP for the United Kingdom and $5.3 \times 10^{-2}$ percent of GDP for the European Union.

Such variation in annual customer savings can be attributed to the fact that the sizes of the markets in which the competition authorities intervene, the scope, and the number of cases can all vary significantly from one year to another and across jurisdictions. Another reason for such variation is that the assumptions and methodologies[2] used for estimating customer savings, for example, regarding the price effect, its duration, and the size of the affected market, vary from one jurisdiction to another,[3] making it hard to compare the results of the different authorities. This is why the Organisation for Economic Co-operation and Development (OECD) has made some proposals intended to increase the convergence of assumptions used by different competition authorities (see box 6.2).

A strength of the customer savings approach is that its bottom-up estimates are closely linked to the important decisions made by the competition authorities.

**TABLE 6.2  Estimates of Annual Customer Savings**
*% of GDP x 10⁻²*

| | 2008 | 2009 | 2010 | 2011 | 2012 | 2013 | 2014 | 2015 | Average, 2008–15 |
|---|---|---|---|---|---|---|---|---|---|
| European Union | 5.1 | 5.9 | 8.9–13.4 | 4.4–6.4 | 2.6–5.7 | 3.8–4.7 | 2.7–5.5 | 1.4–2.8 | 5.3 |
| United States (DoJ + FTC) | 0.6 | 1.8 | 0.6 | 1.4 | 6.1 | 1.0 | 2.7 | 3.3 | 2.2 |
| United Kingdom (CC + OFT) | 2.3 | 2.4 | 1.3 | 1.0 | 0.9 | 1.0 | 0.5 | 0.5 | 1.2 |
| Netherlands (NMA/ACM) | 0.6 | 0.1 | 1.4 | 5.7 | 3.4 | 9.9[a] | 3.9[a] | 1.6[a] | 2.2 |

*Source:* European Commission calculations based on national and European Union sources.

*Note:* ACM = Netherlands Authority for Consumers and Markets; CC = Competition and Markets Authority (former Competition Commission, which also took the responsibilities of the OFT); DoJ = Department of Justice; FTC = Federal Trade Commission; NMA = Netherlands Competition Authority; OFT = Office of Fair Trading.

a. Not comparable with the figures for 2008–12 because of a change in methodology.

## Guiding Principles and Methodology Suggested by the OECD to Calculate Customer Savings

The following principles have been endorsed by the Competition Committee of the Organisation for Economic Co-operation and Development (OECD):

1. Whenever possible, use case-specific information.
2. Assume that no intervention will have a negative impact.
3. Estimate static consumer benefits and when possible also include dynamic ones.
4. Calculate and publish the estimates regularly.
5. Present the results both as an annual figure and as an annual moving average over three years.
6. Present the results by type of decisions (for example, separate the estimated impact of cartel decisions from that of merger decisions).

The OECD also suggests using a simple and easily applicable methodology: the static consumer benefits resulting from each decision are the product of the size of the affected turnover, the price increase avoided, and the expected duration of the price effect. When case-specific information is available on these three elements, this information should be used.

When such information is not available, the OECD suggests using the assumptions shown in table B6.2.1.

TABLE B6.2.1  **Assumptions Proposed by the OECD**

| Indicator | Cartel cases | Merger cases |
| --- | --- | --- |
| Affected turnover | Ex ante turnover of the companies under investigation in the affected market(s) | Ex ante turnover of all firms in the affected market(s) |
| Yearly price effect | Overcharge of 10% | Price increase of 3% |
| Duration | 3 years | 2 years |

*Source:* OECD 2014.

However, its main disadvantage is that customer savings measure only the direct price effects of competition policy interventions. Therefore, these estimates are small when expressed as a percentage of GDP. Moreover, the total effects extend beyond prices and include effects on quality, choice, and innovation. The customer savings estimates also ignore the indirect consequences of the price reduction for the economy as a whole. Most important, they do not account for the deterrent effects of competition policy, which can be very significant (see section 6.3.2). For these various reasons, not all competition authorities in OECD jurisdictions calculate the customer savings resulting from their interventions. Some of them have expressed concern that these estimates oversimplify matters, giving external stakeholders a partial or distorted view of the value and purpose of competition law enforcement. This would argue in favor of using a more comprehensive approach such as the one adopted by this chapter.

### 6.3.2 Deterrent Effects

*Definition and Determinants of Deterrent Effects*

A primary goal of competition policy enforcement is to deter anticompetitive behavior by enterprises, thereby maintaining a level playing field in product markets to the benefit of the end consumer. The deterrent effect of a cartel prohibition, for example, depends on the impact of the decision by the competition authority on the perceived likelihood of getting caught and on the size of the expected fines. For a punishment to be effective in deterring anticompetitive behavior, it needs to be transparent and imposed on the undertakings that committed the infringements.

Cartel prohibitions and fines are supposed to deter new cartel formation, limit overcharges, and reduce the stability of undetected cartels. A number of papers have attempted to address the question of whether current fines are sufficient to deter companies from joining cartels. Most researchers consider that EU antitrust fines are insufficient for cartel deterrence. Motta (2008), however, considers that fines set according to the relevant EU guidelines are not necessarily inadequate for achieving deterrence. Nonetheless, there are other ways to increase deterrence that should be further explored. A system of private rights of action, for example, possibly combined with greater attention to fostering a culture of competition, would be more suited to increase cartel deterrence.

Looking at developments over time, Hyytinen, Steen, and Toivanen (2010) find that at the end of a period during which cartels in Finland were legal (1951–90) almost all manufacturing industries had become cartelized. Similarly, Baker (2003) provides evidence that periods of lax antitrust enforcement in the United States were invariably followed by an increase in anticompetitive behavior. Therefore, stricter enforcement (in whatever form) should also contribute to greater cartel deterrence.

The literature on the deterrent effects of merger control is more limited than that on cartels. In the area of mergers, the deterrent effect is defined as the extent to which companies modify or abandon their merger plans in order to take out anticompetitive elements. However, this is very difficult to measure, as it implies observing the number of mergers deterred by the merger control regime and assessing whether the deterred mergers would have had anticompetitive effects. On the one hand, a strict application of merger control rules may enhance welfare because it deters future anticompetitive mergers (see Nocke and Whinston 2011; Sørgard 2009, 2014). On the other hand, companies may decide not to go ahead with a procompetition merger if merger control rules are applied too strictly. In the end, an appropriate balance needs to be found. The presumption of the literature is that notified mergers are anticompetitive and that therefore a reduction in the number of notified mergers is an indication of a positive deterrent effect of the merger control, which appears to be a strong assumption.

In addition, there is a debate regarding the type of actions (Phase 1 remedies, Phase 2 remedies, or prohibitions) having the greatest deterrent effects. Buccirossi et al. (2008) consider that the most common reasons for abandoning a merger are the risk that it would not be approved and the high cost of remedies. Seldeslachts, Clougherty, and Barros (2009), however, consider that blocked mergers have significant deterrent effects, whereas there is no impact from merger settlements or ongoing monitoring. Duso, Gugler, and Szücs (2013) find that, since the 2004 EU merger control reform, prohibitions have had no deterrent effects, whereas aborted mergers in either Phase 1 or Phase 2 have had such effects. In a more recent paper, Clougherty et al. (2016) find that, of the various EU merger control actions, only Phase 1 remedies have a deterrent effect. These divergent results show that further work is necessary before drawing robust conclusions on the type of actions having the strongest deterrent effects on anti-competitive mergers.

### Measurement of Deterrent Effects

The deterrent effects of a competition policy intervention are difficult to measure because they are not felt immediately and cannot be measured directly. Therefore, there is more work on optimal deterrence from a theoretical perspective than work that tackles the problem of measuring deterrent effects. Nevertheless, attempts have been made to get rough estimates of the deterrent effects of merger control and cartel punishment. These estimates are very often based on surveys directly asking businesses and legal advisers about the deterrent effects of competition authorities' work across different areas (such as cartel policy enforcement or merger control). These surveys have limitations: there is no certainty about the reliability of the information provided by the respondents, and the surveys may be biased. However, this is the only way to obtain direct information on deterrent effects. A summary of the results of recent EU surveys is given in table 6.3.

Surveys of competition lawyers have been used in a number of studies commissioned by competition authorities to evaluate the deterrent effect of their merger decisions. The Twynstra Gudde (2005) study asked competition lawyers in the Netherlands about their follow-up of 475 merger proposals in the period 2000–03. About 6 percent of such proposals were abandoned because of concerns about possible infringements of competition rules, whereas another 12 percent were modified. For each merger enforcement action by the Netherlands Competition Authority, 7.5 mergers are deterred. According to U.K. competition lawyers, four out of five harmful mergers in the United Kingdom are deterred as a result of competition policy enforcement (Deloitte 2007). Many 2-to-1 market consolidations are never even considered, because the authorities would certainly be opposed. Moreover, a survey of companies also conducted by Deloitte shows that for each merger enforcement action by the OFT (U.K. Office of Fair Trading), five mergers are deterred. A more recent survey made by

**TABLE 6.3  Summary of Results of Surveys on Deterrent Effects**

| Source | Method | Conclusion | Number of cases deterred per case investigated/detected |
|---|---|---|---|
| Twynstra Gudde (2005) | Interviews with 16 competition lawyers and companies in the health care, energy, and publishing industries about the follow-up of 475 merger proposals during the period 2000–03. | Six percent of notified mergers are abandoned and 12% modified. | For every merger blocked or remedied, 7.5 are abandoned or modified. |
| Deloitte (2007) | Thirty interviews with competition lawyers, economists, and companies; questionnaire completed by 234 competition lawyers and 202 large firms (200+ employees). Period 2004–06. | According to lawyers, 8% of qualified[a] mergers are abandoned and 7% modified. According to companies, 8% are abandoned and 4% modified. | For every merger blocked or remedied, 5 are abandoned or modified according to lawyers. For every cartel detected, 5 are deterred according to lawyers and 16 are deterred according to companies. |
| London Economics (2011) | Twenty-seven interviews of professionals from legal firms and survey based on questionnaire completed by 501 large firms (200+ employees) and 308 small firms (under 200 employees). Period 2003–11. | Eighteen percent of qualified mergers are abandoned and 15% modified (based on a small sample). | For every merger blocked or remedied, 1.8 are abandoned (based on a small sample). For every cartel detected, 28 are deterred (but only 20% of cartels are detected). |
| SEO (2011) | Online survey completed by 512 companies and 97 advisers on competition law (mainly lawyers) from 2005 to mid-2010. | Thirteen percent of notified mergers are abandoned and 5% modified. | For every cartel detected, 5 are deterred (but only one-third of cartels are detected). |

*Sources:* Baarsma et al. 2012; CMA 2014.

a. A qualified merger is a merger over which the U.K. competition authority could take jurisdiction.

London Economics (2011) finds a lower deterrent effect of 1.8 mergers deterred for each merger enforcement action. Finally, a study carried out for the Netherlands Competition Authority by SEO (2011) reports that 5 percent of notified mergers are modified prior to notification and that 13 percent are deterred in anticipation of a possible intervention by the Netherlands Competition Authority. To sum up, according to these surveys, between 12 and 33 percent of notified/qualified mergers are either abandoned or modified because of concerns about possible infringements of competition rules, and between 1.8 and 7.5 mergers are deterred per merger enforcement action by the competition authorities.

Other research focuses on the effects of enforcement on the observable population of cartels and ultimately attempts to make an inference on how such enforcement might affect the whole population of cartels (including the number of undetected cartels). The validity of this approach depends on the robustness of the established link between the number of detected cartels and the whole population of cartels. Various methods have been used to measure the deterrent effects of cartel policy enforcement actions. For example, Ormosi (2014) uses methods similar to those applied to make inferences about wildlife population characteristics in ecology to determine whether an observed change in the number of detected cartels is caused by a change in the detection rate or by a change in the rate of deterrence. On the basis of this approach, he finds that less than a fifth of EU cartels between 1985 and 2005 were detected. This result is similar to the survey result reported by London Economics (2011). The survey by SEO (2011), however, obtains a detection rate of one-third. The surveys by London Economics (2011) and SEO (2011) have also been used to estimate the ratio of cartels deterred over cartels detected. They find that there are between 5 and 28 cartels deterred per cartel detected.

Using the above survey information to determine the deterrent effects of competition policy enforcement is not straightforward. As highlighted by Ormosi (2014) in the case of cartels, even if the ratio of deterred cartels over detected cartels is 5 to 1, we cannot deduce that the harms from the deterred cartel are five times greater than the competition authorities' estimates of the savings achieved from the detection of cartels. The reason is that the observed sample of cartels detected may not be representative of the full population of cartels. Davies and Ormosi (2013) consider that this sample selection bias is likely to be substantial because the unobserved cases could well be those that are the most harmful. In particular, undetected cartels are likely to be more harmful than the detected ones, because the latter are less sustainable or more prone to whistle-blowers. Similarly, mergers with clear anticompetitive effects are more likely to be discouraged by merger control. Davies and Ormosi estimate that the deterred cartel harms would be between 10 and 30 times what is detected and recorded by competition authorities. For mergers, this multiplying factor ranges between 6 and 17.

In the calculation of the markup shocks, including the deterrent effects of competition authorities' interventions, we have used another, sector-based approach to estimate the deterrent effects (see the subsection titled "Deterrent Effects of Merger and Cartel Decisions" in section 6.5.1). However, we have applied a multiplying factor of 30 as an upper bound for the deterrent effects of cartel decisions and a multiplying factor of 15 as an upper bound for the deterrent effects of merger decisions, taking into account that mergers and cartels with important anticompetitive effects are more likely to be deterred by competition policy enforcement.

## 6.4 QUEST Model

### 6.4.1 Short Description of the QUEST Model

The macroeconomic assessment presented in this chapter is based on an extended version of the European Commission's QUEST III model (see Ratto, Roeger, and in 't Veld 2009), which we adapted for analyzing the potential distributional effects of competition policy. Standard modern macroeconomic models, so-called DSGE models, go in the direction of meeting the requirement of rigorous micro foundations. They also include imperfections in goods and labor markets by modeling these markets as imperfectly competitive. Nevertheless, these models typically lack sufficient detail to make a link between product market reforms and their distributional consequences. We overcome this limitation by introducing two skill groups, low and high skilled, into the DSGE model of Ratto, Roeger, and in 't Veld (2009).

The model version used here is a two-region, open-economy setup calibrated for the EU and the rest of the world. For each region, the model economy is populated by households and final-goods-producing firms, and there is both a monetary and a fiscal authority, both following rule-based stabilization policies. The domestic and foreign firms produce a continuum of differentiated goods. The goods produced in the home country are imperfect substitutes for goods produced abroad. The level of competition among firms is captured by the inverse elasticity of substitution between the goods varieties, which can be directly linked to the markup that firms charge over the marginal cost of production. Competition policy in the model acts as an instrument to decrease these markups and therefore increase competition among the firms.

From the consumers' side, we distinguish between households that are liquidity constrained and consume their disposable income, and non-liquidity-constrained (so-called Ricardian) households that have full access to financial markets. The latter group of households make decisions on financial and real capital investments. The model is a fully forward-looking dynamic model in which all investment decisions are based on the expected future stream of income. Households also differ in terms of their skills and wages. In standard DSGE models, liquidity- and non-liquidity-constrained households earn the same wage, which makes these models less suitable for the purpose of the chapter. In order to measure the distributional consequences of competition policies, we introduce two skill groups into our model with different wages. Additionally, we identify the liquidity-constrained households as low skilled and the non-liquidity-constrained households as high skilled. By using the International Standard Classification of Education (ISCED), we define the share of population with up to lower secondary education (ISCED 2) as low skilled and the rest of the population as high skilled. Specifically, in our calibration for the EU, this means that about 25 percent of the population is classified as low skilled and liquidity constrained while the remaining share is considered high skilled and non-liquidity-constrained at the same time.

We calibrate our model by selecting behavioral and technological parameters so that the model can replicate important empirical ratios such as labor productivity, investment, consumption-to-GDP ratios, the wage share, and the employment rate, given a set of structural indicators describing market frictions in goods and labor markets, tax wedges, and skill endowments. Most of the variables and parameters are taken from available statistical or empirical sources from the literature, and the remaining parameters are tied down by the mathematical relationship of the model equations.

The model closely follows Ratto, Roeger, and in 't Veld (2009). Therefore, the following two subsections will focus on those parts of the model crucial for understanding the transmission mechanism of markup shocks (section 6.4.2) and their distributional consequences (section 6.4.3). In order to focus on the main transmission mechanism, for illustration purposes we present a slightly simplified set of equations from the model in these sections.

## 6.4.2 Modeling the Macroeconomic Effects of Markup Shocks

Competition policy measures are translated into the model as markup shocks, which are interpreted as resulting from interventions made by the competition authority to increase the level of competition among domestic firms. We assume that final goods producers work under monopolistic competition settings and each firm produces a variety of the domestic good that is an imperfect substitute for varieties produced by other firms. Final output of firm $j$ at time $t$ $\left(Y_t^j\right)$ is produced using capital $K_t^j$ and a labor aggregate $\left(L_t^j\right)$ in a Cobb-Douglas technology, subject to a fixed cost $FC_{Y_t}^j$

$$Y_t^j = \left(L_t^j - FC_L^j\right)^\alpha \left(u_t^j - K_t^j\right)^{1-\alpha} - FC_Y^j \tag{6.1}$$

with

$$L_t^j = \left(\Lambda_L^{\frac{1}{\mu}}\left(X_L L_{L,t}^j\right)^{\frac{\mu-1}{\mu}} + \Lambda_H^{\frac{1}{\mu}}\left(X_H L_{H,t}^j\right)^{\frac{\mu-1}{\mu}}\right)^{\frac{\mu}{\mu-1}}, \tag{6.2}$$

where $L_{L,t}^j$ and $L_{H,t}^j$ denote the employment of low- and high-skilled workers by firm $j$, respectively. Parameter $\Lambda$ is the corresponding share parameter ($s \in \{L, H\}$), $X_s$ is the efficiency unit, and $\mu$ is the elasticity of substitution between different labor types.[4] The term $FC_L^j$ represents overhead labor, and $u_t^j$ is the measure of capacity utilization.

The objective of the firm is to maximize the present discounted value of profits:

$$PR_t^j = P_t^j Y_t^j - W_{L,t}^j L_{L,t}^j - W_{H,t}^j L_{H,t}^j - i_t^K P_t^I K_t^j \tag{6.3}$$

where $i^K$ denotes the rental rate of capital.[5]

It can be shown that in a symmetric equilibrium, when $P_t^j = P_t, \forall j$, firms charge a markup over the marginal cost of production (MC):

$$P_t^j = \left(1 + \tau_t^j\right) MC_t^j, \tag{6.4}$$

where $\tau_t^j$ is the price markup, which is defined as a function of the elasticity of substitution $\sigma^d$, and a markup shock $\varepsilon_{mkp,t}$:

$$\tau_t^j = 1/(\sigma^d - 1) + \varepsilon_{mkp,t}. \tag{6.5}$$

In the subsequent analysis we will simulate the effect of competition policies as negative shocks to the price markup via the markup shock component ($\varepsilon_{mkp,t}$) in equation (6.5).

Skill-specific labor demand can be obtained from the first-order condition of the firm's cost minimization problem[6] with respect to labor:

$$P_t^j \frac{\partial Y_t^j}{\partial L_{s,t}} \frac{1}{1+\tau_t^j} = W_{s,t}, s \in \{L, H\}, \tag{6.6}$$

where the marginal product of labor and the markup will jointly determine the optimally chosen level of low- and high-skilled employment level.

To sum up the transmission channel from the firms' (supply) side, the interventions of the competition authority resulting in an increase in competition and a decrease in markups will lead to lower prices (equation (6.4)). Since firms are forward-looking, their demand for labor and capital is based on the expected future stream of profits taking into account the effect of markups on both prices and demand. They take into account the direct effect of markups on future profitability, which is negative because of lower markups, and at the same time they also take into account the increase in future demand for their products due to the lower prices. In order to satisfy the higher demand, firms require more labor and capital. However, the decline of firms' future profitability partly mitigates the increase of demand for input factors, as increased production costs and lower prices can result in shrinking profits accrued by the firms (equation (6.3)).

### 6.4.3 Modeling the Distributional Effects

The model allows investigating the effects of EU merger control and cartel policy interventions not only on standard macroeconomic variables such as GDP and employment, but also on distributional outcomes and second-order effects through examining employment and the wage-distribution across households (i) with different socioeconomic characteristics—in particular skill levels—and (ii) with different income sources (capital ownership, wage earners, and benefit recipients).

We assume that there are two types of households characterized by a skill-income type combination:

1. High-skilled, non-liquidity-constrained (NLC) households whose income sources are wages, transfers, and benefits, and additionally income from capital ownership and the financial market.

2. Low-skilled, liquidity-constrained (LC) households whose income sources are only wages, transfers, and benefits. These households earn lower wages, which is captured by their lower efficiency level in the labor aggregate (equation (6.2)). These households cannot rely on additional income from holding assets (for example, government bonds, physical capital) nor from the firms' profits, as opposed to the non-liquidity-constrained, high-skilled households who can benefit from accessing both financial and physical capital markets.

This setup allows assessing the effects of competition policy on employment and wages across skill-income levels and across income sources by comparing the effect on wages with the effect on profits.

Formally, the household sector consists of a continuum of households $h \in [0,1]$. A share $(1-\varepsilon)$ of these households is not liquidity constrained and is high skilled. They have access to financial markets where they can buy and sell domestic assets (government bonds), and they accumulate physical capital, which they rent out to the final good sector. The remaining share $\varepsilon$ of households is liquidity constrained and low skilled. These households cannot trade in financial and physical assets and consume their disposable income each period. For each skill group we assume that households supply differentiated labor services to their trade unions, which act as wage setters in monopolistically competitive labor markets for each skill group separately. The unions pool wage income and distribute it in equal proportions among their members within each skill group. Nominal rigidity in wage setting is introduced by assuming that the households face adjustment costs for changing wages.

The utility function of households is additively separable in consumption ($C_{h,t}$) and leisure ($1-L_{h,s,t}$). We assume log-utility for consumption and allow for habit persistence (as measured by the parameter $habc$).

$$U\left(C_{h,t}\right) = \left(1 - habc\right)\log\left(C_{h,t} - habc\overline{C_{t-1}}\right). \tag{6.7}$$

Preferences for leisure are given by

$$V\left(1 - L_{h,s,t}\right) = \frac{\omega_s}{1-\kappa}\left(1 - L_{h,s,t}\right)^{1-\kappa}, \textit{for } s \in \left\{L, H\right\}. \tag{6.8}$$

Parameters $\kappa(\kappa > 0)$ and $\omega_s$ are used to calibrate the corresponding Frisch labor supply elasticities.[7] We assume a skill-specific weight ($\omega_s$) on leisure, which is necessary in order to capture differences in labor supply elasticities across skill groups (higher for low skilled and lower for high skilled).

## Non-Liquidity-Constrained (High-Skilled) Households

Non-liquidity-constrained households maximize an intertemporal utility function in consumption and leisure, subject to a budget constraint. These households make decisions about consumption ($C_{h,t}$), and labor supply ($L_{h,t}$), the purchases of investment goods ($I_{h,t}$) and government bonds ($B_{h,t}$), and the renting of physical capital stock ($K_{h,t}$), and receive wage income ($W_{H,t}$), unemployment benefits[8] ($bW_{H,t}$), transfer income from the government ($TR_{h,t}$), and interest income ($i, i_{K,t}$). Hence, non-liquidity-constrained households face the following Lagrangian:

$$\max_{\left\{C_{h,t}, L_{h,H,t}, B_{h,t}, \atop I_{h,t}, K_{h,t}\right\}_{t=0}^{\infty}} V_{i,0} = E_0 \sum_{t=0}^{\infty} \beta^t \left( U\left(C_{h,t}\right) + V\left(1 - L_{h,H,t}\right) \right)$$

$$-E_0 \sum_{t=0}^{\infty} \lambda_{h,t} \frac{\beta^t}{P_t} \left( \begin{array}{l} \left(1 + t_{C,t}\right) P_{C,t} C_{h,t} + B_{h,t} + P_{I,t}\left(I_{h,t}\right) - \left(1 + i_{t-1}\right) B_{h,t-1} \\ -\left(1 - t_{w,H,t}\right) W_{H,t} L_{h,H,t} - b W_{H,t} \left(1 - NPART_{h,t} - L_{h,H,t}\right) - TR_{h,t} \\ -\left(1 - t_K\right)\left(i_{K,t-1} - rp_k\right) P_{I,t-1} K_{h,t-1} - t_K \delta_K P_{I,t-1} K_{h,t-1} - \sum_{j=1}^{J} PR_{j,h,t} \end{array} \right)$$

$$-E_0 \sum_{t=0}^{\infty} \lambda_{h,t} \xi_{h,t} \beta^t \left( K_{h,t} - I_{h,t} - \left(1 - \delta_K\right) K_{h,t-1} \right). \tag{6.9}$$

The budget constraints are written in real terms with the price for consumption, investment ($P_{C,t}, P_{I,t}$), and wages ($W_{H,t}$) divided by GDP deflator ($P_t$). All firms of the economy are owned by non-liquidity-constrained households who share the firms' total profits, $\sum_{j=1}^{J} PR_{j,h,t}$, where $J$ denotes the number of firms. *NPART* denotes the nonparticipation rate, and $b$ is the benefit replacement rate. As shown by the budget constraints, the households pay consumption taxes ($t_{C,t}$), wage income taxes ($t_{w,H,t}$) and $t_K$ capital income taxes, and depreciation allowances ($t_K \delta_K$) after their earnings on physical capital. When investing into tangible capital, the household requires premium $rp_K$ in order to cover the increased risk on the return related to these assets. The final term in equation (6.9) reflects the technological constraint with respect to the accumulation of capital over time.

## Liquidity-Constrained (Low-Skilled) Households

Liquidity-constrained households do not optimize but simply consume their current income at each date. The consumption of household $h$ is thus determined by the net wage income plus benefits and net transfers:

$$(1 + t_{C,t}) P_{C,t} C_{h,t} = (1 - t_{w,L,t}) W_{L,t} L_{h,L,t} + b W_{L,t}(1 - NPART_{h,L,t} - L_{h,L,t}) + TR_{h,t}. \tag{6.10}$$

## Wage Setting

Within each skill group a variety of labor services are supplied that are imperfect substitutes to each other. Thus, trade unions can charge a wage markup $\left(\mu_{s,t}^w\right)$ over the reservation wage.[9] The reservation wage is given as the marginal utility of leisure divided by the corresponding marginal utility of consumption. The relevant net real wage to which the markup adjusted reservation wage is equated is the gross wage adjusted for labor taxes, consumption taxes, and unemployment benefits, which act as a subsidy to leisure. Thus, the wage equation is given as

$$\frac{U_{1-L,h,s,t}}{U_{C,h,s,t}}\left(1+\mu_{s,t}^w\right)=\frac{W_{s,t}\left(1-t_{w,s,t}-b\right)}{P_{C,t}\left(1+t_{C,t}\right)}\,for\,s\in\{L,H\}. \tag{6.11}$$

Finally, to sum up the transmission channels from the households (demand) side, low-skilled liquidity-constrained households, which consume their income every period, can increase their consumption thanks to declining prices and increasing wage income (as firms' labor demand increases, see previous section). High-skilled, non-liquidity-constrained households rely on additional income from holding assets (for example, government bonds, physical capital) and from the firms' profits. Depending on the magnitude of the decline in firms' profits resulting from the lower markups, these households may have a smaller increase in their consumption relative to the liquidity-constrained households.

## 6.5 Model Simulations

### 6.5.1 Calculation of Markup Shocks

#### Method

A database, which was created to calculate customer savings estimates from important merger and cartel decisions by the European Commission, has been used to calibrate the markup shocks applied to the QUEST model. As explained in section 6.3.1, customer savings are obtained by multiplying the estimated reduction in prices resulting from competition policy enforcement decisions in the market concerned by the estimated duration of the price reduction and the size of the market.

The aggregate change in markup ($\Delta MUP$) due to a set $N$ of important competition policy enforcement decisions can be defined as follows:[10]

$$\varepsilon_{mpk}=\Delta MUP_N=\Sigma_{k\in\{K_N\}}\left[\frac{\Delta P}{P_k}\left(1+MUP_k\right)\right]\frac{GO_k}{GO}, \tag{6.12}$$

where $K_N$ is the set of sectors $k$ in which these decisions led to a change in customer prices, $\Delta P/P_k$.

Markup levels are calibrated for the available sectors on the basis of Thum-Thysen and Canton (2015), which extends Roeger's (1995) markup calculation method by including the effects of product market reforms. Equation (6.12) illustrates that the aggregate markup shock moves in line with price shocks in the sectors affected by the European Commission's decisions. However, they are weighted by the relative gross markup in the sector concerned, $(1 + MUP_k)$, and by the share of gross output in sector $k$ in the EU economy as a whole, $GO_k/GO$.

In our simulations the sectors $k$ are defined at the ISIC3 (International Standard Industrial Classification of All Economic Activities, Rev. 3) 2-digit level.

### Direct Effects of Merger and Cartel Decisions

A distinction is made between markup shocks reflecting only the direct effects of merger and cartel decisions and shocks including the deterrent effects as well. In the former case, the price change in each sector $k$ is computed as a weighted average of the price changes in the set of markets affected by European Commission merger and cartel decisions $n$:

$$\frac{\Delta P}{P_k} = \sum_{n \in M_k} \frac{\Delta P}{P_n} MS_{nk} + \sum_{n \in C_k} \frac{\Delta P}{P_n} MS_{nk} \qquad (6.13)$$

where $M_k$ and $C_k$ are the sets of merger and cartel decisions, respectively, affecting sector $k$. For each merger and cartel decision, the European Commission defines a relevant market directly concerned by the decision. In our simulations, the weights $MS_{nk}$ used to calculate the price change at the sector level are defined as the share of the affected turnover in the relevant market of decision $n$ in sector $k$ ($mkt_{nk}$) over gross output in the sector at the 2-digit level ($GO_k$):

$$MS_{nk} = \frac{mkt_{nk}}{GO_k}. \qquad (6.14)$$

As already mentioned in section 6.3.1, we adopt the default assumption that merger and cartel decisions entail price reductions of 3 percent and 10 percent, respectively, in comparison with the counterfactual of no intervention. Equation (6.13) can therefore be reformulated as:

$$\frac{\Delta P}{P_k} = -0.03 \sum_{n \in M_k} MS_{nk} - 0.1 \sum_{n \in C_k} MS_{nk}. \qquad (6.15)$$

Substituting back equations (6.14) and (6.15) in equation (6.12), the markup change associated with the direct effects of merger and cartel decisions can be calculated as follows:

$$\Delta MUP_N = -\frac{1}{GO} \Sigma_{k \in \{K_N\}} \left[ \left( 0.03 \Sigma_{n \in M_k} mkt_{nk} + 0.1 \Sigma_{n \in C_k} mkt_{nk} \right) (1 + MUP_k) \right]. \quad (6.16)$$

### Deterrent Effects of Merger and Cartel Decisions

As shown in section 6.3.1, the direct price effects of competition policy decisions ignore the deterrent effects of such decisions. To take into account these deterrent effects, we make the assumption that, for each important decision by the European Commission, the price reduction covers not only the relevant market directly affected by the decision (the direct effects described above) but also the whole subsector defined at the NACE rev2 (statistical classification of economic activities in the European Community) 4-digit level to which the relevant market belongs. For example, an important airline merger decision with competition concerns covering specific routes only is supposed to have deterrent effects on the whole air passenger transport sector, meaning that other airline companies will be induced to abandon likely anticompetitive mergers. This assumption rests on the idea that the deterrent effects of competition policy interventions are more likely to have spillovers on the companies belonging to the same sector. The assumption has some empirical support: a survey by Deloitte suggests that mergers in the United Kingdom are more likely to be abandoned or modified if there has been a recent inquiry by the U.K. competition authority in the sector (Deloitte 2007; Gordon and Squires 2008).

In the calculation of the markup shocks including deterrent effects, we assume that the deterrent effects will spill over to the whole subsector defined at the NACE rev2 4-digit level to which the market concerned by the competition policy intervention belongs. When making an important merger or cartel decision, the European Commission tends to indicate the NACE rev2 sectors concerned. In order to reflect the deterrent effects in our simulation, the weights $MS_{nk}$ used to calculate the price change in sector $k$ resulting from decisions $n$ are defined as the share of output at the NACE rev2 4-digit level of sector $k$ concerned by decisions $n$ in total output of sector $k$ (defined at NACE rev2 2-digit level). However, because of a lack of information on gross output at the NACE rev2 4-digit level, we use the share of value added at the NACE rev2 4-digit level in total value added at the NACE rev2 2-digit level instead:

$$MS_{nk} = \frac{VA4_{nk}}{VA2_k}. \quad (6.17)$$

In order to avoid implausible multiplication effects for specific small cases, we assume that this value cannot exceed the original value of the affected market by a certain threshold, $T \in \{T_M, T_C\}$, which may differ between merger and cartel decisions:

$$MS_{nk} = \begin{cases} \dfrac{VA4_{nk}}{VA2_k} & if \ \dfrac{VA4_{nk}}{VA2_k} GO_k < T\,mkt_{nk} \\[4mm] \dfrac{T\,mkt_{nk}}{GO_k} & if \ \dfrac{VA4_{nk}}{VA2_k} GO_k \geq T\,mkt_{nk} \end{cases},\tag{6.18}$$

where $VA2_k$ denotes the value added of the 2-digit NACE rev2 sectors corresponding to the ISIC3 sectors used in the model simulations[11] (see sections 6.5.2 and 6.5.3). The thresholds $T_M$ for merger decisions and $T_C$ for cartel decisions have been set at 15 and 30, respectively, in order to be broadly in line with the literature, which shows that the deterred harm could reach up to 17 times the direct harm of a merger decision and 30 times the direct harm of a cartel decision (see section 6.3.2).

The application of the weights $MS_{nk}$ defined in equation (6.18) permits the calculation of markup shock including deterrent effects:

$$\Delta MUP_N^{det} = -\frac{1}{GO}\Sigma_{k \in \{K_N\}}\Big[\big(0.03\Sigma_{n \in M_k}\,MS_{nk}GO_k$$

$$+0.1\Sigma_{n \in C_k}\,MS_{nk}GO_k\big)\big(1+MUP_k\big)\Big].\tag{6.19}$$

*Magnitude and Duration of the Shock*
The direct impact of the European Commission's competition policies can be assessed by aggregating the changes in markup directly resulting from its merger and cartel decisions. Since the price effects following decisions by the European Commission may last more than a year, customers will benefit not only from the interventions in that same year, but also from interventions with a longer duration made in previous years.

In the current exercise we look at decisions that had an impact in 2014, that is, decisions taken in 2012, 2013, and 2014. The decrease in markup $(-\Delta MUP_N)$ associated with decisions by the European Commission in 2014 as well as decisions from earlier years still having an impact in 2014 is computed using equation (6.16) and then summed to arrive at a total effect in 2014 of 0.04 percentage points. This figure includes the direct effects of the European Commission's merger and cartel decisions only.

However, the simulations presented in the present chapter consider not only the direct but also the deterrent effects of merger and cartel decisions. Using equation (6.19) instead of equation (6.16), the decrease in markup $\big(-\Delta MUP_N^{det}\big)$ resulting from the European Commission's decisions in 2012, 2013, and 2014 can be derived: the markup reduction due to 2012 decisions still having an impact in 2014 equals

0.15 percentage points, due to 2013 decisions 0.03 percentage points, and due to 2014 decisions 0.67 percentage points, which add up to an aggregate negative markup shock of 0.85 percentage points in 2014, which corresponds to a 6.65 percent reduction in the markup level.

The magnitude of this shock appears to be reasonable in comparison with the markup shocks reported by simulation studies aimed at assessing the impact of a wider set of competition-friendly structural reforms. For instance, in Varga and in 't Veld (2014) structural reforms aimed at narrowing the gap compared to the average of the three best EU performers in terms of market functioning correspond to an average markup decline across the EU of about 1.5 percentage points.

With respect to the duration of the shock, the assumption is that the effects of important merger and cartel decisions by the European Commission last three years (see above) and that the European Commission will continue its competition policy interventions at the same pace into the foreseeable future. Such a "permanent" markup shock can then be applied to a baseline scenario under which the European Commission would make no merger or cartel decisions. The assumption of a permanent shock reflects the idea that a single competition intervention by the Commission will have little or no enduring effects on company behavior. The deterrent effects of such interventions come from companies' awareness of the existence of a competition authority and the expectation that the authority will continue to act if infringements of competition law occur.

### 6.5.2 Simulations of Macroeconomic Effects

The simulations presented in this section are based on an aggregate negative markup shock of $\varepsilon_{mpk,t} = 0.85$ percentage points (see equation (6.5)) to the QUEST model. The magnitude of the shock reflects both the direct and deterrent effects of the European Commission's merger and cartel decisions. Table 6.4 shows the precise magnitude of the shock considered, both in absolute and relative terms. As described above, we take into account the cumulative "permanent" effects of the Commission's competition policy interventions.

Table 6.5 reports the percentage change of GDP and of selected macroeconomic variables of interest resulting from the above markup shock. The figures reported are in percentage point difference from the unshocked values. Columns report different number of years after the shock.

TABLE 6.4   **Magnitude of Markup Shock**

| $\Delta\varepsilon_{mpk}(pp)$ | mpk level (%) | $\Delta\varepsilon_{mpk}(\%)$ |
|---|---|---|
| −0.847 | 12.7 | −6.654 |

TABLE 6.5  **Macroeconomic Effects of Markup Shock**
*% change after n years*

| Variable | 1 | 5 | 10 | 20 | 50 |
|---|---|---|---|---|---|
| GDP | 0.231 | 0.400 | 0.532 | 0.697 | 0.766 |
| GDP deflator | −0.175 | −0.229 | −0.309 | −0.439 | −0.488 |
| Employment | 0.183 | 0.284 | 0.339 | 0.367 | 0.336 |
| Consumption | 0.239 | 0.353 | 0.484 | 0.637 | 0.699 |
| Investment | 0.375 | 0.777 | 0.949 | 1.150 | 1.241 |
| Labor productivity | 0.048 | 0.115 | 0.193 | 0.328 | 0.428 |

Table 6.5 illustrates that competition policy interventions increase output and raise demand for the factors of production (capital, labor). The combination of price decline and the higher wages associated with increased labor demand and higher labor productivity yields an increase in consumption. Investment is also increasing because the negative direct effect of markups on future profitability is dominated by the positive effect of increasing demand due to lower prices. In terms of GDP we can observe an increase of 0.23 percent after one year. After five years, the effect on GDP almost doubles, increasing to 0.40 percent. This result is in line with Van Sinderen and Kemp (2008), who estimate that the policies of the Netherlands Competition Authority over the 1998–2007 period had a positive GDP effect of 0.3 percent after five years and 0.4 percent after ten years.

Alternatively, the magnitude of the effects on GDP of the European Commission's merger and cartel decisions in 2012 can be put into perspective by comparing the GDP effects with similar studies examining other pro-competition policies. Monteagudo, Rutkowski, and Lorenzani (2012) estimate the economic impact of the implementation of the Services Directive across the EU Member States. It concludes that Member States may achieve about 0.7 percent higher GDP from the Directive if they continue their reform efforts after 10 years, and a 0.8 percent GDP increase in the long run at the EU level. The same study estimates that the introduction of Points of Single Contact in the Member States, a measure which facilitates cross-border service provision, could bring about a 0.13 percent GDP increase after 10 years and up to a 0.2 percent increase in the long run at the aggregate EU level. These results are broadly of the same order of magnitude as the GDP effects reported here. The European Commission (2012) estimates that the EU's ambitious Single Market initiative should result in a 1.8 percent increase in EU GDP and a 1.3 percent increase in employment after 15 years. Although these studies rely on different methodologies, they can help us to compare our results with other actual competition policy–friendly measures. Varga and in 't Veld (2014) find that structural reforms aimed at narrowing the gap in relation to the average of the three best EU performers in terms of market functioning would boost EU GDP by 1.1 percent after 10 years.

### 6.5.3 Simulations of Distributional Effects

In this section we focus on the distributional effects of the European Commission's merger and cartel decisions. As explained in section 6.4.3, we make a distinction between different types of households. Non-liquidity-constrained, high-skilled households work; receive wages, transfers, and benefits; consume and save; own capital; and invest in financial markets. Liquidity-constrained, low-skilled households, whose only sources of income are wages, transfers, and benefits, consume all their resources in each period. Making a distinction between these two types of households allows us to analyze the distributional effects of interventions by competition authorities such as the European Commission.

Table 6.6 reports the percentage change of the main macroeconomic variables describing the relative performance of non-liquidity-constrained, high-skilled households (NLC) and liquidity-constrained, low-skilled households (LC). Variables that refer to a specific household type are expressed in per-household terms. It appears that the markup shock leads to an increased demand for both non-liquidity-constrained and liquidity-constrained labor. Consequently, the wage increase for both types of households is also comparable, but slightly higher for non-liquidity-constrained households.

TABLE 6.6  **Distributional Effects of Markup Shock**
*% change after n years*

| Variable | 1 | 5 | 10 | 20 | 50 |
|---|---|---|---|---|---|
| Aggregate employment | 0.183 | 0.284 | 0.339 | 0.367 | 0.336 |
| NLC | 0.183 | 0.287 | 0.345 | 0.371 | 0.340 |
| LC | 0.185 | 0.275 | 0.313 | 0.348 | 0.322 |
| Aggregate consumption | 0.239 | 0.353 | 0.484 | 0.637 | 0.699 |
| NLC | 0.202 | 0.232 | 0.348 | 0.496 | 0.569 |
| LC | 0.408 | 0.918 | 1.117 | 1.296 | 1.306 |
| Wage income NLC | 0.723 | 1.592 | 1.967 | 2.242 | 2.189 |
| Wage income LC | 0.657 | 1.493 | 1.799 | 2.049 | 2.022 |
| Benefits NLC | −1.781 | −2.775 | −3.453 | −3.681 | −3.194 |
| Benefits LC | −0.421 | −0.457 | −0.581 | −0.640 | −0.430 |
| Transfers NLC | 0.231 | 0.400 | 0.532 | 0.697 | 0.766 |
| Transfers LC | 0.231 | 0.400 | 0.532 | 0.697 | 0.766 |
| Profits NLC | −6.079 | −8.205 | −7.757 | −7.165 | −6.777 |
| Capital income NLC | 1.255 | 1.610 | 1.723 | 1.840 | 1.850 |
| Bonds interest NLC | −0.526 | −0.476 | −0.681 | −0.176 | 0.551 |

*Note:* LC = liquidity-constrained, low-skilled households; NLC = non-liquidity-constrained, high-skilled households.

We also observe a substantial deterioration in profits due to lower markups (a peak deterioration of 8.2 percent after five years), and a decrease in income from financial assets due to lower interest rates on bonds, driven by an accommodating monetary policy responding to decreasing prices. The latter two negative effects are borne only by the non-liquidity-constrained households, who, however, can benefit from an increase in capital income due to a higher demand for production factors.

Following the increase in disposable incomes, households increase consumption by 0.35 percent after five years. The increase in consumption of liquidity-constrained households is particularly prominent because of the fact that in the QUEST model liquidity-constrained households consume all the available income sources and do not save or invest. In the long run non-liquidity-constrained households slowly recuperate their consumption relative to the liquidity-constrained households as their losses from profits and interests on bonds are decreasing.

Unemployment benefits paid to non-liquidity-constrained households are decreasing because they experience a proportionally larger decline in their unemployment rate.[12] As transfer incomes are not linked to unemployment or wages, they increase proportionally at the same rate for both households.

Overall, we can observe that pro-competition policies have important redistributive effects because, while they boost the demand for all types of workers, they significantly reduce profits destined for non-liquidity-constrained households.

The distributional consequences of competition-friendly interventions and product market reforms are not addressed in the previously mentioned studies of Monteagudo, Rutkowski, and Lorenzani (2012), the European Commission (2012), and Varga and in 't Veld (2014). Structural reforms, in particular, tax, labor market, and welfare reforms, have been more frequently analyzed in terms of their distributional effects. Burgert and Roeger (2014), for instance, simulate the macroeconomic impact of tax shifts in the European Commission's QUEST model and show that a tax shift from labor income to consumption redistributes disposable income from capital owners to wage earners. They find that the tax shift is regressive in the short run, but progressive in the long run, if it is enacted by reducing employers' social security contributions, and is progressive already in the short run if it is enacted by reducing personal income taxes. In contrast, our results show that competition-friendly measures can favor poorer households in the short run.

Ahrend, Arnold, and Moeser (2011) present model-based evidence about how the short-term impact of selected macroeconomic shocks is shared across different groups of agents. Unsurprisingly, the authors find that individuals with low incomes, and especially young people, seem in general to lose most from adverse macroeconomic shocks (fiscal consolidation reforms). Stricter product market regulation (for example, stronger entry barriers, less competition-friendly environment) is found to amplify the negative effects of certain shocks for youths and the poorer segments of society. Additionally, more rigid market regulations also had negative income effects on the poor following devaluations and commodity price decreases, and adversely affected poverty in the aftermath of financial crises and fiscal expansion shocks. This evidence is very much in line with the results presented in this chapter, which illustrates how pro-competition policy actions and reforms benefit the poorer segments of society.

## 6.6 Conclusions and Policy Implications

This chapter tries to bridge the gap between the microeconomic estimates of the customer savings associated with important merger and cartel interventions and the longer-term macroeconomic effects of these interventions. It also attempts to measure not only the direct effects of competition policy interventions but also their deterrent effects. Finally, it sheds some light on the distributional impact of competition policy.

The macroeconomic effects of competition policy interventions are assessed by applying markup shocks to a DSGE model, the QUEST model. The markup shocks are calibrated on the basis of the microeconomic customer savings from cartel and merger decisions of the European Commission in 2014 as well as decisions from earlier years still having an impact in 2014. These shocks reflect both direct and deterrent effects of competition policy interventions. The deterrent effects are assessed by assuming that the price effects of the Commission's decisions affect not only the relevant market cited in the decision but also the whole subsector to which this market belongs (subject to thresholds defined in line with the literature on the size of deterrent effects of merger and cartel decisions, respectively). In the QUEST model simulations the markup shock brings about a reduction in prices, which in turn results in higher demand, employment, and GDP growth. Profits are negatively affected.

The results of the simulations show that the total effects (including the deterrent effects) of competition policy interventions on GDP are sizeable: a 0.4 percent increase after five years and a 0.8 percent increase in the long term. This result is very similar to the one obtained in the one other study on the macroeconomic impact of competition policy that we are aware of. Van Sinderen and Kemp (2008) report increases of 0.3 percent and 0.4 percent in GDP after five and ten years, respectively. The competition policy effects are slightly lower than the estimated impact of the implementation of the Services Directive.

The QUEST model also allows assessing the distributional effects of the EU competition policy interventions across households, differentiating between non-liquidity-constrained households (savers and high-skilled) and liquidity-constrained households (low-skilled and consuming all their resources in each period). The simulations show that competition policy has important redistributive effects, with liquidity-constrained households increasing their consumption proportionally more than non-liquidity-constrained households: the liquidity-constrained households increase their consumption four times more than the non-liquidity-constrained households after five years (by 0.92 and 0.23 percent, respectively). This supports the view that competition policy interventions, by lowering prices and—as studied in other work, also by increasing the quality and variety of products—are particularly beneficial for the poorest in the society.

This work can be further refined in different ways. As a first step, alternative simulations will be carried out to test the robustness of the results. For example, the European Commission provides lower and upper bounds for its customer savings estimates, based on different assumptions regarding the price effect of its interventions and their duration. These different assumptions can be used to define different scenarios of markup shocks, which will provide a range of effects of the competition policy interventions. Similarly, different assumptions regarding the deterrent effects of competition policy could be tested, as there is still a high degree of uncertainty regarding the magnitude of these effects. At a later stage, it would be worthwhile to consider the differential effects of competition policy decisions affecting different sectors. However, this would require the use of a macroeconomic model that is disaggregated by sector. In addition, one may want to include an assessment of the macroeconomic effects of other competition policy interventions in the areas of antitrust and state aid control, which are not covered in this chapter.

To conclude, this chapter is a first contribution to a more comprehensive analysis of the impact of competition policy, going beyond the direct price effects and integrating deterrent and longer-term effects. This objective is ambitious and the simulations are reliant on a chain of assumptions, going from the calculation of customer savings and the approximation of the deterrent effects to the specification and calibration of the general equilibrium model. However, these assumptions do not undermine the usefulness of the analysis in getting a better understanding of the role of competition policy in society.

## Notes

1. A Phase 1 merger decision is a decision made within 25 working days following the notification of the merger. If the merger raises competition concerns and cannot be resolved in Phase 1, a Phase 2 merger investigation is opened. Phase 2 is an in-depth analysis of the merger's effects on competition and requires more time (at least 90 working days from the opening of a Phase 2 investigation). Following the Phase 2 investigation, the Commission may either unconditionally clear the merger, or approve the merger subject to remedies, or prohibit the merger if no adequate remedies to the competition concerns have been proposed by the merging parties.

2. See Davies 2013 for a summary of the assumptions made in the four jurisdictions.

3. For example, the Authority for Consumers and Markets in the Netherlands and the U.S. Department of Justice assume that the duration of the effect of a cartel decision is one year, whereas the Competition and Markets Authority in the United Kingdom assumes a duration of six years.

4. Data on skill-specific population shares, participation rates, and wages are obtained from the Labour Force Survey (EUROSTAT). The elasticity of substitution between different labor types ($\mu$) is one of the major parameters addressed in the labor economics literature. We rely on the seminal reference for this elasticity parameter by Katz and Murphy (1992). We use their estimated elasticity of substitution between skilled and unskilled labor, which is about 1.4.

5. Note that following Ratto, Roeger, and in 't Veld (2009), we assume that economic agents (firms and households) face technological constraints that restrict their price and wage setting, investment, employment, and capacity utilization decisions. These constraints are captured by the corresponding adjustment costs, but for easier tractability we omit these terms in the following sections.

6. Note that the term $\frac{1}{1+\tau_t^j}$ represents the Lagrange multiplier, which in a cost minimization problem can be interpreted as the effect on the objective (that is, costs) of relaxing the constraint by one unit (that is, producing one extra unit). This interpretation implies that the Lagrange multiplier equals real marginal cost $\frac{MC_t^j}{P_t^j} = \frac{1}{1+\tau_t^j}$.

7. The Frisch labor supply elasticity is defined as the elasticity of hours worked to the wage rate. In other words, it measures the substitution effect of a change in the wage rate on the supply of labor.

8. Note that $b$ is defined as the benefit replacement rate. Households only make a decision about the level of employment, but there is no distinction on the part of households between unemployment and nonparticipation. It is assumed that the government makes a decision how to classify the nonworking part of the population into unemployed and nonparticipants. The nonparticipation rate (NPART) must therefore be seen as a policy variable characterizing the generosity of the benefit system.

9. The wage markup depends on the intratemporal elasticity of substitution between differentiated labor services within each skill group, and fluctuations in the markup arise because of wage adjustment costs following Ratto, Roeger, and in 't Veld (2009).

10. Note that from equation (6.4) we can express the percentage price change in sector $k$ as $\Delta P_k / P_k = (\Delta(1 + MUP_k)) / (1 + MUP_k) + \Delta MC_k / MC_k$, where $MUP_k$ is the markup $(\tau_t^k)$. Assuming that $\Delta MC_k / MC_k = 0$ and $\Delta(1 + MUP_k) \approx \Delta MUP_k$, we obtain that $\Delta MUP_k = \Delta P_k / P_k (1 + MUP_k)$. Equation (6.12) aggregates the relevant markup changes using the corresponding market shares as weights.

11. The conversion from NACE rev2 classification to ISIC3 is based on the Eurostat RAMON correspondence tables (from NACE rev2 to NACE1.1 and from ISIC3.1 to ISIC3), available at http://ec.europa.eu/eurostat/ramon/relations/index.cfm?TargetUrl=LST_REL as well as on the United Nations conversion tables: http://unstats.un.org/unsd/cr/registry/regdnld.asp?Lg=1 (from NACE1.1 to ISIC3.1).

12. Although the employment effect is the same for each skill group—because the firms require a similar increase of labor input from both of them—the same increase in employment means a much larger decrease in the unemployment of high-skilled workers because their unemployment is much smaller initially.

## Bibliography

Ahrend, Rudiger, Jens Arnold, and Charlotte Moeser. 2011. "The Sharing of Macroeconomic Risk: Who Loses (and Gains) from Macroeconomic Shocks." OECD Economics Department Working Papers 877, OECD Publishing, Paris.

Baarsma, Barbara, Ron Kemp, Rob van der Noll, and Joe Seldeslachts. 2012. "Let's Not Stick Together: Anticipation of Cartel and Merger Control in the Netherlands." *De Economist* 160: 357–76.

Baker, Jonathan. 2003. "The Case of Antitrust Enforcement." *Journal of Economic Perspectives* 17 (4): 27–50.

Bolotova, Yuliya, and John M. Connor. 2006. "Cartel Overcharges: Survey and Meta-analysis." *International Journal of Industrial Organisation* 24 (6): 1109–37.

Buccirossi, Paolo, Lorenzo Ciari, Tomaso Duso, Giancarlo Spagnolo, and Cristiana Vitale. 2008. "A Study on the Effectiveness of Competition Policy." Report prepared by Lear for the Directorate General for Economic and Financial Affairs of the European Commission.

———. 2013. "Competition Policy and Productivity Growth: An Empirical Assessment." *Review of Economics and Statistics* 95 (4): 1324–36.

Burgert, Matthias, and Werner Roeger. 2014. "Fiscal Devaluation: Efficiency and Equity." European Economy, Economic Papers 542, European Union.

Clougherty, Joseph A. 2010. "Competition Policy Trends and Economic Growth: Cross-National Empirical Evidence." *International Journal of the Economics of Business* 17 (1): 111–27.

Clougherty, Joseph, Tomaso Duso, Miyu Lee, and Jo Seldeslachts. 2016. "Effective European Antitrust: Does EC Merger Policy Generate Deterrence?" *Economic Inquiry* 54 (4): 1884–1903.

CMA (Competition and Markets Authority, London). 2014. "Indirect Impact of Competition Policy with a Focus on Deterrence Effects." Internal working paper.

Davies, Stephen. 2013. "Assessment of the Impact of Competition Authorities' Activities." Note submitted to Working Party No. 2 of the Competition Committee, Organisation for Economic Co-operation and Development, February 25.

Davies, Stephen, and Peter L. Ormosi. 2013. "The Impact of Competition Policy: What Are the Known Unknowns?" CCP Working Paper 13–7, Centre for Competition Policy, University of East Anglia, U.K.

Deloitte. 2007. "The Deterrent Effect of Competition Enforcement by the OFT." Report Prepared for the Office of Fair Trading, London.

Duso, Tomaso, Klaus Gugler, and Florian Szücs. 2013. "An Empirical Assessment of the 2004 EU Merger Policy Reform." *Economic Journal* 123 (572): 596–619.

European Commission. 2012. *20 Years of the European Single Market*. Directorate General for Internal Market and Services, European Union.

———. 2013. "Evaluation of Consumer Benefits of EU Merger Control in 2012, Following a New Methodology." Note of the Chief Economist Team, February 7.

Gordon, Fiammetta, and David Squires. 2008. "The Deterrent Effect of UK Competition Enforcement." *De Economist* 156 (4): 411–32.

Hylton, Keith N., and Fei Deng. 2007. "Antitrust around the World: An Empirical Analysis of the Scope of Competition Laws and Their Effects." *Antitrust Law Journal* 74 (2): 271–341.

Hyytinen, Ari, Frode Steen, and Otto Toivanen. 2010. "Cartels Uncovered." CEPR Discussion Paper No. 7761, Centre for Economic Policy Research, London.

Ilzkovitz, Fabienne, and Adriaan Dierx. 2014. "Macro-economic Impact of Competition Policy: Rationale, Implementation and Challenges." Paper presented at the 9th International Conference on Competition and Regulation, Corfu, Greece, July 4–6.

———. 2015. "Ex-post Economic Evaluation of Competition Policy Enforcement: A Review of the Literature." Report prepared for the Competition Directorate General, European Commission.

Katz, Lawrence F., and Kevin M. Murphy. 1992. "Changes in Relative Wages, 1963–1987: Supply and Demand Factors. *Quarterly Journal of Economics* 107 (1): 35–78.

Kee, Hiau Looi, and Bernard Hoekman. 2007. "Imports, Entry and Competition Law as Market Disciplines." *European Economic Review* 51 (4): 831–58.

Kovacic, William E. 2006. "Using Ex Post Evaluations to Improve the Performance of Competition Policy Authorities." *Journal of Corporation Law* 31: 504–47.

Krakowski, Michael. 2005. "Competition Policy Works: The Effect of Competition Policy on the Intensity of Competition—An International Cross-Country Comparison." HWWA Discussion Paper 332, Hamburg Institute of International Economics.

London Economics. 2011. "The Impact of Competition Interventions on Compliance and Deterrence." OFT Report No. 1391, U.K. Office of Fair Trading, December.

Monteagudo, Josefina, Alexander Rutkowski, and Dimitri Lorenzani. 2012. "The Economic Impact of the Services Directive: A First Assessment Following Implementation." European Economy, Economic Papers 456, European Union.

Motta, Massimo. 2008. "On Cartel Deterrence and Fines in the European Union." *European Competition Law Review* 29: 209–20.

Mudde, Jan M. 2012. "The Outcome Effect of European Competition Policy for the Netherlands." Master Thesis under the Supervision of Prof. Dr. J. van Sinderen, Erasmus University, Rotterdam, the Netherlands.

Nocke, Volker, and Michael D. Whinston. 2011. "Dynamic Merger Review." *Journal of Political Economy* 118 (6): 1201–51.

OECD (Organisation of Economic Co-operation and Development). 2014. "Guide for Helping Competition Authorities Assess the Expected Impact of their Activities." DAF/COMP (2014)8.

OFT (U.K. Office of Fair Trading). 2012. "Consumer Benefits from the OFT's Work." OFT Working Paper 1428, OFT, London, June.

Ormosi, Peter L. 2014. "A Tip of the Iceberg? The Probability of Catching Cartels." *Journal of Applied Econometrics* 29 (4): 549–66.

Petersen, Niels. 2013. "Antitrust Law and the Promotion of Democracy and Economic Growth." *Journal of Competition Law and Economics* 9 (3): 593–636.

Ratto, Marco, Werner Roeger, and Jan in 't Veld. 2009. "QUEST III: An Estimated DSGE Model of the Euro Area with Fiscal and Monetary Policy." *Economic Modelling* 26 (1): 222–33.

Roeger, Werner. 1995. "Can Imperfect Competition Explain the Difference between Primal and Dual Productivity Measures?" *Journal of Political Economy* 103 (21): 316–30.

Samà, Danilo. 2013. "The Effectiveness of Competition Policy: An Econometric Assessment in Developed and Developing Countries." MPRA Paper 55360, University Library of Munich; Working Paper 0716, Socioeconomic Institute, University of Zurich.

Seldeslachts, Jo, Joseph A. Clougherty, and Pedro Pita Barros. 2009. "Settle for Now but Block for Tomorrow: The Deterrence Effects of Merger Policy Tools." *Journal of Law and Economics* 52 (3): 607–34.

SEO Amsterdam Economics (Stichting voor Economisch Onderzoek). 2011. "Anticipating Cartel and Merger Control." SEO report for the Netherlands Competition Authority.

Smuda, Florian. 2014. "Cartel Overcharges and the Deterrent Effect of EU Competition Law." *Journal of Competition Law and Economics* 10 (1): 63–86.

Sørgard, Lars. 2009. "Optimal Merger Policy Enforcement vs. Deterrence." *Journal of Industrial Economics* 57 (3): 438–56.

———. 2014. "From Research on Mergers to Merger Policy." *International Journal of the Economics of Business* 21 (1): 37–42.

Thum-Thysen, Anna, and Erik Canton. 2015. "Estimation of Service Sector Mark-Ups Determined by Structural Reform Indicators." European Economy, Economic Papers 547, European Union.

Twynstra Gudde. 2005. "Research into the Anticipation of Merger Control." Report for the Netherlands Competition Authority, October 27.

Van Sinderen, Jarig, and Ron Kemp. 2008. "The Economic Effects of Competition Law Enforcement: The Case of the Netherlands." *De Economist* 156 (4): 365–85.

Varga, Janos, and Jan in 't Veld. 2014. "The Potential Growth Impact of Structural Reforms in the EU: A Benchmarking Exercise." European Economy, Economic Papers 541, European Union.

# 7. Effect of Competition Law on Innovation: A Cross-National Statistical Analysis

**Tim Büthe** and **Cindy Cheng** (Duke University and Hochschule für Politik at the Technical University of Munich, Germany)

Innovation leads to greater diversity of products, higher product quality, and/or lower costs of production and thus has been widely recognized as a key driver of economic growth. Many political economists have long seen innovation, or more precisely the incentive to innovate, as a key benefit of the competition that is a hallmark of a market economy. Accordingly, creating and maintaining this incentive to innovate is a central economic rationale for adopting and maintaining antitrust or competition laws and policies. Empirical analyses of the effect of competition law on innovation, however, are scarce, almost all based on U.S. data, and yield mixed results. This chapter provides the first cross-sectional and panel analyses of the relationship between competition law and innovation at the aggregate, national level for a large number of jurisdictions, including a large sample of developing countries. We find that the adoption of competition laws indeed has a strongly statistically significant and positive effect on the rate of innovation cross-nationally and over time, as measured by the number of patent filings.

Tim Büthe, Associate Professor of Political Science and Public Policy at Duke University; Professor of Political Science and Public Policy, holding the Chair in International Relations, at the Hochschule für Politik (Bavarian School of Public Policy) at the Technical University of Munich. He also is Senior Fellow for the Rethinking Regulation Project at the Kenan Institute for Ethics, Duke University. E-mail: buthe@duke.edu or buthe@hfp .tum.de. Cindy Cheng is a PhD candidate in the Department of Political Science at Duke University. E-mail: ccheng623@gmail.com. The authors appear in alphabetical order; both have contributed equally to this chapter. Tim Büthe's research was supported in part by the U.S. National Science Foundation (Law and Social Sciences Program), under Grant No. SES-1228483 (+ supplement SES-1228483-001). Any opinions, findings, and conclusions or recommendations expressed in this chapter are those of the authors and do not necessarily reflect the views of the National Science Foundation. For fruitful conversations and/or comments on earlier drafts, we thank Edward Balleisen, John Davies, Alexander Kirshner, Georgiana Pop, Daniel Sokol, Duncan Wigan, and attendees of presentations at the World Bank-OECD Inaugural Conference of the Global Expert Network on Competition Policy, Shared Prosperity and Inclusive Growth (Washington, DC, June 2015), the Annual Convention of the International Studies Association (Atlanta, March 2016), and the Strategy Seminar at Duke's Fuqua School of Business (March 2016). For making data available to us, we thank the individuals and institutions listed in note 19, as well as the contributors to the National Science Foundation data project, as noted on the pages of http://www.competitionpolicy.net.

## 7.1 Introduction

Political economists since at least Adam Smith have seen innovation, or more precisely the incentive to innovate, as a key benefit of market competition. Schumpeter (1975 [1942]) challenged this conventional wisdom, arguing that monopolists or dominant firms that are secure in having a large market share are more likely to innovate. But his claim was soon countered by Arrow (1962) and more recent work, suggesting that the original theoretical expectation of a positive relationship between innovation and competition has stronger deductive support, albeit with some qualifications. Implicit in such arguments is that antitrust law or more broadly "competition policy," which seeks to safeguard or increase market competition, should boost innovation.

Empirically, the picture is less clear. Although the relationship between innovation and competition, as measured by the number and size distribution of competitors in a given industry, has been examined at length, empirical analyses of the effect of competition *law and policy* on innovation are few and far between. Existing analyses, almost all using U.S. data, can be summarized as follows: firm- and industry-level analyses of responses to the threat or actuality of antitrust enforcement by economic historians suggest that competition law tends to boost the level of innovation by the targeted firms (or by other firms in the industry)—but the effect does not appear to be uniform or entirely consistent. The few existing statistical papers yield mixed results. Moreover, empirical work on non-U.S. data has been rare so far, with no cross-national or panel data analyses of the effect of competition law and policy on innovation.

We begin with a brief review of the theoretical literature on how variation in market structure, in the level of competition, and specifically variation in competition law and policy might affect innovation. Based on this discussion, we generally expect competition law/policy to foster innovation, but we caution that there are four possible interpretations of a positive relationship between competition law/policy and innovation. After a very brief review of the prior empirical literature, we then present what to the best of our knowledge is the first statistical analysis of the relationship between competition law and innovation for a comprehensive panel of countries, including a large sample of developing countries, as well as Organisation for Economic Co-operation and Development (OECD) countries (in joint and separate analyses). Using two alternative measures of innovation (foreign patent filings in the United States and domestic patent filings across a large number of countries) in cross-sectional and panel analyses, we find that the adoption of competition laws significantly boosts innovation. The final section sets out a broader research agenda for such cross-national analyses.

## 7.2 Theory

Innovation is highly valued in both the public and the private sector. Although particular innovations may engender strong social and/or political resistance and certain innovations can be (ab)used to diminish economic well-being or political freedom (see, for example, Hintze 1975; Levinson 2006; Pavie 2014; Schumpeter 1975 [1942]), the capacity of innovation to increase the productivity of labor and capital makes innovation a key driver of prosperity and economic growth (David 1975; Porter 1990; Solow 1970). Innovation, moreover, promises tangible benefits beyond contributing to abstract aggregates such as gross domestic product (GDP) growth. And, because much innovation is geared toward producing the same goods or services more efficiently, it results in cost savings that allow lower prices, better quality, higher profits, or some combination thereof.[1]

Lower prices at constant quality, better quality at the same price, and/or higher profits are generally valued in the advanced capitalist democracies, but these benefits of innovation are (all else equal) at least as important for developing countries, where poverty is widespread and capital is scarce, because they promise higher standards of living and greater economic opportunity. And fostering innovation may be particularly important for developing countries insofar as it drives the development or adaptation of products, for instance, to climatic conditions that differ from typical OECD country conditions for which "standard" consumer and industrial goods tend to be designed, or to electrical grids that only occasionally supply the stable voltage assumed, for instance, by the devices that are central to "modern" medicine.[2]

For all of the above reasons, promoting innovation is a widely proclaimed goal of public policy—and of the "culture" that managers in the public and private sector are supposed to foster. For the individual enterprise or organization, however, innovation is also costly. Coming up with ideas for enhancing a product, producing it less expensively, or improving work flow cuts into time otherwise spent doing everything in the established way. Developing such ideas into concrete proposals and implementing those changes on a trial basis take additional, often substantial resources, which may in the long run be considered a good investment, but in the short run reduces output and profits. And, for a host of reasons, many innovations that seem like a great idea in theory do not succeed in practice. As a consequence, fostering innovation is a difficult and often elusive goal. As Lerner and Stern wrote on the occasion of the 50th anniversary of the foundational innovation research volume *The Rate and Direction of Inventive Activity*: "despite the critical nature of innovation, much remains unclear as to how nations, firms, and academic bodies can encourage this activity" (Lerner and Stern 2012, 1; see also Priest 2011).

Recent research has generally focused on social and political-legal institutions that might encourage individual market participants to invest in innovation at (close to) socially optimal levels.[3] Competition policy arguably is one such institution.

In the absence of market competition, producers not only may seek to appropriate all of the benefits of innovation for themselves but they may also become complacent, forgoing further innovation (and the short-term costs associated with it). As Porter puts it: "Loss of domestic rivalry is a dry rot that slowly undermines competitive advantage by slowing the pace of innovation and dynamism" (Porter 1990, 170). Conversely, innovation may allow a firm to gain a competitive advantage, enabling it to compete on price or other qualities. Political economists since Adam Smith (and some even before Smith, see De Roover 1951) therefore have seen innovation, or more precisely the incentive to innovate, as a key benefit of market competition. And to the extent that competition law and policy foster competition, we then should also expect competition law and policy to foster innovation.

Schumpeter challenged the conventional wisdom about the relationship between competition and innovation in his magisterial work on capitalism as a process of "creative destruction" (1975, esp. chapter VIII, sections 5–6). To be sure, he shows no sympathy for the "ordinary cartel" that involves no improvements in "the methods of production, organization, and so on," and he grants that market competition can stimulate marginal inventions that yield slightly more efficient ways of producing the same goods or services without the need for significant investments. Yet, he warns that any structure of the market that approximates perfect competition and entails "free entry into every industry" would bring the process of creative destruction to a standstill. "Perfectly free entry into a new field may make it impossible to enter it at all. . . [so much so that] the bulk of what we call economic progress is incompatible with [perfect competition]" because major innovations tend to require major investments that cannot be recouped if there is free entry.

A cursory reading might suggest that Schumpeter is here making the familiar case in favor of intellectual property rights protections, but he goes further than that. He argues that monopolistic or oligopolistic large firms have important and inherent benefits, such as easier access to financing from the retention of their own profits (itself a function of being able to charge prices above marginal costs).[4] What might appear to be anticompetitive structures or behavior thus affords these firms— in Schumpeter's account—the short-term cushion that is necessary to give them the incentive to take the risks entailed in implementing a radical innovation. The need for such a cushion arises from "long-range investing under rapidly changing conditions. . . [being] like shooting at a target that is not only indistinct but moving— and moving jerkily at that." Schumpeter concludes with what might appear to be a call for abandoning antitrust enforcement (though he never uses the term): "It is hence a mistake to base the theory of government regulation on the principle that big business should be made to work as the respective industry would work in perfect competition."[5]

In a widely cited chapter, Kenneth Arrow (1962) implicitly challenged Schumpeter's claim by developing a simple formal model of the incentives to innovate. A monopolist's ability to earn monopoly rents is bound up with the preinnovation production system (similarly, cartel agreements often rely upon the technological status quo ante, for instance to divide up markets or profits). Innovation, even if profitable as such, is there-fore less attractive to incumbent firms in highly concentrated industries than it would be if they were subjected to more competition. A firm that already has a large market share also has less of a chance to gain additional market share through innovation than an otherwise identical firm that is subject to great market competition. Arrow thus restored the neoclassical conventional wisdom that competition is conducive to innovation. He also (in effect) reinforced the expectation that well-designed and well-enforced competi-tion law and policy might foster innovation.

A large body of literature on the economics and political economy of innovation has led to a much more nuanced understanding in the half century since Arrow's piece, though much of that literature still starts from the Schumpeter-vs.-Arrow debate (for example, Ginsburg and Wright 2012; Vickers 2010). Both the advantages of an estab-lished, large incumbent firm in an oligopolistic market, for instance, and the disadvan-tages that such firms face in responding to a new entrant who nonetheless dares to challenge them, have been more carefully specified (see, for example, Bresnahan, Greenstein, and Henderson 2012 for a recent review). At the same time, there are many aspects of the relationship between competition and innovation that "remain uncer-tain or even mysterious" (Lerner and Stern 2012, 1).

Empirically, there is no simple, consistent relationship between market structure and rates of innovation (Cohen 2010), and both Schumpeter and Arrow might have been right: there are strong reasons to believe theoretically that both very high levels of concentration and truly "perfect" competition might be detrimental to innovation. Indeed, many—though not all—recent empirical studies find an "inverted U"–shaped relationship, where innovation is greatest in markets with at least four to five large firms (that is, at an intermediate level of competition, resembling neither perfect com-petition nor monopoly). Similarly, the relationship between firm size and innovation does not appear simple or necessarily linear.

Turning to competition *law and policy*, recent work has sought to overcome the Schumpeter-vs.-Arrow mindset, with Baker (2007, esp. 579–83) and Shapiro (2012, 363ff) arguing that the positions of Schumpeter and Arrow are not as strictly com-peting (that is, incompatible) as they might seem. Specifically, Schumpeter was surely right that the incentive to innovate is affected by the prospects for recapturing the costs of innovation, including possibly through temporary protection from competition to allow capturing rents (Baker 2007, 581; Shapiro 2012, 364). This sug-gests allowing a deviation from the drive for greater competition in the aftermath of innovations that "provide greater value to customers" (Shapiro 2012, 364), usually in the form of intellectual property (IP) or patent rights. At the same time, the theo-retical case for a policy that fosters competition during product development and the production process—in order to spur innovation—remains strong: competition among firms producing close substitutes or developing new products creates strong incentives "to find ways to lower costs, improve quality or develop better products" (Baker 2007, 579).[6] In other words, given intellectual property rights protections that safeguard the innovator's ability to recoup his investments, competition law and policy that encourage rivalry (and create disincentives against firms colluding with each other to protect themselves from market competition) should foster innovation.

While our main contribution in this chapter is empirical, we distinguish four political-economic logics for competition law and policy to boost innovation, which we note here even if our empirical analyses in this chapter do not allow us to distinguish between them. The first two are derived from the conventional wisdom among classical and neoclassical economists laid out above. The third and fourth may be more interesting in that they suggest that competition law might boost innovation even if it fails to actually increase market competition.

1. Competition law may foster innovation simply by making markets more competitive. For firms that want to increase their profits and/or market share, competition between producers creates an incentive to innovate in order to be able to offer the goods or services at lower prices or to differentiate themselves from their competitors on some measure of quality. Since these incentives should apply to all market participants (and can be assumed to be common knowledge), even a status quo–oriented firm, that is, a firm that is perfectly content with its current profits and market share, will under these conditions have incentives to innovate to keep up with its competitors. We will discuss empirical measures of innovation below, but this logic has a straightforward implication for the measure that we use in our statistical analyses, so we note it already: competition law should be associated with a higher number of patent filings (all other things being equal) as innovators seek to safeguard their ability to recoup the costs of innovation, as discussed above.

2. Competition law may foster innovation by lowering barriers to market entry so more people with new ideas will bring them to market. In the process, those innovators may be expected to file patents for ideas and inventions that otherwise would have just remained blueprints in a drawer. Here, as above, the threat of entry by new, innovative competitors also creates incentives for the incumbent firms to innovate, in order to remain competitive (and possibly to deter market entry by new competitors who might otherwise expect that even a minor innovation would allow them to capture a substantial market share from the complacent incumbents).

3. A third possible causal mechanism is less appealing to competition policy "purists" but may be just as important: vigorously enforced competition law creates an incentive for incumbent firms in oligopolistic markets—even and especially if they are engaged in anticompetitive behavior—to avoid the public image of a rent-seeking oligopolist. Incumbent firms can do so by engaging in

cutting-edge innovation and thus avoid becoming a politically attractive target of attention for the enforcement agency. Relatedly, incumbent firms have an incentive to innovate in order to keep the definition of products and markets fluid, thus again dissuading enforcement agencies from focusing attention (and scarce enforcement resources) on the firm and its anticompetitive behavior because enforcement agencies typically seek to address current "live" issues rather than allegations of past violations that are "moot" after the facts on the ground have shifted (see George Priest's discussion of mootness and judicial efficiency, as summarized in Goldstein et al. 2012). To put it differently: competition law creates incentives to innovate because innovation that results in new products allows a firm to practically create new markets, requiring competition regulators to catch up before they can even discern whether the firm is engaged in anticompetitive behavior. Recognizing this possible, additional and distinct causal mechanism (and the next one) is important because it suggests that competition policy might foster innovation even while being ineffective in diminishing anticompetitive behavior.

4. Last but not least (and, anecdotal evidence suggests, quite importantly), effective competition law precludes the use of various practices that firms in many countries have long used to protect themselves from the vagaries of the market. This increases the attractiveness of patents as a potential source of protection from competition, which remains available and legal. To put it differently: competition law creates incentive to innovate because, thanks to patents and other intellectual property rights protections, the innovations provide a firm with an opportunity to reap supracompetitive profits perfectly legally for some time.

## 7.3 Review of the Empirical Literature

Most of the empirical studies in the literature about the effect of competition on innovation use industry-level variation in competition or competitiveness to gain analytical leverage over innovation (using proxy measures of competition at the industry level, such as profitability or the Lerner index of price elasticity of demand). Findings vary; but, although some studies appear to find support for Schumpeter's conjecture that highly concentrated industries or dominant firms are more likely to generate innovation, more of the recent empirical research suggests that greater competition boosts innovation[7]—though at a diminishing rate, as first suggested by Scherer (1967). Indeed, Aghion et al. (2005)—and earlier Kamien and Schwartz (1976)—posited the inverted U–shaped relationship mentioned above, where firms in moderately competitive markets innovate the most, whereas firms in both monopolistic and highly competitive markets exhibit less innovation. Aghion et al. find empirical support for this relationship in U.K. data, measuring innovation by patent registrations, as in our empirical analysis. Bérubé, Duhamel, and Ershov (2012); Carlin, Schaffer, and Seabright (2004); and Polder and Veldhuizen (2012) report similar findings for Canadian, Central and East European, and Netherlandic[8] firms, respectively (see also Tingvall and Poldahl 2006).

Cross-country analyses of the effect of the level of competition on innovation, which take the country or jurisdiction as the unit of analysis, are comparatively rare. They also tend to rely upon rather indirect measures of innovation, such as economic growth—inferring innovation from its assumed (but contested) effects. For example in a cross-sectional analysis of several "indicators of [the] intensity of economy-wide competition," Dutz and Hayri (2000) find that competition has a significantly positive effect on the average annual growth rate of real gross national product (GNP) per capita during 1986–1995—which they interpret as supporting prior sectoral analyses that find that "more competition leads to more innovation" (Dutz and Hayri 2000, ii).[9] Interestingly, one of Dutz and Hayri's proxy measures of market competition, for which they find a clearly positive, statistically significant correlation with innovation (proxied by GNP growth), is a measure of perceived effectiveness of "anti-monopoly" *policy* from the World Economic Forum survey.

Notwithstanding this well-known finding, empirical research on the effect of *competition law* on innovation is even scarcer than national-level analyses of the relationship between competition and innovation. The most direct evidence of the effect of competition policy on innovation comes from case studies of individual firms and sometimes industries, mostly in the United States. Studies of the formation of the American Tobacco Company, for instance, show that attaining a nearly monopolistic position in several of its markets did not stop the innovative drive of this very dynamic trust, but it affected the type of innovations pursued. According to Porter (1969), innovations in technology and management in particular, which lowered costs and could be strategically passed on to consumers, were most common during two moments in time: first, during the early years, when James Buchanan Duke was forging American Tobacco out of multiple competitors, several of which resisted until he convinced them that they would not survive in head-on price competition—and again when antitrust scrutiny raised the prospects of new competitors entering the market.

Indeed, case studies of diverse industries, from traditional basic materials industries and chemicals (DuPont) and steel to consumer and industrial consumption products (lightbulbs, GE) to (relative) high-tech industries such as film (Eastman Kodak), telecommunications (AT&T), and computing (IBM), suggest that it was in numerous cases the increased threat of antitrust intervention (or the consequence of actual enforcement actions) that consciously prompted the leadership of dominant companies in these industries to refrain from the further use of aggressive tactics with which they had previously moved against new innovation-driven entrants into their respective industries—and that this directly contributed to more innovations coming to fruition

(Chandler 1994; Didrichsen 1972; Hart 1998–99; Smith and Hounshell 1985). At the same time, the threat of antitrust enforcement against horizontal mergers involving already dominant firms also appears to have stimulated innovation by the incumbent firms, not just to hold off new competitors but also to find new outlets for capital and managerialist desires for growth in firm size by moving into new products and industries (for example, Mowery and Rosenberg 1998, 13–16, *passim*).

While most of these case studies suggest a causal and clearly positive effect of competition law on innovation, the findings from qualitative research do not provide unqualified support for the argument. The causal mechanisms driving the observed positive effects seem quite varied, and it is often difficult to discern whether the resulting increases in innovation were fortuitous unintended consequences or reliably predictable consequences of a policy intervention. In other words, how indicative of a general pattern are these cases? The question arises, for instance, in light of case studies such as Mazzone and Mingardi's of the European Union (EU) Intel case (2011), which suggest that antitrust enforcement was detrimental to innovation (maybe because the case was, arguably, politically motivated). And it arises a fortiori in developing country contexts, where Rodriguez and Menon (based on consultancy experience in numerous though unspecified developing countries) caution that innovating firms tend to attract the scrutiny of competition law enforcement agencies, so that competition law often suppresses "desperately needed" innovation and entrepreneurship (Rodriguez and Menon 2010, xix, 36, 64, 143). Maybe unsurprisingly, developing country antitrust regulators tend to see it quite differently, expecting an innovation-enhancing role for competition law (for example, Lipimile 2004). In sum, the findings of case studies are mixed.

Statistical analyses seem even more inconclusive—maybe inevitably so, given that there are very few of them. Analyzing U.S. patent filings from 1953 to 2000, Marinova, McAleer, and Slottje (2005) find that higher levels of civil (but not criminal) antitrust enforcement by the U.S. Department of Justice (DoJ) (as a measure of the seriousness of U.S. antitrust enforcement) lead to a significantly higher number of patent filings (and successful filings) during the following year, suggesting that competition law enforcement boosts innovation. By contrast, Young and Shughart (2010), using VAR (vector autoregression) models, find evidence of antitrust enforcement resulting in transitory reductions in labor productivity (using the index of "output per hour" for U.S. business from the U.S. Bureau of Labor Statistics' Major Sector Productivity and Costs Indices), which they interpret as an indication that DoJ antitrust enforcement actions constitute a negative technology shock. Yet Symeonidis (2008) finds essentially the opposite using industry-level data from the United Kingdom from 1954 through 1973. Specifically, he finds that the introduction of anticartel legislation in the United Kingdom in 1956 resulted in significant increases in labor productivity in industries that were previously known to have been heavily cartelized, such as bread and flour confectionery or carpets.

To the best of our knowledge, there are no prior statistical analyses of the effect of competition law or policy on innovation at the national aggregate level, especially not using cross-national or panel data.

## 7.4 Empirical Analysis

### 7.4.1 Measuring Innovation: The Dependent Variable

Measuring innovation entails some well-known challenges (see, for example, Kuznets 1962; Sanders 1962). The most common measures are research and development (R&D) expenditures and patent filings (OECD Secretariat 2010; Smith 2005). Neither measure is perfect. In international comparisons, higher R&D expenditures may be a function of the scarcity of technical talent or a function of inefficiency rather than greater innovation. Reported R&D expenditures may also differ across countries because of tax code rules, and cross-national aggregate data for R&D are available for only a very limited number of countries. Patent filings are no panacea either, especially in light of the "patent wars" of recent years, which have driven firms in many high-tech industries to seek "war chests" of patents to sue or countersue competitors to disrupt their ability to bring a new product to market (or defend against a competitor using this tactic, see Bessen and Meurer 2008; Hall and Ziedonis 2001). In the developing country context, it is also a legitimate question whether innovation at the patentable technological cutting edge is the kind of innovation that most advances their economic development. Nonetheless, patent filings generally are thought to capture variation in innovation across time and space quite well, and data are reasonably readily available (see below).

We use two different measures of patents to assess the relationship between innovation and the adoption of antitrust laws.[10] The first measure is the number of patent applications in the United States in a given year, logged, by the country of residence of the first-named inventor. These data are available as "patent applications by country of origin" from the U.S. Patent and Trademark Office (USPTO) from 1965 to 2014.[11] The second measure is the number of patents applied for by residents of a country in their country of origin, also logged, available from the World Intellectual Property Organization (WIPO) from 1960 to 2014.[12]

U.S. patent applications are an attractive measure of innovation for two reasons. Generally, using patent applications filed in one location helps ensure a uniform standard of review for patent applications and eases comparisons of patents as a unit of account. Moreover, the U.S. patent bureau applies a high standard for patentability, because the United States has for many years been at the forefront of technological innovation (Porter and Stern 2002). Because of its size and relative wealth, the United States also is generally the first jurisdiction of choice for inventors considering filing in a foreign country.

Meanwhile, using data for patents for which inventors or businesses applied in their home countries (to which we will hereafter refer as "WIPO patents" after the organization that collects the data from national patent offices) captures precisely what U.S. patent data cannot. Because patents generally give rights to the inventor only in the country in which the patent is issued,[13] domestic competition law might be expected to most directly affect the incidence of domestic patents. Moreover, if innovation leads to economic growth not only through the profits it generates for the inventor but also through the multiplier effect it may have when it solves real problems confronted by a given society, then in some respects WIPO patents may represent a more robust measure of innovation than U.S. patents. That is, WIPO patents are arguably better at measuring the extent to which technology is being developed to address problems that are specific to the inventor's home country. At the same time, the numbers for WIPO patents may be less strictly comparable across countries than the numbers for U.S. patents if national patent offices vary in the standards they apply, the fees and administrative hurdles that they demand for patent applications, and so on. Given that neither measure is clearly superior, we use and report the results for both (in separate analyses).

### 7.4.2  Measuring Competition Law: Toward International Comparability

Our key interest regarding each country's competition regime (for the purposes of this chapter) is whether the country has a substantively meaningful competition law and for how long such a law has been in effect. The specific empirical measures used in our analyses are based on content analyses of all competition-related statutes that we could identify for 217 jurisdictions, including 195 countries, 15 noncountry jurisdictions, and 7 regional bodies.[14] For this coding work, we used and extended the collection of competition laws by Büthe and Bradford (2012), then reviewed the texts of each jurisdiction's earliest laws with competition-related provisions. To be considered what we here call a "substantively meaningful competition law," the legislation under review had to:

- Have, at least among other things, the declared purpose of fostering or safeguarding market competition in the national economy; and
- Contain, at a minimum, a prohibition of cartels or cartel-like forms of collusion (that is, disallow price-fixing agreements or coordinated reductions in production, market-sharing agreements, and the like).[15]

The first criterion has the intent and effect of excluding from consideration constitutional provisions that might prohibit monopolies, cartels, or market manipulation generically, even if such provisions occur in the context of a general commitment to a market economy.[16] And it excludes from consideration as a country's first "competition law" legislation that applies only to a specific industry or sector, even if for that industry the legislation might provide well-designed and strong competition provisions and even if the legislation is competition-specific.[17] The rationale for these exclusions is in part feasibility: reliably identifying every industry-specific statute for approximately two hundred jurisdictions and assessing the competition provisions possibly contained therein seemed like an impossible task even with tremendous research assistance. The first exclusion criterion is also motivated by an assessment of likely effectiveness: pro-competition constitutional provisions are likely to require additional implementing legislation before they create incentives for innovation, and competition provisions that apply only to a single industry are unlikely to have a measurable effect on economywide measures of innovation.

The second criterion seeks to establish a substantive, readily cross-nationally comparable minimum threshold for what "counts" as a competition law, consistent with recent scholarship by, for example, Gutmann and Voigt (2014) and Peters et al. (2009, 606). The rationale for requiring that a law contain a prohibition of cartels is that we consider a cartel prohibition necessary for competition legislation to have any chance of deterring anticompetitive behavior and safeguarding market competition to the point of creating incentives for innovation.

Austria provides a useful illustration of why imposing this requirement is important: Austria passed one of the first post-WWII "cartel laws" in 1951 (still in semi-sovereign status under joint oversight of the Allied Powers). But this law simply regulated the enforceability of cartel agreements in Austrian courts. Specifically, it required prior notification of a cartel agreement to a government registry before it could be enforced in an Austrian court of law. This registration requirement eventually proved quite important when—in a series of amendments or replacements of the cartel law in 1972, 1988, and 2002—the Austrian government decided to impose increasingly strict constraints on the permissible cartels. But even the 2002 amendment to the 1988 law remained focused on public registration (transparency) and administrative procedures for efficiently obtaining approval for anticompetitive agreements under various conditions. Only in 2005 did the Austrian parliament pass the first law "*against* cartels and other competition-reducing measures" (emphasis added), which indeed contained a clear prohibition of cartels.

Applying these criteria in our review of the specific content of the competition-related provisions of each jurisdiction's pertinent laws, we identified 136 countries, 7 regional bodies, and 7 nonstate jurisdictions that had adopted at least one actual competition law prior to January 1, 2016.[18] To do so, we built on prior work (see, in particular, Büthe 2014, esp. 220f) and supplemented our own reading of the laws' provisions with the discussion of the country's competition regime (or the absence thereof) in a wide range of sources.[19] We then recorded the year when the first competition law that met our selection criteria came into effect.

Even with very explicit criteria, which any legislation had to fulfill to "count" as a competition law, encoding our competition law variable(s) required making a number of judgment calls. One issue was deciding whether to record the year during which a country first enacted a competition law that met the criteria, which might be considered the key moment in time insofar as enacting the law sends a signal to potential innovators, or to record the year when the first competition law came into effect, that is, when its provision became legally binding. The difference matters insofar as a number of countries afforded their business community a period of anywhere between three months and (usually no more than) two years between passing the legislation and having it come into effect. Considering the latter more likely to change the incentives for innovation, we use the latter for the analyses presented in this chapter, but we recorded both years for each law and also conducted the analyses using the year-of-law-enactment variable to ensure that our findings are robust to this choice.

Another key issue was determining which competition law should count as a given country's "first" such law. One option was to count simply the chronologically first legislation that fulfilled our selection criteria. For most countries, this was straightforward, but not for all. The biggest issue was discontinuity. Argentina, Norway, Poland, and South Africa, for instance, all passed a first competition law between World Wars I and II (in 1923, 1926, 1933, and 1933, respectively), but—after an often patchy record of enforcement during the early years—suspended or even revoked the law during the Great Depression or World War II.[20] And it then took them until 1980, 1993, 1987, and 1998, respectively, before these countries passed a new competition law that met the selection criteria *and then continuously kept a qualifying competition law on the books*. A few countries suspended or overruled their initial competition laws at other, later times, usually in response to economic crises (such as Ireland, whose expansive 1958 price control legislation rendered its 1953 competition law moot), or passed a first competition law but failed to pass the implementing secondary legislation that was required for the original law to take effect (such as Colombia, whose 1959 "Ley por la cual se dictan algunas disposiciones sobre prácticas comerciales restrictivas" did not become fully operational until the required secondary legislation was passed in 1992; see OECD 2009). A related phenomenon is observable in Bangladesh. When East Pakistan became the newly independent country of Bangladesh in 1971, it started out with all preindependence Pakistani laws nominally on the books, including the 1970 Monopolies and Restrictive Trade Practices (Control and Prevention) Ordinance; but the applicability of the general principle was contested for laws passed just prior to independence, and experts note that neither the Bangladeshi legislature nor the executive ever acknowledged the 1970 law as applicable in Bangladesh, arguably making the 2012 Bangladeshi Competition Act the first competition law for the country (see, for example, Evrard et al. 2014; Raihan 2015, esp. 5). Given that it is theoretically conceivable that either the chronologically first law or the first continuously-in-effect law (or both) could boost the level of innovation in the country, we encoded both measures to make them available for future research (we call the resulting variables "Years competition law in effect" and "Years competition law continuously in effect," respectively). In the tables below, we initially report results for both, then focus on the latter for which we consider the theoretical rationale to be stronger.

Another important coding decision concerns regional competition regimes. The European Community has long been known for having adopted a competition law and policy long before several of its member states. Yet, while for the EU the question of how to treat such regional competition rules relative to the member states' rules is interesting only for the early years of our panel, it is an increasingly important question for international comparative competition law analysis, because there is a growing number of regional bodies with supranational competition rules, especially in Africa and Latin America. And for a number of regional bodies they are considered increasingly consequential, including the Caribbean Community (CARICOM), which in 2008 set up a supranational agency to enforce the competition rules that it originally adopted in 2001 (effective 2002); the Common Market for Eastern and Southern Africa (COMESA), which in 2013 set up a supranational competition agency to implement its 2004 competition regime; and the West African Economic and Monetary Union (WAEMU/UEMOA), which also is increasingly active in enforcing its 2002/03 competition regime. This raises the difficult question of whether to consider the regional competition rules instead of any national competition law and, if so, whether to "count" the regional rules only for countries that do not have a competition law at the national level.[21] And, if the regional rules are to be used for coding, even for countries with a prior national competition regime, should this already be done for the early years of the regional rules when their status might have been uncertain and enforcement might have made the national competition laws far more meaningful, as in the case of WAEMU and Senegal (see Bakhoum and Molestina 2011; Weick 2010)? Since these questions have no easy, clear answers, we have for the exploratory analyses in this chapter de facto ignored the regional competition regimes and simply analyzed each country's domestic (national-level) competition law. We expect to address this issue in subsequent papers.

Finally, note that, for the analyses reported in this chapter, we focus on the mere existence of a substantively meaningful competition *law* (as defined above), then calculate for each country-year the number of years since the first such law came into (continuous) effect and thus has been legally binding— we code our variables 0 if the country has no competition law yet. We do not here use more differentiated measures of the content of the law, nor do we condition our law duration measure on some metrics of implementation or enforcement, the effectiveness of the jurisdiction's broader competition *policy*, or general measures of rule of law, state capacity, or government effectiveness. Such more differentiated analyses, from which we refrained in this initial, exploratory analysis, because they complicate the statistical analysis, should surely be done in subsequent work.

### 7.4.3 Control Variables

We include in our analyses of the effect of competition law on innovation a number of control variables that have been found to be important predictors of innovation in the most comprehensive previous attempt to statistically model innovation using patent applications (Cheng, Grieco, and Guzman 2014): population, GDP per capita, trade and foreign direct investment (FDI) flows, political institutions, and a measure of state capacity.[22]

Specifically, we include two basic demographic covariates in every statistical model. Population straightforwardly controls for the number of *potential* innovators in each country. We also include population squared to allow for a nonlinear relationship: a larger population surely increases the number of patent filings (ceteris paribus), but it may exhibit diminishing returns in bringing about new, patentable ideas.[23]

We also include one basic economic control variable in every model: GDP per capita (in constant 2005 dollars), to account for a country's level of economic (and thus usually technological) development—and the domestic resources that a given inventor or business may be able to draw upon. We expect a strongly statistically significant positive coefficient.

A surely important aspect of the legal environment—especially in light of how we have operationalized "innovation"—is whether a country has a patent law. It seems likely that having such a law at home will increase the incentives to innovate for a given country's residents such that it will boost U.S. patent registrations by the country's residents. And, for the WIPO measure of patent registrations, having such legislation is presumably a prerequisite for registering "innovations" by the country's residents. For consistency with our competition law measure, however, we do not simply use an indicator ("dummy") variable for whether or not the country has such a law. Instead, for the main analyses, we use the number of years since the country's patent law came into effect as our control variable, thus allowing for the possibility that the effect of an IP-law on innovation increases quasi-linearly over time. The data for this variable was collected from the WIPO Lex database ("Main IP Laws: Enacted by Legislature").[24] The earliest piece of legislation identified by WIPO as providing patent protection for a given country was used.

We also include two additional economic and two political control variables. Trade as a percentage of GDP and net inward FDI flows as a percentage of GDP are included as measures of a country's connection to, and integration into, international markets (Xu and Chiang 2005), even though the theoretical expectation regarding these variables is not entirely clear. On the one hand, increased integration into the world economy may increase the level of competition in a country's economy, providing greater incentives to innovate (see, for example, Blackhurst 1991; Hazledine 1991).[25] On the other hand, greater links with the international community may allow greater technological spillovers across different markets such that greater relative effort is spent on licensing and adaption of international technology as opposed to spurring domestic innovation (Connolly 2003).[26]

A rich body of research has been devoted to investigating how political institutions stimulate or stymie growth (for example, Barro 1996; Przeworski and Limongi 1993). While the specific hypothesized mechanisms differ, the importance of political institutions for growth is no longer in doubt: The nature of a country's political institutions is thought to provide a direct impetus for innovation and growth (Evans 1992) and shape incentives that make it more (or less) likely for individuals to behave in growth-conducive or at least growth-compatible ways (Acemoglu, Johnson, and Robinson 2001). In recognition of this finding, we include a measure of political institutions, polity2, from the Polity IV Project. Polity2 combines a measure of democratic institutional features and an inverted measure of autocratic institutional features, resulting in a variable that has a range from −10 to 10 (where the extreme values identify fully autocratic and fully democratic regimes, respectively). While small unit changes in the polity2 score are substantively difficult to interpret, large unit differences or changes can be fairly unambiguously interpreted, with higher scores indicating more democratic institutions.

Finally, we include a measure of *state capacity* in recognition of the fact that a competent government bureaucracy is a minimum requirement for patents to be meaningful, because they grant public privileges in the form of legal protections. Unfortunately, the exact meaning and therefore every empirical measure of state capacity is contested; recent scholarship mostly treats it as multidimensional, incorporating the degree of bureaucratic professionalization, rule of law, and fiscal capacity (Cárdenas 2010). Our main focus here is on the government's ability to implement and enforce its own policies and laws. Therefore, we use the Worldwide Governance Indicators' (WGI) indicator of government effectiveness, which is designed to capture "perceptions of the quality of public services, the quality of the civil service and the degree of its independence from political pressures, the quality of policy formulation and implementation, and the credibility of the government's commitment to such policies."[27]

### 7.4.4 Methodological Concerns (1): Multicollinearity

As always in multivariate regression, we are concerned about possible multicollinearity, that is, the possibility that two or more variables in our data may be highly correlated with each other, which could negatively affect the validity of our analysis. We investigate this possibility by calculating the variance inflation factor for each of our variables and performing a condition number test on the dataset.

The variance inflation factor provides an estimate of how much the variance of an estimated coefficient is increased because of multicollinearity. A variance inflation factor of 1 indicates that there is no collinearity between variables. The most common rule of thumb is that a variance inflation factor of 10 or above indicates severe multicollinearity problems, though some use thresholds as high as 20 or 40, and others use thresholds as strict as 5 (see O'Brien 2007). For both our raw, nonimputed dataset and our imputed dataset, all variables have variance inflation factors less than 5. For both the nonimputed and imputed data, the WGI Government Effectiveness measure has the highest variance inflation factor, with values of 3.95 and 4.81, respectively.

Many multivariate statistical approaches involve decomposing the correlation matrix of the data into linear combinations of different variables. The linear combinations are chosen so that the first combination has the largest possible variance, the second combination has the next largest variance subject to being uncorrelated with the first combination, the third combination has the third largest variance subject to being uncorrelated with the first and second combinations, and so on. The variance of each of these linear combinations is called the eigenvalue. The condition number test investigates potential multicollinearity in a dataset through a comparison of each eigenvalue to the highest eigenvalue. Having a large ratio indicates that the data can be explained by a smaller number of eigenvectors than the number of independent variables, suggesting multicollinearity in the dataset. As a rule of thumb, a condition number of 30 or greater is an indication of problematic multicollinearity (Belsley, Kuh, and Welsch 1980). Our scaled raw data have a condition number of 7.19 while our scaled imputed data have a condition number of 8.07, well below the threshold of 30.

Overall then, the variance inflation factors and condition numbers for both our raw and imputed data suggest that multicollinearity should not drive the results that we find in our chapter. In our analysis we use both the scaled and unscaled versions of our data and find that our results are robust to both. We present the unscaled results for ease of interpretability.

### 7.4.5 Methodological Concerns (2): Missing Data and Imputation

Missing data is a common problem in cross-national panel analyses, especially analyses that seek to take into account the experience of a broad cross-section of developing countries, which our analysis seeks to do. Missing data is a particular issue for our patent measures. Developing countries are more likely to have missing patent data either because they are less likely to have patents to report or because they are more likely to fail to report their data, for example, due to weak bureaucratic capacity or greater frequency of political and economic crises.[28] Note that, under such conditions, patent levels (that is, the values of the missing data for the dependent variable) are also likely to be low. Indeed, if we compare the means for the U.S. and WIPO patent measures with and without imputed values (compare table 7.2 to table 7.1), we observe that the means with the imputed values are substantially lower.

**TABLE 7.1 Summary Statistics for Full Dataset, with Imputed Values**

| Variable | Mean | SD | Median | Minimum | Maximum | IQR |
|---|---|---|---|---|---|---|
| U.S. patents | $1.25e^3$ | $1.08e^4$ | 9 | 0 | $2.88e^5$ | 76.4 |
| WIPO patents | $4.55e^3$ | $2.72e^4$ | 134 | 1 | $7.98e^5$ | 853 |
| Years competition law in effect | 7.33 | 17.4 | 0 | 0 | 126 | 5 |
| Years competition law continuously in effect | 4.02 | 10.7 | 0 | 0 | 125 | 1 |
| Polity2 | 0.755 | 6.96 | 0 | −10 | 10 | 15 |
| Government effectiveness | −0.133 | 0.855 | −0.344 | −2.45 | 2.43 | 1.11 |
| Years of IP law duration | 8.50 | 14.9 | 0 | 0 | 126 | 12 |
| GDP per capita | $1.00e^4$ | $1.87e^4$ | $2.80e^3$ | 69.6 | $6.33e^5$ | $1.04e^4$ |
| Population | $2.82e^7$ | $1.08e^8$ | $5.71e^6$ | $6.13e^3$ | $1.36e^9$ | $1.63e^7$ |
| Trade (% GDP) | 79.9 | 50.4 | 69.7 | 0.0210 | $5.31e^3$ | 53.9 |
| FDI (% GDP) | 3.15 | 8.01 | 1.63 | −82.9 | 467 | 3.3 |

*Note:* Whenever the size of a value warrants it for the sake of efficiency, we use scientific notation where, for instance, $1.25e^3$ means $1.25 \times 10^3$. Values for mean and standard deviation (SD) are rounded to three significant digits. FDI = foreign direct investment; GDP = gross domestic product; IP = intellectual property; IQR = interquartile range; WIPO = World Intellectual Property Organization.

**TABLE 7.2 Summary Statistics for Nonimputed Data**

| Variable | Mean | SD | Median | Minimum | Maximum | IQR |
|---|---|---|---|---|---|---|
| U.S. patents | $2.39e^4$ | $1.55e^4$ | 13 | 0 | $2.88e^5$ | 171 |
| WIPO patents | $8.35e^4$ | $3.96e^4$ | 201 | 1 | $7.98e^5$ | $1.63e^4$ |
| Years competition law in effect | 7.70 | 17.4 | 0 | 0 | 126 | 7 |
| Years competition law continuously in effect | 4.02 | 10.9 | 0 | 0 | 125 | 1 |
| Polity2 | 0.982 | 7.46 | 2 | −10 | 10 | 16 |
| Government effectiveness | −0.0393 | 1.01 | −0.21 | −2.45 | 2.43 | 1.44 |
| Years of IP law duration | 8.26 | 14.9 | 0 | 0 | 126 | 11 |
| GDP per capita | $9.36e^4$ | $1.56e^4$ | $2.53e^4$ | 69.6 | $1.59e^5$ | $1.04e^4$ |
| Population | $2.85e^7$ | $1.09e^8$ | $5.53e^6$ | $6.13e^4$ | $1.36e^9$ | $1.61e^7$ |
| Trade (% GDP) | 76.6 | 50.5 | 66.7 | 0.0210 | 532 | 53.1 |
| FDI (% GDP) | 3.49 | 9.59 | 1.50 | −82.9 | 467 | 3.63 |

*Note:* Whenever the size of a value warrants it for the sake of efficiency, we use scientific notation where, for instance, $1.25e^3$ means $1.25 \times 10^3$. Values for mean and standard deviation (SD) are rounded to three significant digits. FDI = foreign direct investment; GDP = gross domestic product; IP = intellectual property; IQR = interquartile range; WIPO = World Intellectual Property Organization.

While it has long been common practice to implicitly ignore (or even exacerbate) the problem of missing data through listwise deletion, methodological research suggests that such a strategy leads to biased and inconsistent results—a problem we need to worry about here because, as noted above, our observations with missing data appear to be disproportionately country-years with low values on the dependent variable. To address this problem, social scientists have increasingly used imputation, that is, replacing missing data with "substitute" data (see, for example, King et al. 2001).

The goal of imputation is to replace missing values in such a way that it safeguards against the biased and inefficient estimates and standard errors that listwise deletion often produces. Different imputation methods attack this problem in different ways. They range from the simple mean imputation (in which the missing value is replaced by the mean of the nonmissing values) to the complicated "multiple" imputation (in which multiple substitutes of each missing value are generated from a predictive model of the nonmissing data). Unfortunately, simple imputation models like mean imputation often do little to address bias and inefficiency problems in the data, while more complicated models like multiple imputation often fail to converge (that is, fail to result in a stable estimate for the substitute value) or require considerable computing power and time (for example, Honaker, King, and Blackwell 2011; Van Buuren and Groothuis-Oudshoorn 2011).

The approach that we use in this chapter addresses the crux of the issue, that is, the potential for biased estimates, yet has the benefit of being relatively simple and fast to implement. It entails sampling our imputed values from the joint distribution of the existing data.[29] To account for time trends, we include the three- and five-year lags for each of our variables to impute our data.[30] Following imputation, we then keep only the original unlagged data as the basis for our analysis. This approach, developed by Hoff (2007), has been described in greater detailed in Hollenbach et al. (2014).[31] (Note that for the rest of this chapter, when we refer to the "imputed data," we mean the dataset that combines the original values for the nonmissing data with imputed values for the dataset cells that originally had missing data.) Summary statistics for the data before and after imputation can be found in tables 7.1 and 7.2.

Note that we also conducted all of our analyses using the original dataset with listwise deletion (as well as the imputed dataset). The resulting analyses are substantively quite similar. For purposes of brevity, we present the results using the imputed data for the panel data only, whereas we include the results for both the imputed and nonimputed cross-sectional analysis. The detailed results of the panel analysis using nonimputed data are available upon request.

### 7.4.6 Findings 1: Cross-Sectional Analyses

We begin our investigation of the relationship between competition law and innovation with a cross-national or cross-jurisdictional analysis of the relationship between patent filings and the cumulative number of years since the country's first competition law came into effect.[32] We lag all control variables by five years to account for the lead time between an idea's conception and its patentable realization,[33] and to provide a simple safeguard against reverse causation. We also lag our competition law measure by five years, so that a country is first recorded as having a competition law five years after its first competition law comes into effect. We lag this variable because we would generally expect a change in a country's laws to have an appreciable effect on innovation only after some time.[34]

In table 7.3, we show the resulting estimates for U.S. patents (with imputed data) for the year 2014, the most recent year for which patent data are available. We first estimate a basic ordinary least squares (OLS) model with U.S. patents as the dependent variable and the number of years since the first competition law came into effect chronologically for the full sample of 207 jurisdictions (model 1). We estimate a clearly statistically significant positive coefficient for this measure of competition law, suggesting that countries with a competition law exhibit a higher rate of innovation, which further increases over time. Specifically, each additional year of a country having an antitrust law is associated with a 2.64 percent increase in the number of U.S. patents filed by residents of that country.

TABLE 7.3  **Cross-Sectional Relationship between Competition Law Duration and Logged U.S. Patent Production, 2014 (Imputed Data)**

| Variable | Model 1 | Model 2 | Model 3 | Model 4 |
|---|---|---|---|---|
| Years competition law in effect | **0.0264** | **0.0295** | | |
| | $(6.17e^{-3})$ | $(6.94e^{-3})$ | | |
| Years competition law continuously in effect | | | 0.0496 | 0.0412 |
| | | | (−0.0103) | (−0.0115) |
| Polity2 | −0.0178 | −0.0212 | −0.0201 | −0.0150 |
| | (−0.0196) | (−0.0192) | (−0.0195) | (−0.0193) |
| Government effectiveness | **1.19** | **0.911** | **1.17** | **0.911** |
| | (−0.197) | (−0.203) | (−0.195) | (−0.206) |
| Years IP law in effect | **0.022** | **0.0144** | **0.0253** | **0.0141** |
| | $(5.78e^{-3})$ | $(6.63e^{-3})$ | $(5.59e^{-3})$ | $(6.72e^{-3})$ |
| Log GDP per capita | 0.216 | 0.141 | 0.195 | 0.154 |
| | (−0.111) | (−0.109) | (−0.110) | (−0.111) |
| Population | **$2.09e^{-8}$** | **$1.82e^{-8}$** | **$2.09e^{-8}$** | **$2.00e^{-8}$** |
| | $(3.37e^{-9})$ | $(3.41e^{-9})$ | $(3.31e^{-9})$ | $(3.38e^{-9})$ |
| Population squared | **$-1.27e^{-17}$** | **$-1.03e^{-17}$** | **$-1.24e^{-17}$** | **$-1.14e^{-17}$** |
| | $(2.66e^{-18})$ | $(2.68e^{-18})$ | $(2.63e^{-18})$ | $(2.67e^{-18})$ |
| Trade (% GDP) | $-1.29e^{-3}$ | $2.36e^{-3}$ | $-4.96e^{-4}$ | $2.39e^{-3}$ |
| | $(2.54e^{-3})$ | $(2.53e^{-3})$ | $(2.54e^{-3})$ | $(2.58e^{-3})$ |
| FDI (% GDP) | $-8.44e^{-3}$ | $-8.25e^{-3}$ | $-7.78e^{-3}$ | −0.0114 |
| | (−0.0166) | (−0.0184) | (−0.0165) | (−0.0186) |
| Intercept | 0.590 | 0.785 | 0.521 | 0.646 |
| | (−0.925) | (−0.907) | (−0.915) | (−0.922) |
| $N$ | 207 | 184 | 207 | 184 |
| Adjusted $R^2$ | 0.694 | 0.542 | 0.714 | 0.528 |
| AIC | 730 | 633 | 726 | 638 |
| BIC | 767 | 669 | 762 | 674 |

Note: Whenever the size of a value warrants it for the sake of efficiency, we use scientific notation where, for instance, $1.25e^3$ means $1.25 \times 10^3$. Standard errors in parentheses. Bold parameter estimates indicate statistical significance at the 5 percent level. All estimates are rounded to three significant figures. AIC = Akaike Information Criterion; BIC = Bayesian Information Criterion; FDI = foreign direct investment; GDP = gross domestic product; IP = intellectual property; $N$ = number of observations (here: countries); adjusted $R^2$ = adjusted $R$ squared (goodness of fit measure).

We worry, however, that the much higher number of patents filed by inventors from developed (OECD) countries could be driving these results. So, in model 2, we reestimate the same empirical model using only data from the 184 developing countries and jurisdictions in our dataset.[35] The positive statistical relationship between the years a competition law has been in effect and innovation not only holds but is even stronger for the developing country subsample: the results suggest that a one-year increase in the duration of an antitrust law is associated with a 2.95 percent increase in U.S. patent applications from those developing countries.

In models 3 and 4, we then reestimate these basic cross-sectional models of U.S. patents (as the dependent variable) but with our second measure of competition law duration as the key independent variable, that is, the number of years for which a competition law has been in continuous effect. We continue to find a positive and significant statistical relationship, both when considering all countries (model 3) and when restricting the sample to developing countries (model 4). Substantively, we find that each additional year of a continuously-in-effect competition law is associated with a 4.96 percent and 4.12 percent increase in U.S. patents, respectively.

All results shown so far are based on using 2014 U.S. patent data for the dependent variable. Do the results hold for earlier years? Figure 7.1 shows the coefficient estimates

**FIGURE 7.1  Coefficient Plot: Estimated Effect of Competition Law Duration on Logged U.S. Patent Production, 1965–2014 (Cross-Sectional Analyses, Imputed Data)**

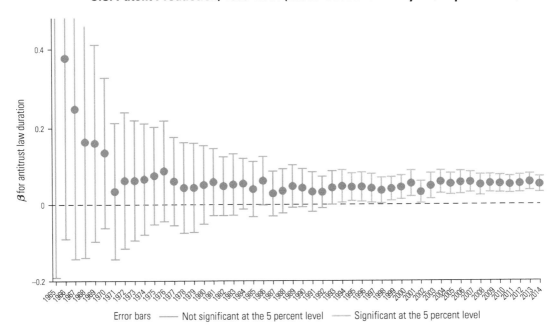

for our main independent variable of interest, the number of years for which an antitrust law has been continuously in effect, based on conducting the cross-sectional analyses in table 7.3 separately for each year in our dataset using logged U.S. patents as the dependent variable (model 3). These estimates are strikingly consistent over time, suggesting that there has been a statistically (and substantively) significant positive relationship across countries at least since the early to mid-1990s. In fact, the magnitude of the estimated effect remains very similar going back as far as the early 1970s, but, because of much wider confidence intervals for the early years, the earlier estimates miss the conventional $p<0.05$ threshold for statistical significance.

Yet what is the concrete, substantive meaning of these coefficient estimates? Put another way, we might want to know: How many more patent filings do, for instance, the 2014 estimates suggest we should expect in a country with a competition law, compared to a country without such a law? The estimated coefficient gives only a partial sense of this substantive effect, because the coefficients indicate the estimated marginal effect for an additional year of having a competition law continuously in effect, whereas for countries with a competition law the actual values taken by this variable have of course increased over time. Figure 7.2 gives a sense of the implied substantive effect over time by showing (for all the years for which the competition law-duration variable was statistically significant) the additional patent registrations predicted as a consequence of a 1 standard deviation increase in the competition law-duration variable (while keeping all other variables at their mean for the given year).[36]

**FIGURE 7.2   Estimated Substantive Effect for Years with Statistically Significant Effect**

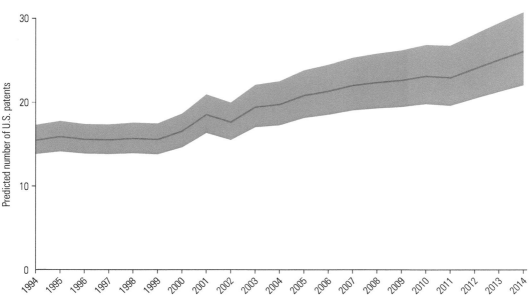

A Step Ahead

Next we turn to the cross-sectional estimates using WIPO patents as the dependent variable in table 7.4. We estimate the same models for 2014 WIPO patents as we estimated for U.S. patents in table 7.3, based on the full sample of 208 countries (model 5), then the subsample of developing countries only (model 6), using the first competition law measure (number of years since the chronologically first competition law). Model 7 then shows the estimates using the continuously-in-effect competition law measure for the full dataset; model 8 shows only the corresponding estimates for the developing countries' sample. Again we find that there is a strong positive and significant relationship between antitrust competition and patent production across the different measures for antitrust as well as for the different subsets of data.

TABLE 7.4   **Cross-Sectional Relationship between Competition Law Duration and Logged WIPO Patent Production, 2014 (Imputed Data)**

| Variable | Model 5 | Model 6 | Model 7 | Model 8 |
|---|---|---|---|---|
| Years competition law in effect | **0.0228** ($7.92e^{-3}$) | **0.0317** ($9.71e^{-3}$) | | |
| Years competition law continuously in effect | | | **0.0472** ($-0.0118$) | **0.0662** ($-0.0157$) |
| Polity2 | $-0.0367$ ($-0.0256$) | $-0.0472$ ($-0.0269$) | $-0.0392$ ($-0.0251$) | $-0.0481$ ($-0.0261$) |
| Government effectiveness | **0.715** ($-0.258$) | 0.396 ($-0.285$) | **0.688** ($-0.253$) | 0.365 ($-0.279$) |
| Years IP law in effect | 0.0135 ($7.55e^{-3}$) | $6.42e^{-3}$ ($9.28e^{-3}$) | **0.0153** ($7.25e^{-3}$) | $6.12e^{-3}$ ($9.10e^{-3}$) |
| Log GDP per capita | 0.0859 ($-0.145$) | $5.22e^{-3}$ ($-0.153$) | 0.0508 ($-0.143$) | $4.41e^{-3}$ ($-0.150$) |
| Population | **$2.59e^{-8}$** ($4.14e^{-9}$) | **$2.56e^{-8}$** ($4.78e^{-9}$) | **$2.33e^{-8}$** ($4.17e^{-9}$) | **$2.64e^{-8}$** ($4.58e^{-9}$) |
| Population squared | **$-1.61e^{-17}$** ($3.28e^{-18}$) | **$-1.55e^{-17}$** ($3.75e^{-18}$) | **$-1.38e^{-17}$** ($3.32e^{-18}$) | **$-1.57e^{-17}$** ($3.62e^{-18}$) |
| Trade (% GDP) | $-3.86e^{-3}$ ($3.32e^{-3}$) | $7.01e^{-4}$ ($3.55e^{-3}$) | $-2.96e^{-3}$ ($3.27e^{-3}$) | $1.52e^{-3}$ ($3.49e^{-3}$) |
| FDI (% GDP) | 0.0150 ($-0.0217$) | 0.0169 ($-0.0258$) | 0.0152 ($-0.0213$) | 0.0160 ($-0.0252$) |
| Intercept | **3.32** ($-1.20$) | **3.28** ($-1.27$) | **3.40** ($-1.18$) | **3.03** ($-1.25$) |
| N | 208 | 184 | 208 | 184 |
| Adjusted $R^2$ | 0.473 | 0.326 | 0.492 | 0.352 |
| AIC | 845 | 757 | 837 | 750 |
| BIC | 882 | 792 | 874 | 785 |

Note: Whenever the size of a value warrants it for the sake of efficiency, we use scientific notation where, for instance, $1.25e^3$ means $1.25 \times 10^3$. Standard errors in parentheses. Bold parameter estimates indicate statistical significance at the 5 percent level. All estimates are rounded to three significant figures. AIC = Akaike Information Criterion; BIC = Bayesian Information Criterion; FDI = foreign direct investment; GDP = gross domestic product; IP = intellectual property; N = number of observations (here: countries); adjusted $R^2$ = adjusted R squared (goodness of fit measure); WIPO = World Intellectual Property Organization.

We again investigate whether our cross-sectional results for 2014 WIPO patents are consistent across time or merely an aberration. In figure 7.3, we plot the coefficient estimates for our main independent variable of interest, the number of years for which an antitrust law has been continuously in effect, this time from models using logged WIPO patents as the dependent variable. We continue to find a robust relationship between antitrust law and innovation as far back as the early to mid-1990s. Moreover, substantively, this relationship is even stronger when using WIPO patents as the dependent variables than using U.S. patents.

In our cross-sectional analyses, we thus generally find for the last twenty years evidence of a positive and significant relationship between the number of years since an antitrust law has been passed and the number of patents filed by citizens of the country (U.S. patent data) and within a given country (WIPO data) for both our measure of the time since a country's chronologically first competition law and the continuously-in-effect measure of competition law duration. Across both U.S. patents and WIPO patents, we also find that the continuously-in-effect measure of competition law is substantively even stronger than the chronologically first measure. Model 8 for example, suggests an increase by as much as 6.62 percent in the number of WIPO patents filed in developing countries, with every additional year of an antitrust law continuously having been in effect (compared to the 3.17 percent increase for a

**FIGURE 7.3**   **Coefficient Plot: Estimated Effect of Competition Law Duration on Logged WIPO Patent Production, 1965–2014 (Cross-Sectional Analyses, Imputed Data)**

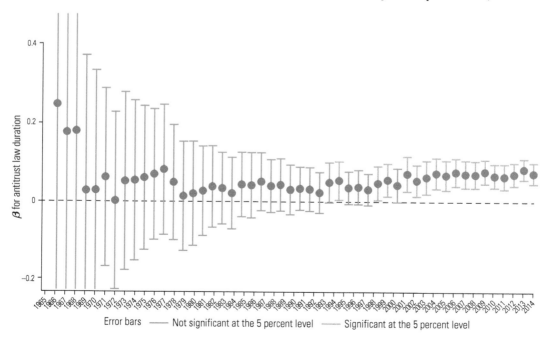

A Step Ahead

chronologically first antitrust law estimated in model 6). We thus focus our subsequent panel analysis on the continuously-in-effect measure though the positive and statistically robust relationship between the chronologically-first measure and patent filings still largely holds. Note also that the positive and significant effect still holds even when we restrict the analysis to non-OECD countries, and is sometimes even stronger.

In table 7.5 we show, for comparison, the estimates for the exact same models as in tables 7.3 and 7.4 using our original, nonimputed data with listwise exclusion in one table. On the whole, the results are slightly weaker than those reported with the imputed

**TABLE 7.5**  **Cross-Sectional Relationship between Competition Law Duration and Logged Patent Production, 2014 (Nonimputed Data)**

| | U.S. patents | | | | WIPO patents | | | |
|---|---|---|---|---|---|---|---|---|
| Variable | Model 9 | Model 10 | Model 11 | Model 12 | Model 13 | Model 14 | Model 15 | Model 16 |
| Years competition law in effect | **0.0165** | **0.0270** | | | 0.0143 | **0.0344** | | |
| | $(6.52e^{-3})$ | $(8.02e^{-3})$ | | | $(9.52e^{-3})$ | $(-0.0128)$ | | |
| Years competition law continuously in effect | | | **0.0353** | **0.0394** | | | **0.0388** | **0.104** |
| | | | $(-0.0127)$ | $(-0.0165)$ | | | $(-0.0149)$ | $(-0.0235)$ |
| Polity2 | $-4.87e^{-3}$ | $-0.0129$ | $-6.85e^{-3}$ | $-3.73e^{-3}$ | $-0.0349$ | $-0.0591$ | $-0.0396$ | $-0.0728$ |
| | $(-0.0231)$ | $(-0.0247)$ | $(-0.0230)$ | $(-0.0252)$ | $(-0.0357)$ | $(-0.0410)$ | $(-0.0346)$ | $(-0.0377)$ |
| Government effectiveness | **1.08** | **0.742** | **1.04** | **0.746** | 0.511 | $-0.0901$ | 0.466 | $-0.117$ |
| | $(-0.290)$ | $(-0.349)$ | $(-0.291)$ | $(-0.366)$ | $(-0.458)$ | $(-0.611)$ | $(-0.445)$ | $(-0.563)$ |
| Years IP law in effect | **0.0171** | 0.0195 | **0.0220** | 0.0188 | $4.64e^{-3}$ | $3.92e^{-3}$ | $7.05e^{-3}$ | $4.23e^{-3}$ |
| | $(7.83e^{-3})$ | $(-0.0112)$ | $(7.55e^{-3})$ | $(-0.0115)$ | $(-0.0116)$ | $(-0.0181)$ | $(-0.0109)$ | $(-0.0167)$ |
| Log GDP per capita | **0.788** | **0.732** | **0.745** | **0.742** | **0.711** | **0.691** | **0.638** | **0.633** |
| | $(-0.177)$ | $(-0.193)$ | $(-0.176)$ | $(-0.200)$ | $(-0.270)$ | $(-0.317)$ | $(-0.265)$ | $(-0.293)$ |
| Population | **$2.37e^{-8}$** | **$2.10e^{-8}$** | **$2.36e^{-8}$** | **$2.27e^{-8}$** | **$2.63e^{-8}$** | **$2.68e^{-8}$** | **$2.32e^{-8}$** | **$2.75e^{-8}$** |
| | $(3.45e^{-9})$ | $(3.78e^{-9})$ | $(3.42e^{-9})$ | $(3.85e^{-9})$ | $(4.80e^{-9})$ | $(6.17e^{-9})$ | $(4.90e^{-9})$ | $(5.61e^{-9})$ |
| Population squared | **$-1.43e^{-17}$** | **$-1.21e^{-17}$** | **$-1.40e^{-17}$** | **$-1.31e^{-17}$** | **$-1.59e^{-17}$** | **$-1.58e^{-17}$** | **$-1.33e^{-17}$** | **$-1.58e^{-17}$** |
| | $(2.67e^{-18})$ | $(2.91e^{-18})$ | $(2.66e^{-18})$ | $(2.97e^{-18})$ | $(3.75e^{-18})$ | $(4.78e^{-18})$ | $(3.85e^{-18})$ | $(4.37e^{-18})$ |
| Trade (% GDP) | $1.66e^{-3}$ | $6.10e^{-3}$ | $2.49e^{-3}$ | $5.99e^{-3}$ | $-5.24e^{-4}$ | $7.13e^{-3}$ | $4.25e^{-4}$ | $7.41e^{-3}$ |
| | $(3.46e^{-3})$ | $(3.95e^{-3})$ | $(3.49e^{-3})$ | $(4.13e^{-3})$ | $(5.28e^{-3})$ | $(6.70e^{-3})$ | $(5.16e^{-3})$ | $(6.17e^{-3})$ |
| FDI (% GDP) | $-0.0320$ | $-0.0119$ | $-0.0309$ | $-0.0171$ | $-0.0168$ | $5.53e^{-3}$ | $-0.0170$ | $-6.15e^{-4}$ |
| | $(-0.0200)$ | $(-0.028)$ | $(-0.0199)$ | $(-0.0287)$ | $(-0.0304)$ | $(-0.0476)$ | $(-0.0296)$ | $(-0.0435)$ |
| Intercept | **$-4.32$** | **$-4.55$** | **$-4.26$** | **$-4.68$** | $-1.72$ | $-2.83$ | $-1.38$ | $-3.00$ |
| | $(-1.57)$ | $(-1.75)$ | $(-1.55)$ | $(-1.83)$ | $(-2.32)$ | $(-2.83)$ | $(-2.26)$ | $(-2.61)$ |
| $N$ | 106 | 84 | 106 | 84 | 97 | 74 | 97 | 74 |
| Adjusted $R^2$ | 0.809 | 0.702 | 0.811 | 0.681 | 0.575 | 0.449 | 0.595 | 0.530 |
| AIC | 360 | 289 | 359 | 295 | 404 | 322 | 399 | 310 |
| BIC | 389 | 316 | 388 | 322 | 432 | 347 | 427 | 336 |

*Note:* Whenever the size of a value warrants it for the sake of efficiency, we use scientific notation where, for instance, $1.25e^3$ means $1.25 \times 10^3$. Standard errors in parentheses. Bold parameter estimates indicate statistical significance at the 5 percent level. All estimates are rounded to three significant figures. AIC = Akaike Information Criterion; BIC = Bayesian Information Criterion; FDI = foreign direct investment; GDP = gross domestic product; IP = intellectual property; $N$ = number of observations (here: countries); adjusted $R^2$ = adjusted $R$ squared (goodness of fit measure); WIPO = World Intellectual Property Organization.

data, but the results are still significant and robust across these different specifications with the exception of model 13 (the counterpart to model 5). This model estimates the relationship between WIPO patents and the chronologically first measure of competition law. However, the results for competition law duration do hold for the raw, non-imputed data for other cross-sections and subsets of the data (results available on request). For example, a one-year increase in the continuously-in-effect measure of antitrust law duration is associated with a 3.9 percent increase in WIPO patent data (model 15).

Finally, although the control variables are not the main focus of this chapter, a brief discussion of the relationship between our control variables and our measures of innovation is warranted. In tables 7.3 and 7.4, we can see that our estimates are remarkably consistent across our two different measures of patents, U.S. patents and WIPO patents; our two different main independent variables of competition law duration; and for our two sets of countries, all countries and developing countries. Perhaps most important for public policy and international organizations are the estimates suggesting that state capacity, as measured by the WGI's government effectiveness variable, is an important, positive facilitator of innovation. An increase of 1 unit of the measure of state capacity, which is about equivalent to its interquartile range (see table 7.1), is associated on average with a 100 percent increase in patent production across countries. Meanwhile, population and population squared are also significant predictors of innovation, with diminishing returns to population increases (as evidenced by the negative sign on the population squared estimate).

Interestingly, there is no significant effect estimated between log GDP per capita and patent production, which is highly surprising given the existing literature. The results of our panel analyses suggest a potential reason for this result (see below).

### 7.4.7 Findings 2: Panel Analyses

While cross-sectional evidence is illuminating, we are also interested in understanding how the relationship between competition law and innovation may change over time. Indeed, our estimates of the cross-sectional models suggest that time dependencies may affect the estimation results (as both the parameter estimates and significance levels change across time). To model these dependencies, we employ a random effects model for 208 countries from 1965 to 2014.[37] Note that random effects models can lead to biased estimates because of correlations between different levels of data. For our dataset, the particular concern is that correlations between time-variant variables (for example, GDP per capita) and time-invariant measures (for example, a country dummy) may lead to biased estimates: while GDP per capita does change over time, its change is not independent of the country in question. That is, we do not expect a country with a GDP per capita comparable to the United States one year to subsequently have a GDP per capita comparable to Zimbabwe the next year. Thus, although time-variant measures may change, they may still be highly correlated with time-invariant measures, and thereby bias the subsequent estimates.

We circumvent these problems by using Bell and Jones' (2015) method for estimating both "within" and "between" effects in a single random effect model. There is then no longer any risk of endogeneity because, under this method, we explicitly separate each variable into its time-variant and time-invariant components. We do so by demeaning each variable to measure its time-varying component (the "within" effect) and use the mean of each variable per country to measure its time-invariant component (the "between" effect). The demeaned within effect now has an overall mean of 0, and as such by definition the correlation between the within and the country-level random effect is 0, which addresses the concern of a potential correlation among different levels of data. Such a specification also allows us to differentiate between the effect of competition law on the level of innovation over time ("within" each country) and the effect of differences in competition law (duration) on the level of innovation across countries ("between" the countries). The results of this analysis are shown in table 7.6.[38]

The estimates shown in table 7.6 suggest that the positive and significant relationship between antitrust law that has continuously been in effect and innovation is robust to panel analysis. Moreover, we find evidence of a positive and significant relationship both across countries (the estimated between effect) and within countries over time (the estimated within effect). The estimated between effect suggests that, on average across countries, countries with longer continuous experience of having a competition law produce more innovation than countries with a short history of having a competition law (even at the end of the time covered by our analyses). Meanwhile the estimated within effect suggests that countries with competition laws experience increases in innovation over time (all other things being equal) on average.

While the between effect is more robust for WIPO patents (models 19 and 20), the within effect is more robust for U.S. patents (models 17 and 18). The results also largely hold across all countries as well as the subset of non-OECD developing countries. Note, however, that the between effect of the continuously-in-effect competition law is not significant for U.S. patents with regard to developing countries (model 18) nor is the within effect of the continuously-in-effect competition law significant for WIPO patents (model 19). Using various other subsets of developing countries (not shown here but available upon request) the within effect of the competition law variable is generally more robust for U.S. patents than the between effect. Meanwhile, the results of model 19 aside, there is generally robust support for a positive and significant relationship for both the within and between effect for the continuously-in-effect competition law variable with regard to WIPO data for models using various other subsets of developing countries (not shown here but available upon request).

TABLE 7.6 **Panel Estimates of the Relationship between Competition Law Duration (Continuously in Effect) and Logged Patent Production with Year and Country Random Effects (Imputed Data)**

| Variable | U.S. patents | | WIPO patents | |
|---|---|---|---|---|
| | Model 17 | Model 18 | Model 19 | Model 20 |
| Years competition law continuously in effect (between) | **0.0318** (−0.0158) | 0.0126 (−0.0177) | **0.0326** (−0.0142) | **0.0918** (−0.0241) |
| Years competition law continuously in effect (within) | **0.0348** ($3.02e^{-3}$) | **0.0420** ($4.09e^{-3}$) | $5.30e^{-3}$ ($3.68e^{-3}$) | **0.0148** ($5.09e^{-3}$) |
| Polity2 (between) | **−0.0791** (−0.0209) | **−0.0527** (−0.0200) | **−0.0565** (−(0.0269) | −0.0485 (−0.0272) |
| Government effectiveness (between) | **2.29** (−0.284) | **1.48** (−0.318) | **1.52** (−0.368) | 0.542 (−0.434) |
| Years IP law in effect (between) | **0.0184** ($7.24e^{-3}$) | $-2.19e^{-3}$ ($8.84e^{-3}$) | $-4.25e^{-3}$ ($9.39e^{-3}$) | **−0.0242** (−0.0121) |
| Log GDP per capita (between) | −0.180 (−0.118) | −0.0701 (−0.113) | −0.0561 (−0.153) | 0.0989 (−0.155) |
| Population (between) | **$2.04e^{-8}$** ($3.39e^{-9}$) | **$1.62e^{-8}$** ($3.26e^{-9}$) | **$2.10e^{-8}$** ($4.37e^{-9}$) | **$2.01e^{-8}$** ($4.45e^{-9}$) |
| Population squared (between) | **$-1.66e^{-17}$** ($3.29e^{-18}$) | **$-1.24e^{-17}$** ($3.15e^{-18}$) | **$-1.61e^{-17}$** ($4.25e^{-18}$) | **$-1.46e^{-17}$** ($4.30e^{-18}$) |
| Trade (% GDP) (between) | **$-6.39e^{-3}$** ($2.62e^{-3}$) | $-2.07e^{-3}$ ($2.58e^{-3}$) | **−0.0149** ($3.37e^{-3}$) | **$-8.70e^{-3}$** ($3.52e^{-3}$) |
| FDI (% GDP) (between) | 0.0201 (−0.0300) | $6.19e^{-3}$ (−0.0278) | 0.0698 (−0.0389) | 0.0583 (−0.0379) |
| Polity2 (within) | **−0.0103** ($3.17e^{-3}$) | **$-9.66e^{-3}$** ($3.56e^{-3}$) | **−0.0238** ($3.93e^{-3}$) | **−0.0261** ($4.44e^{-3}$) |
| Government effectiveness (within) | **0.506** (−0.0401) | **0.513** (−0.0444) | **0.331** (−0.0494) | **0.376** (−0.0551) |
| Years IP law in effect (within) | **0.0313** ($2.02e^{-3}$) | **0.0338** ($2.47e^{-3}$) | **0.0319** ($2.51e^{-3}$) | **0.0409** ($3.08e^{-3}$) |
| Log GDP per capita (within) | **0.467** (−0.0247) | **0.451** (−0.0267) | **0.367** (−0.0306) | **0.350** (−0.0333) |
| Population (within) | **$1.02e^{-8}$** ($1.32e^{-9}$) | **$9.73e^{-9}$** ($1.43e^{-9}$) | **$1.41e^{-8}$** ($1.61e^{-9}$) | **$1.30e^{-8}$** ($1.78e^{-9}$) |
| Population squared (within) | **$-2.63e^{-18}$** ($7.64e^{-19}$) | **$-2.34e^{-18}$** ($8.20e^{-19}$) | **$-5.69e^{-18}$** ($9.33e^{-19}$) | **$-5.24e^{-18}$** ($1.02e^{-18}$) |
| Trade (% GDP) (within) | $-7.50e^{-4}$ ($5.44e^{-4}$) | $-8.56e^{-4}$ ($5.92e^{-4}$) | $7.69e^{-4}$ ($6.74e^{-4}$) | $5.76e^{-4}$ ($7.36e^{-4}$) |
| FDI (% GDP) (within) | $2.59e^{-3}$ ($1.63e^{-3}$) | $2.75e^{-3}$ ($1.79e^{-3}$) | **$5.51e^{-3}$** ($2.02e^{-3}$) | **$5.84e^{-18}$** ($2.22e^{-3}$) |
| Intercept | **4.63** (−0.997) | **3.38** (−0.990) | **6.24** (−1.29) | **4.15** (−1.35) |
| N | 8,717 | 7,567 | 8,767 | 7,567 |
| Countries | 207 | 186 | 208 | 186 |

*Note:* Whenever the size of a value warrants it for the sake of efficiency, we use scientific notation where, for instance, $1.25e^3$ means $1.25 \times 10^3$. Standard errors in parentheses. Bold parameter estimates indicate statistical significance at the 5 percent level. All estimates are rounded to three significant figures. FDI = foreign direct investment; GDP = gross domestic product; IP = intellectual property; $N$ = number of observations (here: country-years); WIPO = World Intellectual Property Organization.

Substantively, the estimated between effects are similar in size to the effects estimated in the cross-sectional models in tables 7.3 and 7.4 and sometimes even larger. For example, a one-year increase of the between effect of a continuously-in-effect competition law is associated with a 9.2 percent increase in the number of WIPO patents cross-nationally for the subset of developing countries (model 20). Meanwhile, a one-year increase of the within effect of a continuously-in-effect competition law is associated with a 4.2 percent increase in the number of patents for that particular country for the subset of developing countries (model 18).

Finally, with regard to the estimates for the control variables, we find that state capacity has an important conditioning effect on innovation both across countries (between effect) and within countries (within effect), with the cross-country effect being the larger of the two. The effect of population on innovation levels also continues to be significant, like in the cross-sectional models, for both the cross-country and within-country levels, but again with diminishing returns.

Logged GDP per capita is found to have a strong positive relationship with innovation for the within-country level (based on the within effect estimates from the panel analysis). Recall that we expected but did not find this relationship with our cross-sectional analyses. The results of the panel analysis suggest that this may be because logged GDP per capita's effect on innovation is largely a within-country one, something that a cross-sectional analysis would not pick up. However, we should also note that our cross-sectional models using raw, instead of imputed, data, presented in table 7.5, does find a strong positive relationship between log GDP per capita and innovation—future work should probe the robustness of these findings.

Polity2 is also found to be negatively related to innovation for both the within and between effects, which differs from our cross-sectional findings that found a null effect. This negative correlation is surprising, given the literature on autocracy and property rights; future work should investigate whether it is robust to the use of other measures and, in particular, whether more differentiated, fine-grained measures are needed to capture the effect of political-economic institutions on innovation.

## 7.5 Conclusions and Policy Implications

Maintaining and increasing incentives for innovation has long been recognized as a—possible and hoped-for—benefit of a well-designed and implemented competition policy. Fostering innovation has become an even more important goal of competition policy with the rise of endogenous growth theory and the increasing emphasis on dynamic efficiency as well as on dynamic effects in antitrust analysis (see Kovacic and Shapiro 2000, esp. 57f).[39] But the increased focus on innovation is not just a function of advanced economic analysis. Competition law scholars and practitioners alike have in recent years emphasized fostering innovation as a goal of competition policy in developing countries (for example, Fox 2007), and developing countries such as

Kenya (2010) and Tanzania (2003) even explicitly note promoting innovation as an objective in their national competition laws.

This chapter reports what to the best of our knowledge are the first statistical analyses across countries and over time (1965–2014) of the effect of having a substantively meaningful competition law on aggregate (national) levels of innovation. Measuring innovation using two types of patent data,[40] we find a robust, strongly statistically significant positive correlation with the length of time for which a country has had a competition law (after a five-year lag). This core finding also holds in analyses restricted to developing countries. In separate annual cross-sectional analyses, we find a strongly significant correlation from the early to mid-1990s onward (and a more weakly significant but still positive effect for prior years). And, in panel analyses, we find evidence of substantively meaningful competition laws boosting innovation both across and within countries over time.

The analyses reported here should be regarded as exploratory, indicative of the promise of a new research agenda rather than conclusive on their own. In future work, we intend to differentiate among competition regimes by their effectiveness—for which we hope to consider the existence of a competition agency and various measures of enforcement—and, maybe most important, to examine more systematically the political and legal context of the world's many competition regimes, rather than "just" to additively include a measure of each country's IP law duration and a generic measure of government effectiveness.[41] Consistent with Büthe and Mattli's (2011) and Büthe's (forthcoming) call for the analysis of institutional configurations instead of context-detached analyses of particular institutions, we would expect the effectiveness of a country's competition law in boosting innovation to depend at least in large part on the availability of supporting institutions in the country, such as rule of law and state capacity. The findings reported here suggest that such research will surely be worthwhile.

Indeed, the findings reported here are quite remarkable on their own, given the number of scholars who have pointed out that if antitrust law is "to enhance scientific and technological progress [it] requires careful case-by-case analysis and delicate implementation" (Hart 1998–99, 76)—the kind of detailed economic analysis that, according to Gerber (2015), most developing country agencies are hard pressed to conduct on a large scale. Yet we find that the adoption and continuous existence of a competition law, on average, both substantively and statistically significantly increases the rate of innovation.

## Notes

1. Different mixes of these efficiency gains of course imply very different distributional outcomes, and many scholars and practitioners advocate competition policy precisely as a way to ensure that such gains are widely shared (for example, Fox 2011). This important issue for the politics of competition policy is, however, beyond the scope of this chapter.

2. See, for instance, the efforts to spark such innovations by Robert Malkin and his colleagues at the EngineeringWorldHealth project (http://www.ewh.org, last accessed January 18, 2016).

3. This focus on macro-context is partly a response to the generally poor results of industrial policies, where policy makers sought to support industries with high innovation and growth potential, which proved an often-impossible task.

4. Baker (2007, 578) notes additional possible advantages of large and/or oligopolistic firms, which are not as susceptible to being made redundant by well-functioning markets as the financing advantage that Schumpeter put front and center.

5. Schumpeter discusses this in terms of shop-floor implementation of new technologies, only, but presumably the feasibility of implementation directly drives actual innovation, unless we assume that there is a readily available sea of innovations with the cost of implementation the only serious constraint.

6. Shapiro (2012, 365) adds to this the "Synergy Principle," which places value on the combination of assets that have the potential to enhance innovation capabilities (where the whole is greater than the sum of the parts) as a guideline for merger reviews.

7. For a recent review, see Cohen 2010. For a wealth of historical, as well as contemporary illustrations, see Baumol 2002.

8. Per World Bank style, "Netherlandic" is used instead of "Dutch."

9. Similarly, Sakakibara and Porter (2001), for instance, interpret their finding of a positive correlation between the level of competition at the industry level (measured as market-share instability) and trade performance (measured by world export share) as an indication that competition fosters innovation.

10. In particular, we use as our dependent variable what the U.S. Patent and Trademark Office calls "utility patents." These are issued "for the invention of a new and useful process, machine, manufacture, or composition of matter, or a new and useful improvement thereof" and represent approximately 90 percent of recently issued patents. See http://www.uspto.gov/web/offices/ac/ido/oeip/taf/patdesc.htm (last accessed October 21, 2016) for a description of different patent types.

11. See the USPTO website, http://www.uspto.gov/web/offices/ac/ido/oeip/taf/appl_yr.htm (last accessed May 15, 2015). We use the number of patent applications instead of the number of patent grants because a substantial amount of time may elapse between the time when a patent is applied for and the final decision of whether to grant it or not, and we are interested in whether antitrust law stimulates innovation—patent application should track more closely when the new idea was conceived than the grant of a patent. We also considered using citation-weighted patents to better capture the underlying innovativeness of each patent (see Kogan et al. 2012), but unfortunately, for many years, this measure is available for fewer than 30 countries, making it impossible to conduct separate statistical analyses by year or separate analyses for countries in the developing world.

12. WIPO patent application data for 1980 to 2014 are available at the WIPO website, http://ipstats.wipo.int/ipstatv2/?lang=en (last accessed May 15, 2015 with the selection: "1a – Direct applications" and "Resident and abroad count by applicant's origin (equivalent count)." WIPO patent data prior to 1980 are available on the WIPO patent statistics home page: http://www.wipo.int/ipstats/en/statistics/patents/ (last accessed October 21, 2016). For some countries, the data for the number of patent applications in the inventor's country of origin actually reach back as far as 1883. However, given the data availability of the covariates, we restrict our analysis to 1960–2014.

13. Note however that the process of obtaining a patent in another country is facilitated if one's home country and the country in which one wishes to obtain the patent are both signatories of the Patent Cooperation Treaty.

14. We follow Gleditsch and Ward (1999) in distinguishing between countries and noncountry jurisdictions that nonetheless have sufficient legislative and judicial autonomy to be considered

as separate (potential) competition regimes. The 15 noncountry jurisdictions included in our dataset (and in some analyses) are Bermuda; Cayman Islands; Faeroe Islands; French Polynesia; Greenland; Guernsey; Hong Kong SAR, China; Isle of Man; Jersey; Macao SAR, China; New Caledonia; Sint Maarten (the Netherlandic part of the Caribbean island of St. Martin); Turks and Caicos Islands; the British Virgin Islands; and the West Bank and Gaza. We were able to obtain data for at least some variables and some years for each of these jurisdictions.

15. In detailed spreadsheets that are available upon request, we recorded for each country the specific legislation and its specific provisions on which we based our coding decisions, that is, how a given competition statute fulfilled each of the two criteria.

16. For instance, the Bahraini constitution of 1973 in Article 98 prohibits monopolies unless "granted by law and for a limited time." Article 314 of the 2009 Bolivian constitution states "Private monopolies and oligopolies are prohibited, as well as any other form of association or public or private legal agreement by Bolivian or foreign persons, who attempt to control and have exclusivity over production of and commercialization of goods and services." Neither qualifies as a competition law based on our first exclusion criterion.

17. Bahrain, China, and Singapore, for instance, adopted laws or regulations for the telecommunications industry, which included competition provisions (supposedly to constrain monopoly or collusion) before they passed a general competition law; the former Yugoslav Republic of Macedonia and Singapore also had sector-specific competition rules for energy and for media prior to their adoption of a national competition law.

18. For a new, spatial analysis of the underlying near-global diffusion process of antitrust law, see Büthe and Minhas (2015).

19. Sources consulted include all "peer reviews" conducted under the auspices of the OECD and the Competition and Consumer Protection Policies Programme of the United Nations Conference on Trade and Development (UNCTAD), for which a country's competition law and policy is reviewed by competition agency officials and independent experts from several other countries, resulting in an often detailed written report; Keith Hylton's Antitrust World Wiki; William Kovacic's World Competition Law and Policy Database at George Washington University (http://www.gwclc.com/World-competition-database.html); UNCTAD's collection of competition laws; the U.S. Federal Trade Commission's unofficial database of competition laws; national competition agency websites; and journals that publish the texts of competition laws in translation (sometimes accompanied by a brief legislative history), such as the *European Competition Law Review*; as well as published works discussing comparative data, such as Gutmann and Voigt 2014; Kronthaler 2007, 2010; Voigt 2009; and Waked 2010; and a large number of country-specific articles, chapters, and books. We thank all these scholars, practitioners, and institutions for making their data available to us.

20. These pre-1945 competition laws are discussed, among other things, in Gerber (2010, esp. 163–65) and Baskoy (2008, 57–59), as well as in the respective countries' peer reviews.

21. There are, for instance, as of January 2016, eight COMESA member states that currently have no domestic competition law that meets the criteria, yet the common market competition rules apply: the Comoros, the Democratic Republic of Congo, Djibouti, Eritrea, Libya, South Sudan, Sudan, and Uganda.

22. Data for population, GDP per capita, trade as a percentage of GDP, and net FDI flows as a percentage of GDP were retrieved from the World Bank's World Development Indicators (WDI) database; according to WDI metadata, the version we used was uploaded to the WDI server on December 22, 2015. Cheng, Grieco, and Guzman (2014) use the Fraser Institute's rating of a country's business environment; for our purposes a measure of government effectiveness has a more compelling theoretical rationale. In future analyses, we also plan to use alternative measures of rule of law and/or government/state capacity.

23. Porter and Stern (2002) use the logged form of population in order to account for potential nonlinearities. We find that using population and population squared leads to better model fit as measured by AIC scores and $R^2$.

24. Last accessed January 2016 at: http://www.wipo.int/wipolex/en/results.jsp?countries=&cat_id=1.

25. For a critique of this neoclassical optimism, see Büthe 2014, esp. 215–19.

26. Grossman and Helpman (1991) also support this view indirectly by showing that the returns to technologies produced in developed countries are reduced by imitators in developing countries—who thus devote resources to imitation instead of devoting it to innovative activity of their own.

27. The quote is from Kaufmann, Kraay, and Mastruzzi (2010, 4). The WGI government effectiveness indicator is created by combining perception-based governance data sources from a wide variety of stakeholders, including governments, business and nongovernmental organizations, and academic experts. The construction of this variable is done in a way that maintains the cardinality of the underlying data, weighs the different components by their relative precision but also accounts for the potential uncertainty of the resulting indicator (see Kaufmann, Kraay, and Mastruzzi 2010). Data for the government effectiveness indicator are available at: http://www.govindicators.org (last accessed October 21, 2016).

28. Communication between the authors and the WIPO Economics and Statistics Division, which also supplies the data for U.S. patents, on this subject was as follows: "WIPO collects data from national offices. Normally, for indicators based on collected data, a blank cell may indicate either a missing value or zero count. Unfortunately, we do not maintain a document showing which offices did not supply us data in the past, or that the data is missing."

29. While a marginal distribution describes the probability of realizing an outcome for a single random variable, a joint distribution describes the probability of realizing multiple outcomes for multiple random variables. As such, each imputed value is estimated in a way that takes into account its relationship with all variables in the dataset.

30. Only Polity was not estimated with lags as the stickiness of Polity scores leads to poor performance in the copula imputation.

31. Actual implementation of the missing imputation was done using the "sbgcop" package (Hoff 2012) using the R statistical software.

32. Note that the cross-sectional regressions for nonimputed data are available only for the years 1996, 1998, 2000, and 2002–14 because of the limited availability of the WGI's government effectiveness variable. However, the results for these years are consistent with those found for the imputed data.

33. We also have run the statistical analyses using shorter and even slightly longer lags. The estimated results remain qualitatively the same when we do so.

34. As a result of this five-year lag, we drop two jurisdictions from our analysis—Sint Maarten and South Sudan. They became countries in 2010 and 2011, respectively, and as such neither has been a country for long enough to be included in our analysis. Therefore, while we document the status of competition law for 210 countries, we include only 208 jurisdictions in our analysis. Note also that we exclude the United States from our analysis when the dependent variable is U.S. patents. We do so to address the likelihood that U.S. applicants may have different resources and incentives to file U.S. patents than foreign applicants do.

35. For these analyses, we exclude all years of the 24 "original" 1960/61 OECD member states, that is, the 20 founding members (Austria, Belgium, Canada, Denmark, France, Germany, Greece, Iceland, Ireland, Italy, Luxembourg, the Netherlands, Norway, Portugal, Spain, Sweden, Switzerland, Turkey, the United Kingdom, and the United States) plus the 4 countries that joined by 1973: Australia, Finland, Japan, and New Zealand. Since the United States was already omitted from models 1 and 3 in table 7.3, the number of observations only declines by 23.

36. To focus on the estimated effect of a 1 standard deviation increase in the competition law duration variable, we use for all of figure 7.2 the 2014 coefficient estimates (that is, the estimates for the most recent year, and thus a year for which the estimated coefficient for the competition law variable is, if anything, low) but apply them to the original, raw data from the earlier years.

37. The years covered by these analyses were dictated by the data availability for U.S. patents. While WIPO patents are available even earlier, to facilitate a comparison of our analyses of U.S. and WIPO patents, we limit our WIPO analysis to the 1965–2014 range as well.

38. The panel estimates in table 7.6 are based on estimating a linear model. We also explored nonlinear estimation of the panel data, using maximum likelihood estimation using either a Poisson or Negative Binomial model, but these model estimates were highly unstable.

39. For a critical view of these developments, see Ginsburg and Wright 2012.

40. U.S. patent registrations by a country's residents and domestic patent registrations (by residents) as reported to WIPO.

41. As noted, we also intend to examine regional (supranational) competition regimes, which are increasingly overlapping with national competition regimes.

## Bibliography

Acemoglu, Daron, Simon Johnson, and James A. Robinson. 2001. "The Colonial Origins of Comparative Development: An Empirical Investigation." *American Economic Review* 91 (5): 1369–1401.

Aghion, Philippe, Nick Bloom, Richard Blundell, Rachel Griffith, and Peter Howitt. 2005. "Competition and Innovation: An Inverted-U Relationship." *Quarterly Journal of Economics* 120 (2): 701–28.

Arrow, Kenneth J. 1962. "Economic Welfare and the Allocation of Resources for Invention." In *The Rate and Direction of Inventive Activity: Economic and Social Factors*, 609–25. Princeton, NJ: Princeton University Press for the National Bureau of Economic Research.

Baker, Jonathan B. 2007. "Beyond Schumpeter vs. Arrow: How Antitrust Fosters Innovation." *Antitrust Law Journal* 74 (3): 575–602.

Bakhoum, Mor, and Julia Molestina. 2011. "Institutional Coherence and Effectiveness of a Regional Competition Policy: The Case of the West African Economic and Monetary Union." In *Competition Policy and Regional Integration in Developing Countries*, edited by Josef Drexl et al., 89–115. Cheltenham, U.K.: Edward Elgar.

Barro, Robert J. 1996. "Democracy and Growth." *Journal of Economic Growth* 1 (1): 1–27.

Baskoy, Tuna. 2008. *The Political Economy of European Union Competition Policy: A Case Study of the Telecommunications Industry*. London: Routledge.

Baumol, William J. 2002. *The Free-Market Innovation Machine: Analyzing the Growth Miracle of Capitalism*. Princeton: Princeton University Press.

Bell, Andrew, and Kelvyn Jones. 2015. "Explaining Fixed Effects: Random Effects Modeling of Time-Series Cross-Sectional and Panel Data." *Political Science Research and Methods* 3 (1): 133–53.

Belsley, David A., Edwin Kuh, and Roy E. Welsch. 1980. *Regression Diagnostics: Identifying Influential Data and Sources of Collinearity*. New York: Wiley.

Bérubé, Charles, Marc Duhamel, and Daniel Ershov. 2012. "Market Incentives for Business Innovation: Results from Canada." *Journal of Industry, Competition and Trade* 12 (1): 47–65.

Bessen, James, and Michael J. Meurer. 2008. *Patent Failure: How Judges, Bureaucrats, and Lawyers Put Innovators at Risk*. Princeton: Princeton University Press.

Blackhurst, Richard. 1991. "Trade Policy Is Competition Policy." In *Competition and Economic Development*, edited by Kurt Stockman and Louis Emmerij, 253–58. Paris: OECD.

Bresnahan, Timothy F., Shane Greenstein, and Rebecca M. Henderson. 2012. "Schumpeterian Competition and Diseconomies of Scope." In *The Rate and Direction of Inventive Activity Revisited*, edited by Josh Lerner and Scott Stern, 203–76. Chicago: University of Chicago Press.

Büthe, Tim. 2014. "The Politics of Market Competition: Trade and Antitrust in a Global Economy." In *Oxford Handbook of the Politics of International Trade*, edited by Lisa L. Martin, 213–32. New York: Oxford University Press.

————. Forthcoming. "Agent-Centric Historical Institutionalism as a Theory of Institutional Change: The Politics of Regulating Competition and Mergers in the European Union, 1955–2010." *International Organization* (forthcoming, conditionally accepted).

Büthe, Tim, and Anu Bradford. 2012. "The Law and Politics of Antitrust in Open Economies." Proposal for collaborative research submitted to the Law and Social Sciences Program of the National Science Foundation, January.

Büthe, Tim, and Walter Mattli. 2011. *The New Global Rulers: The Privatization of Regulation in the World Economy*. Princeton: Princeton University Press.

Büthe, Tim, and Shahryar Minhas. 2015. "The Global Diffusion of Competition Law: A Spatial Analysis." Paper presented at the 6th Meeting of the UNCTAD Research Partnership Platform, 6th United Nations Conference to Review the Set of Multilaterally Agreed Equitable Principles and Rules for the Control of Restrictive Business Practices, Geneva, July 10.

Cárdenas, Mauricio. 2010. "State Capacity in Latin America." *Economia* 10 (2): 1–45.

Carlin, Wendy, Mark Schaffer, and Paul Seabright. 2004. "A Minimum of Rivalry: Evidence from Transition Economies on the Importance of Competition for Innovation and Growth." *Contributions to Economic Analysis and Policy* 3 (1): 1–43.

Chandler, Alfred Dupont. 1994. "The Competitive Performance of U.S. Industrial Enterprises since the Second World War." *Business History Review* 68 (1, special issue on "Competitiveness and Capital Investment: The Restructuring of U.S. Industry, 1960–1990"): 1–72.

Cheng, Cindy, Joseph Grieco, and Ana Guzman. 2014. "International Military Conflict and National Technological Innovation." Unpublished manuscript, Duke University, November.

Cohen, Wesley M. 2010. "Fifty Years of Empirical Studies of Innovative Activity and Performance." In *Handbook of the Economics of Innovation*, edited by Bronwyn H. Hall and Nathan Rosenberg, 129–213. Amsterdam: Elsevier.

Connolly, Michelle. 2003. "The Dual Nature of Trade: Measuring Its Impact on Imitation and Growth." *Journal of Development Economics* 72 (1): 31–55.

David, Paul A. 1975. *Technical Choice Innovation and Economic Growth: Essays on American and British Experience in the 19th Century*. Cambridge, U.K.: Cambridge University Press.

De Roover, Raymond. 1951. "Monopoly Theory prior to Adam Smith: A Revision." *Quarterly Journal of Economics* 65 (4): 492–524.

Didrichsen, John. 1972. "The Development of Diversified and Conglomerate Firms in the United States, 1920–1970." *Business History Review* 46 (2): 202–19.

Dutz, Mark A., and Aydin Hayri. 2000. "Does More Intense Competition Lead to Higher Growth?" Policy Research Paper 2320, World Bank, Washington, DC.

Evans, Peter. 1992. "The State as Problem and Solution: Predation, Embedded Autonomy, and Structural Change." In *The Politics of Economic Adjustment: International Constraints, Distributive Conflicts, and the State*, edited by Stephan Haggard and Robert Kaufman, 139–81. Princeton: Princeton University Press.

Evrard, Sébastien J., John C. Lin, David Longstaff, Nicolas Taylor, Peter Wang, Hiromitsu Miyakawa, and Yizhe Zhang. 2014. "Bangladesh." *Jones Day Antitrust and Competition: Asia in Focus* (Spring).

Fox, Eleanor M. 2007. "Economic Development, Poverty and Antitrust: The Other Path." *Southwestern Journal of Law and Trade in the Americas* 13 (2): 211–36.

————. 2011. "Competition, Development, and Regional Integration: In Search of a Competition Law Fit for Developing Countries." In *Competition Policy and Regional Integration in Developing Countries*, edited by Josef Drexl et al., 273–90. Cheltenham, U.K.: Edward Elgar.

Gerber, David J. 2010. *Global Competition: Law, Markets, and Globalization*. New York: Oxford University Press.

———. 2015. "Adapting the Role of Economics in Competition Law: A Developing Country Dilemma." In *Economic Characteristics of Developing Jurisdictions: Their Implications for Competition Law*, edited by Michal S. Gal et al., 248–64. Cheltenham, U.K. and Northampton, MA: Edward Elgar.

Ginsburg, Douglas H., and Joshua D. Wright. 2012. "Dynamic Analysis and the Limits of Antitrust Institutions." *Antitrust Law Journal* 78 (1): 1–22.

Gleditsch, Kristian S., and Michael Ward. 1999. "A Revised List of Independent States since the Congress of Vienna." *International Interactions* 25 (4): 393–413.

Goldstein, Lisa P., Michael J. Mortorano, Scott Stemetzki, and Wesley E. Weeks. 2012. "Antitrust in High-Tech Industries: Conference Report from the George Mason Law Review's Fifteenth Annual Symposium on Antitrust Law." *George Mason Law Review* 19 (5): 1071–96.

Grossman, Gene M., and Elhanan Helpman. 1991. *Innovation and Growth in the Global Economy*. Cambridge, MA: MIT Press.

Gutmann, Jerg, and Stefan Voigt. 2014. "Lending a Hand to the Invisible Hand? Assessing the Effects of Newly Enacted Competition Laws." Manuscript, University of Hamburg, February.

Hall, Bronwyn H., and Rosemarie Ham Ziedonis. 2001. "The Patent Paradox Revisited: An Empirical Study of Patenting in the U.S. Semiconductor Industry, 1979–1995." *Rand Journal of Economics* 32 (1): 101–28.

Hart, David M. 1998–99. "Antitrust and Technological Innovation." *Issues in Science and Technology* 15 (2 Winter: Meeting New Challenges for U.S. Industry): 75–81.

Hazledine, Tim. 1991. "Trade Policy as Competition Policy." In *Canadian Competition Law and Policy at the Centenary*, edited by R. Shyam Khemani and W. T. Stanbury, 45–60. Halifax: Institute of Research on Public Policy.

Hintze, Otto. 1975. "Military Organization and the Organization of the State." In *The Historical Essays of Otto Hintze*, edited by Felix Gilbert, 178–215. New York: Oxford University Press.

Hoff, Peter. 2007. "Extending the Rank Likelihood for Semiparametric Copula Estimation." *Annals of Applied Statistics* 1 (1): 265–83.

———. 2012. "sbgcop: Semiparametric Bayesian Gaussian Copula Estimation and Imputation." R package version 0.975. http://CRAN.R-project.org/package=sbgcop.

Hollenbach, Florian, Nils Metternich, Shahryar Minhas, and Michael D. Ward. 2014. "Fast and Easy Imputation of Missing Social Science Data." Unpublished manuscript, Duke University.

Honaker, James, Gary King, and Matthew Blackwell. 2011. "Amelia II: A Program for Missing Data." *Journal of Statistical Software* 45 (7): 1–47.

Kamien, Morton I., and Nancy L. Schwartz. 1976. "On the Degree of Rivalry for Maximum Innovative Activity." *Quarterly Journal of Economics* 90 (2): 245–60.

Kaufmann, Daniel, Aart Kraay, and Massimo Mastruzzi. 2010. "The Worldwide Governance Indicators: Methodology and Analytical issues." Policy Research Working Paper 5430, World Bank, Washington, DC.

Kenya, Republic of. 2010. "The Competition Act: Act No.12 of 2010." Available online at http://www.wipo.int/wipolex/en/details.jsp?id=11301 (last accessed October 21, 2016).

King, Gary, James Honaker, Anne Joseph, and Kenneth Scheve. 2001. "Analyzing Incomplete Political Science Data: An Alternative Algorithm for Multiple Imputation." *American Political Science Review* 95 (1): 49–69.

Kogan, Leonid, Dimitris Papanikolaou, Amit Seru, and Noah Stoffman. 2012. "Technological Innovation, Resource Allocation, and Growth." NBER Working Paper Series 17769, National Bureau of Economic Research, Cambridge, MA.

Kovacic, William E., and Carl Shapiro. 2000. "Antitrust Policy: A Century of Economic and Legal Thinking." *Journal of Economic Perspectives* 14 (1): 43–60.

Kronthaler, Franz. 2007. *Implementation of Competition Law in Developing and Transition Countries: Theoretical and Empirical Considerations.* Baden-Baden, Germany: Nomos Verlagsgesellschaft.

———. 2010. "Factors Influencing the Implementation of Recently Enacted Competition Laws: An Empirical Analysis." *International Research Journal of Finance and Economics* 51: 71–87.

Kuznets, Simon. 1962. "Inventive Activity: Problems of Definition and Measurement." In *The Rate and Direction of Inventive Activity: Economic and Social Factors,* edited by Richard R. Nelson, 19–43. Princeton, NJ: Princeton University Press for the National Bureau of Economic Research.

Lerner, Josh, and Scott Stern, eds. 2012. *The Rate and Direction of Inventive Activity Revisited.* Chicago: University of Chicago Press.

Levinson, Mark. 2006. *The Box: How the Shipping Container Made the World Smaller and the World Economy Bigger.* Princeton: Princeton University Press.

Lipimile, George K. 2004. "Competition Policy as a Stimulus for Enterprise Development." In *Competition, Competitiveness and Development: Lessons from Developing Countries.* Geneva: United Nations Conference on Trade and Development.

Marinova, Dora, Michael McAleer, and Daniel Slottje. 2005. "Antitrust Environment and Innovation." *Scientometrics* 64 (3): 301–11.

Mazzone, Luca, and Alberto Mingardi. 2011. "Innovation, Competition and Antitrust: An Examination of the Intel Case." *Economic Affairs* 31 (2): 68–75.

Mowery, David C., and Nathan Rosenberg. 1998. *Paths of Innovation: Technological Change in 20th-Century America.* New York: Cambridge University Press.

O'Brien, Robert. 2007. "A Caution Regarding Rules of Thumb for Variance Inflation Factors." *Quality and Quantity* 41: 673–90.

OECD (Organisation for Economic Co-operation and Development). 2009. *Colombia—Peer Review of Competition Law and Policy.* Paris: OECD.

OECD Secretariat. 2010. *Measuring Innovation: A New Perspective.* Paris: OECD.

Pavie, Xavier. 2014. "The Importance of Responsible Innovation and the Necessity of 'Innovation-Care.'" *Philosophy of Management* 13 (1): 21–42.

Peters, Anne, Lucy Koechlin, Till Förster, and Gretta Fenner Zinkernagel, eds. 2009. *Non-state Actors as Standard Setters.* Cambridge, U.K.: Cambridge University Press.

Polder, Michael, and Erik Veldhuizen. 2012. "Innovation and Competition in the Netherlands: Testing the Inverted-U for Industries and Firms." *Journal of Industry, Competition and Trade* 12 (1): 67–91.

Porter, Michael E. 1990. *The Competitive Advantage of Nations: Creating and Sustaining Superior Performance.* London: Macmillan.

Porter, Michael E., and Scott Stern. 2002. "National Innovative Capacity." In *Global Competitiveness Report 2001–2002,* edited by Klaus Schwab, Michael Porter, and Jeffrey Sachs, 102–19. New York: Oxford University Press.

Porter, Patrick G. 1969. "Origins of the American Tobacco Company." *Business History Review* 43 (1): 59–76.

Priest, George L. 2011. "Advancing Antitrust Law to Promote Innovation and Economic Growth." In *Rules for Growth: Promoting Innovation and Growth through Legal Reform,* edited by Robert E. Litan and the Kauffman Task Force on Law, Innovation, and Growth, 209–22. Kansas City, MO: Ewing Marion Kauffman Foundation.

Przeworski, Adam, and Fernando Limongi. 1993. "Political Regimes and Economic Growth." *Journal of Economic Perspectives* 7 (3): 51–69.

Raihan, Abdullah. 2015. "New Enacted Competition Law of Bangladesh and Major Challenges." Presentation at the South Asia Economic Summit: "Making Growth Inclusive and Sustainable in South Asia." Islamabad, Pakistan, December 7–8.

Rodriguez, A. E., and Ashok Menon. 2010. *The Limits of Competition Policy: The Shortcomings of Antitrust in Developing and Reforming Economies*. Austin, TX: Wolters Kluwer Law & Business.

Sakakibara, Mariko, and Michael E. Porter. 2001. "Competing at Home to Win Abroad: Evidence from Japanese Industry." *Review of Economics and Statistics* 83 (2): 310–22.

Sanders, Barkev S. 1962. "Some Difficulties in Measuring Inventive Activities." In *The Rate and Direction of Inventive Activity: Economic and Social Factors*, edited by Richard R. Nelson, 53–83. Princeton, NJ: Princeton University Press for the National Bureau of Economic Research.

Scherer, Frederic M. 1967. "Market Structure and the Employment of Scientists and Engineers." *American Economic Review* 57 (3): 524–31.

Schumpeter, Joseph A. 1975 (1942). *Capitalism, Socialism and Democracy*. 3rd ed. (First published in 1942; 3rd edition first published in 1950.) New York: Harper & Row.

Shapiro, Carl. 2012. "Competition and Innovation: Did Arrow Hit the Bull's Eye?" In *The Rate and Direction of Inventive Activity Revisited*, edited by Josh Lerner and Scott Stern, 361–405. Chicago: University of Chicago Press.

Smith, J. K., and David Hounshell. 1985. "Wallace H. Carothers and Fundamental Research at Du Pont." *Science* 229 (4712): 436–42.

Smith, Keith. 2005. "Measuring Innovation." In *The Oxford Handbook of Innovation*, edited by Jan Fagerberg, David C. Mowery, and Richard R. Nelson, 148–77. New York: Oxford University Press.

Solow, Robert M. 1970. *Growth Theory: An Exposition*. Oxford, U.K.: Oxford University Press.

Symeonidis, George. 2008. "The Effect of Competition on Wages and Productivitiy: Evidence from the United Kingdom." *Review of Economics and Statistics* 90 (1): 134–46.

Tanzania, United Republic of. 2003. "The Fair Competition Act, 2003." Available online, e.g., from UNCTAD at http://unctad.org/Sections/ditc_ccpb/docs/ditc_ccpb_ncl_Tanzania_en.pdf.

Tingvall, Patrik Gustavsson, and Andreas Poldahl. 2006. "Is There Really an Inverted U-shaped Relation between Competition and R&D?" *Economics of Innovation and New Technology* 15 (2): 101–18.

Van Buuren, Stef, and Karin Groothuis-Oudshoorn. 2011. "mice: Multivariate Imputation by Chained Equations in R." *Journal of Statistical Software* 45 (3): 1–67.

Vickers, John. 2010. "Competition Policy and Property Rights." *Economic Journal* 120 (544): 375–92.

Voigt, Stefan. 2009. "The Effects of Competition Policy on Development: Cross-Country Evidence Using Four New Indicators." *Journal of Development Studies* 45 (8): 1225–48.

Waked, Dina I. 2010. "Antitrust Enforcement in Developing Countries: Reasons for Enforcement and Non-enforcement Using Resource-Based Evidence." Paper for the 5th Annual Conference on Empirical Legal Studies. http://ssrn.com/abstract=1638874.

Weick, Daniel P. 2010. "Competition Law and Policy in Senegal: A Cautionary Tale for Regional Integration?" *World Competition* 33 (3): 521–40.

Xu, Bin, and Eric Chiang. 2005. "Trade, Patents, and International Technology Diffusion." *Journal of International Trade and Economic Development* 14 (1): 115–35.

Young, Andrew Thomas, and William F. Shughart. 2010. "The Consequences of the U.S. DoJ's Antitrust Activities: A Macroeconomic Perspective." *Public Choice* 142 (3–4): 409–22.

# Glossary

**Markup:** The difference between the cost of a good or service and its selling price.

**Monopsony/Oligopsony:** An oligopsony is a market in which the number of buyers is small. A monopsony is where there is only one buyer. This allows the buyer(s) to exert buying power over the sellers, especially if the number of sellers is large, and can effectively drive down prices.

**Price-cost margin:** The difference between the price of a good and its marginal cost of production as a fraction of its price. It is often used as an indicator of market power.

**Pro-competition regulations:** Regulations that are designed to achieve public policy objectives while minimizing the extent to which the regulations (i) reinforce dominance or limit entry; (ii) set rules that are conducive to collusive outcomes or increase costs to compete in the market; and (iii) discriminate against certain players, distort the level playing field, or protect vested interests. Pro-competition regulations can also include regulations that are set with the explicit objective of increasing entry or the degree of rivalry in a market. Examples include access regulations for essential facilities, setting of interconnection rates in the case of the telecommunications sector, use-it-or-lose-it provisions for the use of scarce resources, and regulations on the provision of information to consumers or regulations to reduce consumer switching costs.

**Product Market Regulation (PMR) indicators:** References to product market regulation used as an explanatory variable in various studies relate to the Organisation for Economic Co-operation and Development's PMR indicators. The PMR indicators assess the extent to which public policies promote or inhibit market forces in several areas of the product market. The methodology for calculating PMR indicators focuses on specific restrictions of a country's regulatory framework both economywide and in key sectors of the economy. Information is available on a number of topics including electricity, gas, telecommunications, postal services, transport, water, retail distribution, professional services, administrative requirements for business start-ups, treatment of foreign parties, and others, such as governance of public-controlled enterprises or antitrust exclusions and exemptions. The PMR indicators reflect restrictive elements that affect the incentive or ability of firms to compete and that are embedded in formal laws and regulations.

**Total factor productivity:** The efficiency with which firms turn all inputs into outputs.